Total English

UPPER INTERMEDIATE

Teacher's Book with Resource Disc

Araminta Crace
with Fiona Gallagher

Contents

Photocopiable class activities and teaching notes

Photocopiable video activities and answer key

Progress tests with answer key and audio

Achievement tests with answer key and teaching notes, audio and audioscripts

Printable version of Class CD audioscripts and videoscripts

What's new about *New Total English*?

What makes *New Total English* different from – and better than – the first edition? Firstly, don't worry – we haven't thrown the baby out with the bathwater! We haven't changed everything. We've listened to what you said you liked about the first edition and have kept the most popular features. You'll certainly recognise the look, the format and some integral features from the first edition: the Lead-in pages, the easy-to-use lessons, the comprehensive Reference and Review and practice sections, the popular video clips. Changing to the new edition won't mean that you have to get to grips with a completely new course.

Real solutions to real needs

Some things <u>are</u> different, however. We've looked at every aspect of the course and tried to find solutions for some of your real needs. We've improved the flow of many of the lessons in the Students' Book, integrating more Can do statements and making sure that they all have clear 'outcomes'. We've also given more space to important aspects of language learning such as vocabulary, writing and listening. There's a free online Vocabulary Trainer with each level to help learners memorise new words and phrases; a complete Writing bank at the back of the Students' Book, covering different text types and writing sub-skills as well as new semi-authentic listening extracts to help students gain confidence in dealing with features such as redundancy, hesitation and ungrammatical speech. And, as you'd expect with a new edition, we've given the grammar, vocabulary and pronunciation syllabus a complete overhaul as well as updating much of the content.

New digital components

We've also included new digital components in the course package. The ActiveBook component features the Students' Book pages in digital format and includes integrated audio and video as well as interactive exercises for students to do in class or at home. The ActiveTeach component will help you get the most out of the course with its range of interactive whiteboard software tools and *MyTotalEnglishLab* will help students get better results with its range of interactive practice exercises, progress tests and automatic gradebook.

To sum up, we've kept all the best ingredients of the first edition, improved other features and added exciting new digital components to make *New Total English* an even better package. We hope you and your students will continue to enjoy using it.

The *New Total English* author team

Course package

Students' Book with ActiveBook and DVD

The *New Total English* Students' Books with ActiveBook and DVD are divided into 10–12 units that contain approximately 80–120 hours of teaching material. Each unit contains a balanced mix of grammar, vocabulary, pronunciation and skills:

- clear aims and objectives linked to the CEFR (Common European Framework of Reference)
- revised grammar, vocabulary and pronunciation syllabus
- new reading, listening and video material
- new Writing bank with model texts and focus on sub-skills
- revised and extended Pronunciation bank

ActiveBook:

- digital version of Students' Book with interactive activities and integrated audio and video
- video clips can be selected when you use the ActiveBook in your computer, or play it in a DVD player

Students' Book with ActiveBook, DVD and MyLab

Packaged with the *New Total English* Students' Book with ActiveBook and DVD, *MyTotalEnglishLab* provides students with everything they need to make real progress both in class and at home:

MyTotalEnglishLab:

- interactive exercises with feedback
- regular progress and achievement tests
- automatic marking and gradebook

Class CDs

The *New Total English* Class CDs contain all the recorded material from the Students' Books.

Workbook and Audio CD

The *New Total English* Workbooks contain further practice of language areas covered in the corresponding units of the Students' Books:

- extra grammar, vocabulary, skills and pronunciation exercises
- regular Review and Consolidation sections
- audioscripts and accompanying Audio CD
- with and without key versions available

Teacher's Book with Resource Disc

The *New Total English* Teacher's Books provide all the support teachers need to get the most out of the course:

- background notes and instructions on how to exploit each unit
- suggestions for warm-up and extension activities

Resource Disc:

- extensive bank of photocopiable and printable classroom activities
- editable and printable progress and achievement tests
- audio and video scripts

ActiveTeach and DVD

The *New Total English* Teacher's Books will be further enhanced by the ActiveTeach component which features:

- Students' Book in digital format with all the material from the ActiveBook
- all the material from the Resource Disc
- interactive whiteboard software tools
- video clips can be selected when you use the ActiveTeach in your computer, or play it in a DVD player

Vocabulary Trainer

The *New Total English* Vocabulary Trainer is a new online learning tool designed to help students revise and memorise key vocabulary from the course.
Check this exciting new component out on
www.newtotalenglish.vocabtrainer.net

Website

New Total English has its own dedicated website. In addition to background information about the course and authors, the website features teaching tips, downloadable worksheets, links to other useful websites as well as special offers and competitions. Join us online at
www.pearsonlongman.com/newtotalenglish

Each unit of the *New Total English* Students' Books has the same structure:

* **Lead-in page**
  - acts as a springboard into the topic of the unit and engages learners' interest.
  - introduces essential vocabulary related to the topic so that learners start with the same basic grounding.

* **Input lessons**
  - three input lessons, thematically linked, offering interesting angles on the unit topic. Lessons are double-page at lower levels and triple-page at Intermediate and above.
  - each input lesson leads towards a Can do learning objective in line with the CEFR Can do statements.
  - each 90-minute lesson focuses on a specific grammar area and includes vocabulary and skills work.
  - each unit usually contains at least two reading texts, a substantial listening element (including semi-authentic listenings) and pronunciation work.
  - How to... boxes develop students' competence in using language, in line with the CEFR.
  - Lifelong learning boxes offer tips and strategies for developing learners' study skills.

* **Communication page**
  - revises language taught in the previous three lessons in a freer, more communicative context.
  - each communication task practises a range of skills and has a measurable goal or outcome.

* **Vocabulary page (Intermediate and above)**
  - focuses on vocabulary systems and word-building.
  - helps learners to expand and develop their vocabulary.

* **Reference page**
  - summarises the main grammar points covered in each unit and provides a list of key vocabulary.
  - helps learners to catch up if they miss lessons and is an essential revision tool.

* **Review and practice page**
  - provides a range of exercises to consolidate key grammar and vocabulary covered in the unit.
  - can be used to check progress, enabling teachers to identify areas that need further practice.

* **Writing bank**
  - provides models and tips on how to deal with different types of writing (reports, emails and so on).
  - provides guidance on different writing sub-skills such as formality, connotation and paragraph construction.

* **Pronunciation bank**
  - provides a list of English phonemes, guidance on stress, connected speech and intonation.
  - summarises the pronunciation points covered in each unit of the Students' Book.

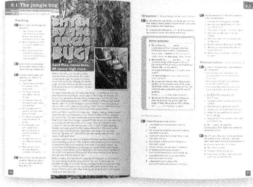

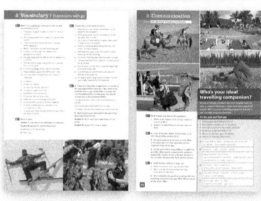

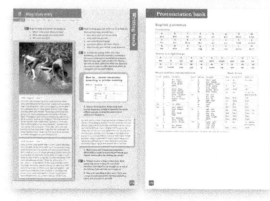

A range of support components help you get the most out of each unit:

- **Students' Book with ActiveBook and DVD**
  - digital version of Students' Book with interactive activites.
  - integrated audio for Students' Book listening activities (including Reference pages and pronunciation activities).
  - wide variety of video clips (including drama, documentary and comedy) which can be selected when you use the ActiveBook in your computer, or play it in a DVD player.
  - interactive video activities.

- **Workbook with Audio CD**
  - consolidation of work covered in the Students' Book.
  - extensive practice of grammar, vocabulary and skills, including pronunciation.
  - regular Review and consolidation sections.
  - can be used in class or for self-study.

- **Students' Book with ActiveBook and MyLab**
  - interactive Workbook with instant feedback and automatic marking.
  - progress and achievement tests with automatic marking and gradebook.

- **Teacher's Book with Resource Disc**
  - provides step-by-step teaching notes including ideas for warmers and extension activities.
  - includes background notes and tips for dealing with particularly difficult language points.
  - Resource Disc features an extensive bank of photocopiable and printable classroom activities as well as editable and printable progress and achievement tests.

- **ActiveTeach**
  - digital version of the Students' Book to be used in class.
  - video clips that can be selected when you use the ActiveTeach in your computer, or play it in a DVD player.
  - all the material from the Teacher's Book Resource Disc.
  - a range of interactive whiteboard software tools.

- **Vocabulary Trainer**
  www.newtotalenglish.vocabtrainer.net
  - new online learning tool designed to help students revise and memorise key vocabulary from each unit of the course.

- **Website**
  www.pearsonlongman.com/newtotalenglish
  - features background information about the course and authors as well as teaching tips, downloadable worksheets and links to other useful websites.

Grammar

New Total English places a lot of emphasis on providing learners with the grammar 'building blocks' they need to communicate confidently. It aims to give learners a thorough foundation in grammar and, at the same time, provides plenty of structured and free practice. Each unit deals with grammar in a broadly similar way:

• Clear presentation and analysis

Each lesson has a clear grammar aim which is stated at the top of the page. Lessons are double-page at lower levels and triple-page at Intermediate and above. New language items are presented in context via reading and/or listening texts and grammar rules are then analysed and explained via the Active grammar boxes, which are a key feature of each lesson. *New Total English* takes a 'guided discovery' approach to grammar and learners are actively invited to think about grammar and work out the rules for themselves.

Active grammar

1 *An original comic book **was bought** for $1.5million.*
   *Someone **bought** an original comic book for $1.5million.*

2 *One of Michael Jackson's gloves **was bought** by 36-year-old Hong Kong businessman Hoffman Ma.*
   *36-year-old Hong Kong businessman Hoffman Ma **bought** one of Michael Jackson's gloves.*

Meaning

We use the passive when we want ...

A to talk about actions, events and processes when who or what causes the action, event or process is unknown or unimportant. This is often the case in writing (or more formal speech).

B to put the focus of what is important at the beginning of the sentence and need to change the sentence to do so.

Form

verb *to be* + past participle

• Varied, regular practice

Once learners have grasped the important rules, all new language is then practised in a variety of different ways so that learners are able to use the grammar with confidence. Practice activities include form-based exercises designed to help learners manipulate the new structures as well as more meaningful, personalised practice. Additional grammar practice exercises can be found in the Review and practice sections at the end of each unit as well as in the Workbooks and *MyTotalEnglishLab*. This component, which features the Workbook exercises in digital format, also provides learners with extra guidance, tips and feedback. The Teacher's Book provides a lot of guidance on how to deal with tricky grammar points. It also contains a Resource Disc with an extensive bank of printable and photocopiable classroom grammar activities which are designed to practise the language in freer, more communicative contexts.

• Easily accessible reference material

In addition to the explanations contained in the Active grammar boxes, there is a Reference section at the end of each unit which provides a summary of the grammar rules as well as extra language notes and examples. Audio recordings of the rules and examples are available on the ActiveBook and ActiveTeach components.

Vocabulary

New Total English recognises the central role that vocabulary plays in successful communication. The emphasis is on providing learners with high-frequency, useful vocabulary which is regularly practised and revised. New vocabulary is presented and practised in a variety of different ways.

• Lead-in pages

Each unit starts with a Lead-in page which provides a springboard into the topic of each unit. Featuring a variety of attractive picture prompts and related exercises, the Lead-in pages are designed to help teachers elicit vocabulary that learners already know as well as pre-teach essential vocabulary for the rest of the unit.

• Topic-based vocabulary

Each unit focuses on useful vocabulary relating to the topic of the lessons as well as vocabulary arising from the listening and reading texts. Items are generally presented in context and practised through a variety of exercises.

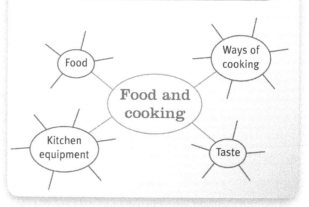

Additional vocabulary practice is provided in the Review and practice sections of the Students' Book and in the practice exercises in the Workbook. Photocopiable vocabulary activities are also available on the ActiveTeach and on the Resource Disc which accompanies the Teacher's Book.

• Vocabulary pages (Intermediate and above)

At the lower levels there is a lot of emphasis on building learners' knowledge of high-frequency words and phrases as well as common lexical sets. Learners are introduced to collocation work at a very early stage and from intermediate level onwards, there is a greater emphasis on vocabulary systems and word-building.

• Vocabulary Trainer

Each level of *New Total English* is accompanied by a Vocabulary Trainer. This unique online learning tool focuses on the key vocabulary in each unit and helps learners memorise new words and phrases.

Speaking

The key aim for most learners is spoken fluency. However, most learners find it difficult to talk about topics which hold no interest for them and many cannot express themselves easily without support. *New Total English* develops spoken fluency in a number of ways – by giving learners discussion topics they want to talk about; by setting up situations where they are motivated to communicate in order to complete a specific task; by providing clear models and examples of how to structure discourse and by encouraging them, wherever possible, to express their own ideas and opinions.

• Fresh angles on familiar topics

Topics in *New Total English* have been chosen for their intrinsic interest and relevance. Obscure topics, i.e. those which are only likely to appeal to a minority audience, have been avoided and discussion questions have been deliberately chosen to encourage learners to draw on their own lives and experience. Inevitably, many of the topics have been covered in other ELT coursebooks but wherever possible, we have tried to find a fresh angle on them.

• Structured speaking activities

Many of the lessons in *New Total English* culminate in a structured final speaking activity in the form of a survey, roleplay etc. Learners are given time to prepare what they are going to say and prompts to help them. The activities often involve pair and group work to maximise learners' opportunities to speak in class. Many of the structured speaking activities are linked to the CEFR Can do statements.

• How to... boxes

There are regular How to... boxes throughout the course which focus on the words and expressions learners need to carry out specific functions, e.g ordering food in a restaurant.

How to... give and check instructions

Use sequence words	_____ , you make a pancake mix.
	_____ , you fry lots of pancakes.
	_____ , you bake it in the oven.
Give detailed instructions/ suggestions	**You must make** _____ it's not too *thick.*
	You should be _____ *not to put too much spinach mix in one layer.*
	The _____ **thing is** *not to overcook it at this point.*
Check instructions	**Is that** _____ *there are lots of layers?*
	So you _____ *you pour the sauce over the whole thing?*
	So it _____ **like** *there are quite a lot of layers?*

• Communication pages

Communication pages feature at the end of each unit and engage learners in a variety of problem-solving tasks and activities. These give learners practice in a number of different skills including speaking.

• Photocopiable class activities

The photocopiable activities on the ActiveTeach and on the Resource Disc are also specifically designed to promote speaking practice.

Pronunciation

New Total English pays particular attention to pronunciation, which is integrated into lessons which present new language. The pronunciation syllabus includes word and sentence stress, intonation and connected speech. The Pronunciation bank at the back of the Students' Books provides a summary of all pronunciation points in the book as well as a list of English phonemes, guidance on intonation and weak forms. The ActiveTeach includes audio to accompany the Pronunciation bank. There is additional pronunciation practice in the Workbooks and Workbook Audio CD.

Listening

Listening is one of the most difficult skills to master and *New Total English* places particular emphasis on developing learners' confidence in this area. Listening texts include short scripted dialogues as well as longer, unscripted semi-authentic listenings. There is additional listening practice in the Workbooks and the video clips on the ActiveBook and ActiveTeach components further enhance learners' confidence in understanding the spoken word.

• Scripted listening activities

Scripted listening activities include short dialogues as well as longer extracts including conversations, interviews and stories. There are lots of simple 'Listen and check your answer' exercises as well as longer, more challenging extracts where learners have to listen for specific information.

• Semi-authentic listening activities

As well as the more traditional scripted listening activities, *New Total English* also includes a range of semi-authentic listening texts, i.e. recordings of one or more people speaking in an unprepared, unscripted way, although they are aware of the relevant level and therefore have adapted their own language to a certain extent accordingly. Learners benefit from listening to a semi-authentic recording because the spontaneity of spoken English means that it is full of false starts, hesitations, redundancy and 'ungrammatical' sentences. Learners need to be aware of these features and they need to develop confidence in dealing with them in order to cope with listening in the 'real world'.

• Video clips

New Total English provides a video clip to accompany each unit of the Students' Book. The videos feature a range of authentic material from a variety of different sources including short films and clips from TV documentaries and drama. The video clips expose learners to real English and are designed to motivate learners to 'raise their game' in terms of developing their listening skills.

To make the material more accessible to learners, photocopiable activities for each video clip are available on the ActiveTeach and on the Resource Disc. There are additional interactive video exercises on the ActiveBook and ActiveTeach which students can complete in class or at home.

The video clips are available on the ActiveBook which accompanies each Students' Book and on the ActiveTeach. You can select the video clips when you use the discs in your computer, or you can play them in a DVD player.

Reading

Many learners need to be able to read texts in English – for their studies, for work or simply for pleasure – and *New Total English* recognises that reading is an extremely important skill that can have a beneficial effect on all aspects of language learning including vocabulary, spelling and writing.

New Total English encourages learners to read as much as possible – in most units there are at least two substantial reading texts – and care has been taken to introduce students to as wide a range of text types as possible, from simple forms and advertisements to short texts from newspapers and magazines.

Reading texts are accompanied by a range of activities that are designed to check comprehension as well as develop key reading skills such as reading for gist, reading for specific information, guessing the meaning of words from the context and so on.

• Choice of texts

As with the listening material in *New Total English*, texts have been chosen for their intrinsic interest as well as for their usefulness in providing a vehicle for the particular grammar and vocabulary points in focus. Many of the texts have been adapted from authentic, real-life sources such as magazines and websites, and where texts have been adapted or graded, every effort has been made to remain faithful to the orignal text type in terms of content and style.

• Exploitation of texts

Each reading text in *New Total English* is accompanied by a number of exploitation exercises that have been carefully selected to develop learners' reading skills. Activities include comprehension and vocabulary work as well as practice in dealing with different reading sub-skills such as reading for gist. There are also a number of jigsaw readings where learners work together and share information.

---

12 Check your ideas by reading the story.

Student A: read story 1 on page 149.

Student B: read story 2 below.

Story 2

An ambitious burglar broke into a vast mansion on Millionaires' Row at Bel Air, Los Angeles. He went through the house room by room, putting anything of value that he could see and carry in the large bag he'd brought with him. Having completely filled his bag, he decided it was time to leave.

He started to realise that he wasn't sure of the way out but moved on quickly, through a large dining room, past an indoor gym and through another room filled with exotic parrots. By now, he was beginning to panic. Then, having run through a large library and a small room full of art, he began to get quite desperate.

• Length and complexity

The length and complexity of the reading texts in *New Total English* get more challenging as the course progresses. At lower levels, the texts are very short and the emphasis is on training learners to read for specific information. At higher levels, learners are introduced to a a greater range and variety text types and more emphasis is placed on textual analysis.

Writing

In these days of electronic media, it is easy to forget that writing is not simply speech written down – effective writing has all sorts of conventions that differ from speech and that are necessary to learn in one's own language as well as in a foreign language.

New Total English pays particular attention to the important skill of writing. One of the most important new features of the revised edition is the Writing bank at the back of each Students' Book which contains 10–12 lessons that focus on different types of writing – emails, blogs, formal and informal letters and so on. Each lesson also provides additional advice and guidance on different writing sub-skills such as formality, connotation and paragraph construction.

• Model text types

Each Writing bank lesson has a Can do statement which refers to the written output that students complete at the end of the lesson. The lesson usually starts with a warmer that engages students in the topic. Learners then go on to focus on a model of the text type and in most cases, there is some comprehension work to ensure that students are familiar with the content before they start working on the format and related sub-skills. The lesson always finishes with a contextualised written output.

• Writing sub-skills

One of the most important aspects of the Writing bank is that it examines the sub-skills of writing in detail. This is important as it helps learners to build on and develop their writing skills, rather than simply providing practice in writing. Among the sub-skills covered are punctuation, grammatical cohesion, paragraphing and features such as varying the vocabulary used to both enhance interest and ensure lexical cohesion.

• How to... boxes

How to... boxes are a particular feature of the Writing bank. They usually focus on a particular sub-skill of writing and in some cases on written conventions, such as email or letter layout, appropriate formality of language for the text type or order of presentation of the content (such as in a review).

How to... write a successful CV

Promote yourself in a positive way	I have _____ problem-solving skills. I provided a _____ service to customers.
Include appropriate details	I am looking for a _____ trainee position. I worked in a _____ team sometimes under pressure.
Write concisely and clearly	I enjoy the dedication and _____ of karate. Spanish (_____) and French (good).

Learner training

New Total English places a strong emphasis on learner training and good study habits are encouraged and developed via the Lifelong learning boxes which are featured in many lessons. The Lifelong learning boxes provide useful tips and suggestions on how to continue learning outside the classroom.

Revision and testing

There are plenty of opportunities for revision in *New Total English* and language is constantly recycled throughout the course. At the end of every unit, there are special Review and practice pages which take the form of mini-progress checks, enabling learners to identify areas where they might need further practice. Interactive versions of the activities on these pages are available on the ActiveBook and ActiveTeach. The Workbook and accompanying Audio CD provide further practice in grammar, vocabulary and skills covered in the corresponding Students' Book. The Workbook is available in with key and without key versions.

For learners who are really serious about making rapid progress in English, *MyTotalEnglishLab* provides the perfect solution. This exciting component features the Workbook exercises in digital format as well as tips and feedback on common errors.

Regular progress and achievement tests are provided on the ActiveTeach, Resource Disc and *MyTotalEnglishLab*. *MyTotalEnglishLab* also includes automatic marking and a gradebook.

New Total English and exams

The table below shows how the different levels of *New Total English* relate to the University of Cambridge ESOL main suite examinations in terms of the language taught and the topics covered.

Starter	Builds foundation for KET
Elementary	Useful for KET
Pre-Intermediate	Useful for PET
Intermediate	Useful for FCE
Upper Intermediate	**Useful for FCE**
Advanced	Useful for CAE

While *New Total English* is not an examination preparation course, a student who has, for example, completed the Upper Intermediate level would have sufficient language to attempt the Cambridge ESOL FCE (First Certificate in English) examination. Many of the exercises in the *New Total English* Students' Books and other components are similar in format to those found in the Cambridge ESOL main suite examinations but specific training is required for all EFL examinations and we would strongly recommend this.

New Total English and the CEFR

New Total English is correlated to the CEFR (Common European Framework of Reference). Please see the *New Total English* website: **www.pearsonlongman.com/newtotalenglish** for details of CEFR Can do statements for each level of the course.

CEFR	
A1	Starter
A2	Elementary
B1	Pre-intermediate
B1+	Intermediate
B2	**Upper Intermediate**
C1	Advanced

Students' Book contents

Students' Book contents

14

1 Connect

Overview

CEFR Can do objectives
1.1 Take part in a conversation and make small talk
1.2 Express your opinion and manage a conversation
1.3 Talk about obligations and abilities
Communication Talk about past and present members of your family
Writing bank Write personally, highlighting the significance of experiences

CEFR Portfolio ideas
a) In pairs, write a list of as many things as you can that you have in common. Try to think of interesting or unusual things (e.g. having the same zodiac sign).
b) Imagine your partner is looking for a new flatmate. Introduce yourselves and try to get to know each other. Try to make a good first impression. Use the language in the How to... box on page 10 and record it on video.
c) Create a family tree for you and your relatives. Under each name, include notes containing details of their personality, hobbies and any other interesting information.
d) You have returned from a language course. Write to a friend describing it. Include details of the school, social activities, your accommodation, etc.

Lead-in

OPTIONAL WARMER
Write the following headings on the board: *family relationships* and *non-family relationships*. Ask Ss to decide under which heading these words should go: *colleague* and *cousin* (cousin = family relationships; colleague = non-family relationships). Give Ss one minute to brainstorm words under each heading in pairs.

1 ▶ Ss look at the photos and discuss what they think the relationships could be between the people.

Suggested answers
Main photo: an extended family (aunts, uncles, cousins, etc.)
Top photo: sisters or close friends
Middle photo: colleagues
Bottom photo: friends or neighbours

2 ▶ Focus Ss on the words from the box. Elicit the meanings of these expressions: *partner* (someone you are having a serious relationship with); *step-sister* (a girl or a woman whose father or mother has married your father or mother); *half-brother* (a brother who is the child of only one of your parents); *sibling* (a brother or sister); *acquaintance* (someone you know, but not very well); *soulmate* (someone you feel close to because you share or understand the same emotions and interests); *close friend* (someone you are good friends with). Focus Ss' attention on the hyphens in *step-sister* and *half-brother*.

▶ Ask Ss to talk in pairs about two of the people from the box and their relationship with them.

▶ Get feedback from various Ss. Ask: *How many of you are closest to a sibling? How many to a friend?*

3a ▶ Ask Ss to read the sentences, focus on the underlined phrases and try to work out what they mean. Do the first one as a whole class, especially if Ss are not used to this type of exercise. Ss read Sentence 1. Ask: *Is the speaker a confident or a shy person?* (shy) *What do you think 'come across as' might mean?* (to give an impression to others based on the way you behave) *What word(s) help you guess the meaning?* (but I'm shy really).

▶ Ss complete the rest of the exercise individually. Check the answers with the whole class.

Answers
1   seem to be
2   meet by chance
3   make people think well of you when they first meet you
4   have similar attitudes and views on things
5   stay in contact with
6   make decisions about people based on what they look like
7   talking in person
8   like someone as soon as you meet them for the first time

b ▶ Ss discuss the sentences in small groups. Elicit opinions during whole class feedback.

1.1 First impressions

In this lesson, Ss read a website where various people give their views about the importance of making a good first impression. Ss practise greetings and making small talk.

OPTIONAL WARMER

Ask Ss to talk in pairs and compare and contrast the following situations: going to a party where you know almost everyone and going to a party where you know hardly anyone; sitting beside someone you have never met before at a dinner party and sitting next to your best friend; accepting a lift from a colleague to a work meeting you don't know well and driving alone.

Reading

1 ▶ Ask Ss to look at the photo. Elicit where the people are (a garden party) and whether the people know each other well or not (they are standing quite far apart so they probably don't know each other well). Ask Ss to compare the relationship between the people at the front of the photo and the people behind them (the people standing behind are closer and might be good friends).

▶ Ss look at the four situations and decide which one might apply to the photo. They then discuss with a partner the type of things they might talk about in each situation (e.g. *I would talk about my boss with work colleagues but not with new neighbours*; *I would talk about public transport in my area to both new neighbours and classmates*, etc.). Get feedback from the whole class, focusing on the topics that could be discussed in each of the situations.

2 ▶ Ask Ss to read the website and answer the question. Let them compare with a partner.

Suggested answers
Ana: shy, nervous
Mark: likes meeting new people, confident
Jelena: nervous but aware that others are feeling
          nervous too

---

3 ▶ Ss read the website again and answer the questions.

Answers
1   a few seconds
2   she thinks it is a good way to start a conversation
3   she feels more confident when she is wearing clothes
    she feels good in
4   yes, they form an instant opinion about people
5   he doesn't like it when people are either too formal or
    informal when they meet people for the first time
6   to treat people as you want them to treat you
7   no, she thinks it is important not to dominate the
    conversation and to listen to other people.

---

4 ▶ Ss discuss the questions in pairs. Go round the class monitoring their conversations and note down any errors you hear which you may like to deal with during feedback.

Grammar | overview (1): the present and future

5 ▶ Explain to Ss that you are going to quickly review present and future verb forms. Ss should be fairly familiar with this grammar already.

▶ Ss match the underlined verbs in the sentences to the uses in the Active grammar box. Ss compare their answers with a partner, then get feedback from the whole class.

Answers
1   e)   3   i)   5   b)   7   j)   9   h)
2   g)   4   a)   6   d)   8   f)   10 c)

▶ Focus Ss' attention on the difference between state and active verbs. Ask: *Which of the following are state verbs: run, speak, believe, own, buy, remember, laugh, understand?* (*believe, own, remember, understand*). Explain that we do not usually use state verbs with continuous forms. If you feel that Ss are ready, write the following sentences on the board: *The rose smells beautiful* and *I am smelling the rose*. Ask Ss to distinguish between the two uses of *smell* (the first is the state of the rose, not an action and the second is the action of someone smelling the rose).

6 ▶ Ss find and correct the mistakes in pairs. Get feedback from the whole class, asking Ss to identify the use from the Active grammar box for each correct sentence. Explain to Ss that it is often possible to use both *will* and *going to* in order to make predictions; it depends on how sure the speaker is that something will happen.

Answers
1   I'll make (h)
2   He's meeting (f)
3   She always arrives (a)
4   I'm going to study (i)
5   My cousin is living (e)
6   I'm going to have (j)
7   I like (b)
8   He's listening (d)

7a ▶ You could start the discussion by asking various Ss questions about the first topic (e.g. *Do you live in this area? Where are you staying while you are doing this course? How do you get here? Do you have your own room?* etc.).

b ▶ Get feedback from the whole class. For large classes, Ss can work in big groups (8–10 students) for this activity.

8 ▶ Focus students on the Lifelong learning box. Point out that good language learners notice things about language and think about the choice of words used in texts and conversation. Ss read the Lifelong learning box and discuss the questions with a partner.

▶ Encourage Ss to notice the choice of language used by native speakers, thinking about why a particular grammatical form was used (or not used) and what its use implies about the speaker's attitude.

Possible answers

1 In a), the speaker is making an instant decision based on their first impression. In b), the speaker is giving advice. In c), the speaker has thought about what they plan to do at the next party.

2 In a), *I'm going to avoid you.* In b), *Don't talk down to them.* In c), *I'll do that.*

3 In a), *I'm going to avoid you* could be used if the speaker has a sure intention of doing this. In b), *Don't talk down to them* could be used for stronger advice. In c), *I'll do that* could be used if the plan is just an idea and less thought through.

Vocabulary | ways of speaking

OPTIONAL LEAD-IN

Tell Ss you are going to focus on an imaginary new word: *blutted*. Write or say the following sentence: *My friend leaned over and 'blutted' her news in my ear because she didn't want the other people on the bus to hear what she was saying.* Ask Ss: *Is 'blutted' a verb, a noun or an adjective?* (a regular verb 'to blut' with an -ed ending). Then ask: *What do you think 'blutted' means?* (speak quietly). Ask: *How do you know?* (we know it is a verb in the past tense and the surrounding context helps with the meaning: *didn't want others to hear, did it in someone's ear*, etc.).

---

9 ▶ Explain to Ss that you are going to focus on verbs and expressions which describe different ways of speaking. Ss find the words in the box in the website on page 8. Tell them they cannot use their dictionaries but they must use the surrounding words to guess what the verbs and expressions mean. Ss compare their answers with a partner.

Answers

chat: have an informal conversation

gossip: talk about other people and what is happening in their lives

make small talk: talk about unimportant things, often to someone you don't know very well

greet someone: say hello

give someone a compliment: make a remark that expresses approval or admiration about someone

boast: tell others how good/successful you are

mumble: speak indistinctly

speak up: ask someone to speak more loudly

talk down to someone: speak in a superior, patronising way to someone

stumble over your words: make mistakes when speaking or not speaking clearly, perhaps due to nervousness or shyness

---

10a ▶ Ss choose the best option for each of the sentences. Ss compare their answers with a partner.

Answers

1 chatting
2 give them a compliment
3 make small talk
4 mumbled
5 talking down
6 stumble over my words
7 greeting
8 Boasting
9 speak up
10 Gossiping

---

b ▶ Ss discuss the ten statements with a partner. Get feedback from the whole class, focusing on two or three of the statements which might generate most discussion.

▶ If you are moving on to exercise 11a, leave statement 3 till last and use this as a transition to the listening text in exercise 11a. Ask Ss: *Who thinks hobbies and the weather are the best topics for making small talk? What other topics are good for making small talk?*

Speaking

OPTIONAL LEAD-IN

Direct Ss' attention to the box of words. Ask Ss: *Are these topics good for making small talk?* Elicit ways of starting/continuing a conversation using these topics (e.g. travel – *How long did it take you to get here today?* weather – *The weather has been lovely recently, hasn't it?*). Write Ss' suggestions on the board. Then Ss discuss topics/phrases with a partner and decide which they would or wouldn't use.

11a ▶ ● 1.2 Ask Ss to read through the questions then play the recording. Ss listen and answer the questions.

Answers

1 waiting for a Spanish lesson to start
2 yes, because they agree to go home together afterwards
3 hobbies (learning Spanish); work; travel; where you live; how you feel

---

b ▶ Focus Ss on the How to... box. Play the recording again. Ss listen and note an additional phrase for each heading. Get feedback from the whole class.

Answers

Greet someone: *Pleased to meet you; A pleasure to meet you too.*

Try to find out what you have in common: *Did you come by bus? What's your job? What do you do? What about you?*

Sound interested in the person: *That sounds fun!*

Finish the conversation politely: *It's been really nice talking to you.*

► Focus on the stress and intonation patterns of these phrases and demonstrate how to use your voice to sound interested and polite. Ss practise saying the expressions.

12a ► Give Ss a few minutes to prepare what they might say in a conversation with someone they haven't met before. Focus on the headings and expressions from exercise 11b.

b ► Ss work in pairs. Try to ensure that each student is working with someone they haven't met/worked with before. Ss practise meeting and starting conversations.

c ► Ss and give each other feedback on their first impressions and how they might improve their small talk skills.

OPTIONAL EXTENSION

Tell Ss to imagine they are at a party where they have to meet and spend three minutes talking to at least five people they don't know. Ss mingle in large groups or as a whole class. Signal to Ss when each three-minute stage begins and finishes. After each three-minute conversation, Ss move on to talk to someone new.

1.2 Family ties

In this lesson, Ss listen to a radio programme about an usual family of jugglers, the Boehmers. They read an article about birth order and its effects on career choices and personality and then discuss key issues relating to this topic.

Listening

The Boehmer family is the world's largest family of jugglers and has won a number of awards, performing all over the US and beyond. They have been performing to audiences with their varied juggling, gymnastics and unicycling skills for over a decade.

OPTIONAL WARMER

Introduce the idea of circus skills with the class. Elicit different types of circus skills and write them on the board (e.g. *juggling, tightrope walking, acrobatics, trapeze, plate-spinning, clowns, knife-throwing, fire-eating*). Ss discuss the following questions with a partner: *Have you even seen these circus skills in action? Which ones do you like/not like to watch? Why/Why not? Can you do any of these skills?*

1a ► Ss look at the photo and discuss what they think the Boehmer family does.

b ► ● 1.3 Tell Ss they are going to hear the recording twice. The first time, they must listen to get the general idea of the text. Then they will listen a second time for more detail.

► Ss look through the questions. Then play the recording. Ss listen and answer the questions. Then they compare with a partner.

Answers
1 eleven
2 They are the largest family of jugglers in the world.
3 They love it.

---

2 ► Ss read through the more detailed questions. Then, play the recording again. Ss listen and answer the questions. Then they compare with a partner.

Answers
1 His job meant he had to travel a lot and he found long periods in hotel rooms boring so he decided to take up a new hobby and teach himself how to juggle.
2 Larry demonstrated his juggling to his children and they wanted to learn too.
3 At an amusement park.
4 He was born with only one arm but is a champion juggler in his own right.
5 Anybody can do it if they practise and persist at it.

3a ▶ Tell Ss that they are going to focus on some of the expressions from the radio programme. Ask Ss to look at the underlined expressions in the audioscript on page 162 and work out what they might mean. Remind Ss that using the context and the sentences around the expressions will help them. Get feedback from the whole class.

Answers
juggle several tasks at once: to be able to do several
    things at the same time
take up a new hobby: to begin a new pastime activity
only too happy about that: was very willing to do it
it all went from strength to strength: got better and better
they picked up on different things: learn easily
to put your mind to it: to make a firm decision to do
    something and focus on it

b ▶ In pairs, Ss summarise what they heard on the radio programme using the phrases in exercise 3a as appropriate. Encourage them not to include every detail but just to give a summary of the most important points.

4 ▶ Ss discuss the four questions in small groups of three or four.

Grammar | overview (2): the past

5a ▶ Ss read the extract and identify the underlined verb forms. Quickly review the positive, negative and interrogative forms for the Past Simple, Past Continuous and Past Perfect Simple.

Answers
Past Simple: *taught, went, showed*
Past Continuous: *was working, was feeling*
Past Perfect Simple: *had spent, had mastered*

b ▶ Ss match the tenses with their uses. Then they compare answers in pairs.

Active grammar
1 A
2 C
3 B

▶ Draw Ss' attention to the Reference on page 19. Give Ss time to read through the section relating to this language point. Answer any questions that might arise. Alternatively, Ss could read this for homework.

6 ▶ Ss choose the correct form in order to complete the sentences. Ss check answers with a partner.

Answers
A
1 was living
2 wanted
3 had taken
B
4 were waiting
5 had started
6 bought

7a ▶ Ss complete the story by using the correct form of the verbs in brackets. Then they compare with a partner.

Answers
1 had heard   7 went
2 hadn't thought   8 realised
3 were living   9 had given
4 had   10 didn't know
5 started   11 had learned
6 were working   12 were growing up

b ▶ Ss write sentences about themselves using the prompts given.

c ▶ Ss compare their sentences with a partner.

Reading

OPTIONAL LEAD-IN
Give the four corners of the room the following titles: *oldest child*; *middle child*; *youngest child*; *only child*. Ss go to the corner which corresponds to their place in their family. Ss then discuss the questions in exercise 8 with other students in the same corner. If there is only one student in a corner, allow them to choose another birth-order group to join.

8 ▶ Ss discuss the questions in pairs. Get feedback from the whole class and ask: *How many of you feel it is best to be the oldest/youngest/middle/only child in a family?*

9 ▶ Explain to Ss that they are going to read the article twice. The first time, they will read very quickly, just to get the general idea of the article. They will then have an opportunity to read the article again more slowly and in more detail. Direct Ss to the summaries in exercise 9 before they read. Give Ss two minutes to get an overview of the article and choose the best summary.

Answer
3

10a ▶ Ss read the article again and decide if the statements are true or false. Encourage them to underline the part of the article which tells them the answers. Ss compare their answers in pairs.

Answers
1 T
2 T
3 F
4 F
5 T

b ▶ Ss discuss the statements. Encourage them to justify their opinions with examples from their own family or a family they know. Elicit opinions and examples from two or three Ss during feedback.

OPTIONAL EXTENSION

Write the following definitions on the board. Ask Ss to find words in the article which correspond to each definition.

1 *what you think/hope will happen (paragraph 2 – expectations)*
2 *wanting to keep someone safe from harm or danger (paragraph 3 – protective)*
3 *the negative part or disadvantage of something (paragraph 3 – downside)*
4 *a positive opinion about someone or something (paragraph 4 – approval)*
5 *doing something which might have dangerous or harmful consequences (paragraph 5 – risk-taking)*
6 *deliberately not obeying rules or people in authority (paragraph 6 – rebellious)*
7 *to be in a tight space between two other things (paragraph 7 – sandwiched)*

Vocabulary | making adjectives from nouns

11 ▶ Write these words on the board: *intellect* and *intellectual*. Ask: *Which one is a noun and which is an adjective?* (*intellect* = noun; *intellectual* = adjective). Focus Ss' attention on the table and ask them to complete the missing words. Ss check their answers in the article.

Answers

1	intellectual	5	responsible
2	artistic	6	success
3	jealousy	7	frustrating
4	loneliness	8	skilful

12 ▶ Ss complete the sentences with the most appropriate word from the table. Ss compare their answers with a partner.

Answers

1	skill	5	intellectual
2	artistic	6	jealous
3	lonely	7	frustration
4	responsibility	8	successful

Speaking

13a ▶ ● 1.4 Play the recording. Ask Ss to decide what the topic of conversation is and whether the speakers agree or disagree with each other.

Suggested answer
They are discussing relationships between older and younger siblings and attitudes of parents to children depending on their position in the family. They disagree on whether younger children look up to an older sibling and on whether parents are more liberal towards younger children.

b ▶ Ss focus on the language in the How to... box. Play the recording again. Ss listen and complete the sentences in the box. Ss check answers in pairs, then as a whole class.

Answers
What do you <u>think</u> about that?
So, you're the <u>middle</u> child then?
That's not the <u>experience</u> that I had …
I think it's quite <u>similar</u>.
That's quite <u>interesting</u>.
I <u>suppose</u> it must be the case for some …

Pronunciation | intonation: sounding tentative

OPTIONAL LEAD-IN

Write the following sentences on the board: *Only children are lonely.* and *Parents are very strict on the oldest child.* Say the first sentence as a statement you firmly believe and the second in a more tentative way, using a wider range of intonation, dragging out words a little more and pausing between words. Ask Ss: *Which statement do I feel more confident about?* Say the two statements again, being more tentative about the first. Ask: *Which do I feel more confident about now? How do you know?* Elicit how we use our voice to convey we are tentative/sure about things.

14a ▶ ● 1.5 Play the recording. Ss listen and decide which extracts are more confident statements and which are more tentative. Ss compare their answers with a partner.

Answers
confident: 2, 3
tentative: 1, 4

b ▶ Play the recording again. Ss read the underlined parts of the audioscript on page 162 as they listen.

▶ Ss practise saying the sentences with a partner.

OPTIONAL EXTENSION

In pairs, Ss take turns to say one of the sentences from exercise 15 in either a confident or a tentative way. The other student must guess whether they are sure/not very sure about what they are saying in each case.

15 ▶ Before starting the discussions, ask Ss to read through the five sentences individually and to decide how strongly they agree/disagree with each one using a scale of 1 to 10. Ss then discuss two of the statements they feel strongly about in small groups. Encourage them to use expressions from the How to... box and to be conscious of their intonation as they speak.

▶ Get feedback from the whole class, focusing on the statements which the Ss disagreed most strongly about.

1.3 Mobile connections

In this lesson, Ss will read about the increased use of mobile phones in Japan and some of the implications of this, particularly for children. Ss discuss these issues and practise talking about their obligations and abilities in relation to keeping in touch with friends and family.

Mobile phones, instant communication and new technology are dominating people's lives more and more. While there are clearly many benefits from these innovations, there are also potential disadvantages, which we don't yet fully understand.

Reading

OPTIONAL WARMER

Ask Ss to take out their mobile phones and show them to a partner. They explain to each other why they chose this particular phone (colour, mobile provider, range of Apps, etc.); what ringtones they have chosen; what they have chosen as the screensaver for their phone.
If a student doesn't have a mobile phone, they can explain why not.

1 ▶ Ss discuss the questions in small groups. Ask for two or three opinions from the whole class. In whole class feedback, elicit the advantages and disadvantages of mobile phones for children.

2 ▶ Read through the topics with the class. Ss then read the article and tick the topics which are referred to. Ss check answers in pairs, then as a whole class.

Answers
1, 3, 6, 7, 9, 10

3 ▶ Ss read the article again and make brief notes about each of the topics ticked in exercise 2. Ask Ss to stop after they have made notes about the first topic so that you can give feedback and demonstrate to Ss the level of detail required. Ss then complete the rest of the exercise individually. Then Ss compare answers with a partner.

Answers
1 one third of 4–15-year-olds in Tokyo; over half of Japanese high-school students
3 'lifestyle', parents, to keep in touch with friends
6 22% talk at least 10 times a day; 45% send at least 10 messages a day
7 mobile phones may lead to superficial rather than genuine conversations and affect the quality of relationships
9 children read less
10 increased health risk for children from using handsets

OPTIONAL EXTENSION

Write the following sentence on the board: *There are a number of worrying issues that have arisen from the increasing use of mobile phones among young people.* Explain that this is the first sentence in a short summary of the article. Ss use their notes from exercise 3 to practise the skill of summary writing. First, Ss identify the main points of the article. They must only choose three or five points. Ss discuss which points they have chosen with a partner.
Then Ss write one paragraph in which they summarise the main points of the article beginning with the sentence on the board. Remind Ss to only include the main points and not too much detail.
Tips for summary writing:
1 identify the main points first;
2 avoid repeating sentences/phrases directly from the original text – make notes of the main points and try to explain the idea in your own words;
3 organise your ideas in a clear and logical way;
4 do not include examples, quotations or additional details from the text in the summary;
5 keep the summary brief – try to use fewer words than in the original to describe the main points;
6 do not give your own opinion in the summary.

4 ▶ Ss discuss the questions in small groups. Elicit Ss' opinions during whole class feedback.

OPTIONAL EXTENSION

If Ss have access to the Internet, they could do a mini-project to find out more predictions about how mobile phones will change in the next five years. Ask them to think about the following topics: usage; design; banning phones in cinemas, etc.
Ss report back on their findings in the next class.

Vocabulary | keeping in touch

5a ▶ Ss find the verb phrases in the article and use the surrounding sentences to work out what the different phrases with touch mean. Do not give feedback yet.

b ▶ Ss work with a partner to answer the two questions. Get feedback from the whole class on the meaning of these verb phrases.

Answers
1 *to stay in touch*; *to keep in touch* (to maintain contact)
2 *to be in touch/to be out of touch* (to be in/out of contact with someone)
to get in touch/to lose touch (to contact someone/to no longer be in contact with someone)
to touch base means to contact friends or home just to check for any news

6a ▶ Ss delete the incorrect word from each sentence. Then they compare answers with a partner.

Answers					
1	of	4	am	7	base
2	in	5	in		
3	the	6	be		

b ▶ Ss read the sentences again and tick which ones are true for themselves. Point out that they can change the wording of the other sentences to make them true.

c ▶ Ss discuss their sentences with a partner. Encourage Ss to ask for and give details about how they feel about keeping in touch/losing touch/touching base with friends and family.

OPTIONAL EXTENSION

Write the following headings on the board: *Mobile phones on the bus/train*; *mobile phones while driving*; *mobile phones on holiday*; *mobile phones in the cinema/classroom*; *mobile phones at the dinner table/while talking to someone else*. Ss discuss their views on mobile phone etiquette for these situations. Encourage Ss to use phrasal verbs from exercise 5a when describing their views. Get feedback from the class about any rules for using mobile phones.

Grammar | obligation and ability

OPTIONAL LEAD-IN

Write the following modal verbs on the board: *can, can't, have to, don't have to, should, shouldn't, must, mustn't*. Ask Ss to make sentences using one of the modal verbs as you call out the following situations: *pay for calls by monthly bill* (e.g. you don't have to pay for calls by monthly bill); *charge the battery regularly* (e.g. you have to charge the battery regularly); *use the Internet* (you can use the Internet on your phone); *text friends during class* (e.g. you shouldn't text friends during class); *turn off your phone* on an airplane (e.g. you must turn off your phone on an airplane).
After demonstrating one or two cues and answers, extend this activity by dividing the class into two teams. Each team thinks of five situations relating to mobile phones. Then, each team takes turns to call out a situation and the other team makes a correct sentence using a modal verb.

7a ▶ Ss complete headings A and B in the Active grammar box.

Active grammar

A general ability – present
B obligation – present

b ▶ 🌐 1.6 Play the recording. Ss listen and answer the questions.

Answers

1 Her parents bought her a phone because they worried about her when she was out.
2 She likes having a phone and she feel safer because she can keep in touch with her parents.

c ▶ Focus Ss on the underlined verbs in the audioscript on page 162. Ss then complete the remaining headings in the Active grammar box. Then they compare with a partner.

Active grammar

C general ability – past
D ability in the past on one specific occasion
E obligation – past

▶ Remind Ss how to form sentences using modal verbs for present and past time.

▶ Focus Ss on the Reference section on page 19.

8 ▶ Ss rewrite the sentences by replacing the underlined words with verbs from the Active grammar box. Ss compare their answers with a partner.

Answers

1 ... should do more exercise.
2 ... I could/was able to read when I was three.
3 ... didn't have to wear a uniform when I was at school.
4 ... have to/should turn your phone off in the cinema.
5 ... shouldn't have apologised to her so late.
6 ... was able to make her understand the problem.
7 ... I had to eat things I didn't like.
8 ... mustn't use your phone during the performance.

Pronunciation | connected speech (1)

9a ▶ Ss look at the sentences. In pairs, Ss decide on the main stress, consonant–vowel and consonant–consonant connections for each one.

b ▶ 🌐 1.7 Play the recording. Ss compare their answers with a partner and take turns to say the sentences to each other.

Answers

2 I couldn't phone them.
3 I was able to phone from there.
4 I know I should've been more careful.
5 I wasn't able to tell them where I was.
6 You have to phone me when you get there.
7 He had to get in touch with his boss.
8 A: Could you speak English when you were five?
   B: Yes, I could.

▶ Focus Ss on the section on Connected speech in the Pronunciation bank on page 161.

10a ► Read through the list with the whole class. Tell Ss to choose five of the prompts and write them a clue to the answer on five separate pieces of paper. Remind Ss not to write or say which piece of information is being referred to, as the idea is for other Ss to guess the prompt.

b ► Ss read the example dialogue before they start. Remind Ss to give the clues in a jumbled order. Ss take turns to look at their partner's words and ask questions in order to elicit which prompt each clue refers to. Encourage Ss to use the language from the Active grammar box during this activity.

OPTIONAL VARIATION

Ss do this as a mingling activity. Ss stand up and walk around the room and show their clues to different Ss. They ask questions and try to guess which prompt the clues refer to. They can only make one guess for each clue. Give a one-minute time limit for each partner change. Ss try to guess as many prompts as possible in the time given and note down the number they got right each time. The winner is the student with the highest number of correct guesses.

1 Vocabulary | phrasal verbs

In this lesson, Ss listen to a conversation and focus on a number of common phrasal verbs, their meaning and their form. Ss use the phrasal verbs to talk about people and relationships.

OPTIONAL WARMER

Write the following sentences on the board.
1   I _take after_ my father – we're both really lazy!
2   My brother always _takes_ my things out of my room.
Ask Ss to discuss in pairs what the verbs mean and which one is a phrasal verb (_take after_ is a phrasal verb – it means to look or behave like someone in your family; _take_ is not a phrasal verb).

1 ► Focus Ss' attention on the photo. Elicit what the relationship between the two women might be (close friends or sisters; they are sitting close together and leaning towards each other). Explain that they are the sister and girlfriend of Tim.

🔘 1.8 Play the recording. Ss read as they listen to the dialogue. Then they answer the two questions and compare with their partner.

Answers
1   Kevin
2   her friend Sally

2a ► Ss work in pairs and think about the meaning of the underlined phrasal verbs in exercise 1. Ss look at the example and write similar short definitions of the verbs.

b ► Ss check their definitions using an English–English dictionary. Ss compare definitions with a new partner. Get feedback from the whole class.

Answers
to look up to – to admire and respect someone
to grow up – to develop from being a child to being an adult
to show off – to try to make people admire you and think you are clever, funny
to bring up – to look after children until they are adults
to get on – to have a good relationship with someone
to go out – to have a romantic relationship with someone
to split up – to end a marriage or a relationship
to fall out – to have a quarrel
to make up – to become friends with someone again after an argument

► Remind Ss that a good English–English dictionary helps with the following points: meaning (giving a definition and often an example); grammar (including, in the case of phrasal verbs, whether it is transitive [T] or intransitive [I]); pronunciation (stress, sounds and number of syllables).

3 ▶ Ss correct the mistakes in each sentence. Then they compare answers with a partner.

> **Answers**
> 1   going out ~~with?~~
> 2   get on with
> 3   made ~~it~~ up
> 4   bringing us up
> 5   looks up to you
> 6   take ~~them~~ after
> 7   grow ~~out~~ up
> 8   fallen out with
> 9   show ~~on~~ off
> 10 split ~~it~~ up

4a ▶ Read through the sentences with the class. Ask them to decide which of them are true for themselves and to change the others to make them true.

b ▶ Ss compare and discuss their sentences with a partner. Encourage Ss to ask for and to give additional information during the discussion (e.g. *Who do you get on best with in your family? Why? Do you spend a lot of time together? How are you and your Dad similar?*, etc.) Get feedback from the whole class by asking each pair to report back about the most interesting sentence discussed.

1 Communication

In this lesson, Ss listen to a man talking about his family tree. They talk about their own family history and describe family members in detail.

> A family tree is a kind of 'map' of the members of a family and how they are connected back through the generations. In recent years, genealogy, or tracing your own family tree, has become a very popular hobby.

> **OPTIONAL WARMER**
> Draw the family tree of a famous family on the board, using only first names, e.g. Homer (father), Marge (mother), Bart, Lisa, Maggie (three children). Ask Ss: *Who are this famous family?* (The Simpsons). Elicit other famous families (e.g. the British royal family; the Gellers from the TV show *Friends*). Ss prepare a family tree for a famous family with a partner. Ask one or two Ss to draw the family tree on the board using only first names. The whole class guesses which family it is.

1a ▶ ⬤ 1.9 Explain to Ss that they are going to listen to a man talking about his family tree. The photos represent some of the people from his family. Focus Ss' attention on the photos. Ask Ss speculate briefly as to who the people could be.

▶ Play the recording. Ss listen and identify who the people in the photos are.

> **Answers**
> Left photo: Cicely and John
> Middle photo: Leon
> Right photo: Aunt Sue

b ▶ Play the recording again and ask Ss to complete the family tree. Ss compare answers with a partner.

> **Answers**
> (from top down) John, Julian, Sue, Leon

2a ▶ Ss to draw their own family tree going back to at least their grandparents (or further back if they want to), using the one in exercise 2 as a model. Tell Ss not to show their family tree to other Ss at this stage.

b ▶ Ss take turns to describe their family trees to each other. One student draws the family tree as they listen to their partner describe their family. When Ss have finished drawing their partner's family tree, they should compare theirs with the original and check how much they have drawn correctly.

3a ▶ Ss choose two people in their family tree to focus on, one from the present and one from the past. Ss think about various details of their lives and prepare what they will say about them.

b ▶ Each student takes turns to describe a family member to their partner, giving lots of details about their lives. Encourage Ss to ask each other questions.

OPTIONAL EXTENSION

Draw the following chart on the board. Ss work in small groups and discuss the three questions in relation to their immediate and extended families.

	Immediate family	Extended family
How many people?		
Who you are closest to?		
How often you get together?		

---

1 Review and practice

1 ▶

Answers

1	go	5	Does the moon go
2	I'm listening	6	speaks
3	doesn't usually rain	7	don't know
4	He's playing	8	is staying

2 ▶

Answers

1 'm going to get
2 'll pass
3 'm meeting
4 's going to hurt
5 'll get

3 ▶

Answers

1 ... while I was watching
2 ... he had left.
3 ✓
4 ... had broken the kitchen window.
5 ... was following me
6 ... had arranged to do

4 ▶

Answers

1	both	5	were able to
2	can't	6	can
3	was able to	7	wasn't able to
4	both	8	both

5 ▶

Answers

1 should have
2 mustn't
3 had to
4 doesn't have to
5 should
6 didn't have to
7 shouldn't have
8 must

6 ▶

Answers

1 fell ~~on~~ out
2 seen eye ~~on~~ to eye
3 ~~frustrated~~ frustration
4 comes ~~up~~ across as
5 ~~make~~ take after
6 ~~jealous~~ jealousy
7 ~~have~~ get on really well
8 he shows ~~out~~ off

1 Writing bank

1 ▶ Ss read the email and answer the questions.

Answer
1   Friends who haven't seen each other for a long time.
2   Fernanda's brother

2 ▶ Ss read the email again and answer the questions.

Answers
1   how she made contact with her friend; news about work; questions about her friend's life
2   informal language

3a ▶ Ss look at the 'informal' features in the How to... box and find examples in the email.

Answers
1   Love it!
2   So some of my news
3   you know
4   or something
5   What's he up to?
6   'cos (because)
7   :-D
8   Fernanda!!
9   all those years ago!!

b ▶ Ss discuss the questions in pairs. Get feedback from the whole class.

Suggested answers
Friends. It would not be appropriate to write a formal letter in this way.

4 ▶ Ss write the email.

Overview

Lead-in	**Vocabulary:** Travel
2.1	**Can do:** Talk in detail about your experiences **Grammar:** Present Perfect Simple and Continuous **Vocabulary:** Describing situations and feelings **Speaking and Pronunciation:** Connected speech (2) **Reading:** Bitten by the jungle bug!
2.2	**Can do:** Ask for information and give detailed answers **Grammar:** Questions **Vocabulary:** Weather **Speaking and Pronunciation:** Connected speech: linking sounds **How to...** add detail **Reading:** Guide to Bhutan **Listening:** Visiting Bhutan
2.3	**Can do:** Express opinions about places and make comparisons **Grammar:** Modifying comparatives **Vocabulary:** Verb phrases about moving/travelling **Speaking and Pronunciation:** **How to...** describe two things which change together **Reading:** On the move!
Vocabulary	Expressions with *go*
Communication	**Can do:** Ask and answer questions in an interview
Writing bank	Write about recent news in a blog **How to...** choose vocabulary according to precise meaning
Extra resources	ActiveTeach and ActiveBook

CEFR Can do objectives
2.1 Talk in detail about your experiences
2.2 Ask for information and give detailed answers
2.3 Express opinions about places and make comparisons
Communication Ask and answer questions in an interview
Writing bank Write about recent news in a blog

CEFR Portfolio ideas
a) Write a fact file similar to the one on page 26 for a 'A trip deep into the Amazon Jungle'. Include details about the weather, what clothes to bring, the landscape, wildlife, food, accommodation, what to do and see, etc.
b) You are part of the organising committee for a conference on tourism. Think of two places you know well in your country. These have been selected as possible venues for the conference. Prepare a presentation comparing and contrasting the two venues in terms of accommodation, facilities and entertainment, transport, etc.
c) A local radio station has a show where people phone in. Today's topic is 'My favourite place in the world'. Take turns being the caller and the DJ. Ask for and give details about the place and why it is so important to you.

Lead-in

OPTIONAL WARMER
Write on the board: *Methods of transport*. Elicit as many different methods of transport as Ss can think of and write them on the board. Encourage them to include more unusual ones, e.g. *glider, rickshaw, camel*. Ask Ss: *Which of these methods of transport have you tried? When? Did you enjoy it? Would you do it again? Why/Why not?*

---

1 ▶ Ss discuss the questions in pairs.

Suggested answers
Main photo: the Antarctic
Top photo: the Grand Canyon, US
Middle photo: local markets, South America
Bottom photo: underwater, Great Barrier Reef

---

2 ▶ ⬤ 1.10 Read through the questions with the class. Play the recording. Ss listen and answer the questions.

Answers
1 She saw her friend's holiday photos.
2 To learn Spanish and get used to being away from home.
3 She found it hard because she experienced culture shock; everything was very different; lots of things went wrong and she was homesick.
4 She loved it.

---

3 ▶ Ask Ss to read through the sentences before they listen. Encourage them to guess what the missing words might be. Play the recording again. Ss listen and complete the expressions. Ss compare answers with a partner and guess what the meanings might be.

Answers
1 *to have itchy feet*: to want to go somewhere new or do something different
2 *went as an independent traveller*: to travel on your own, not as part of an organised group or tour
3 *wandering around*: to walk slowly around an area, usually without clear direction or purpose
4 *bitten by the travel bug*: to have a strong urge to travel to new places
5 *experienced real culture shock*: to feel confused or anxious when you visit a place that is very different from the one you are used to
6 *was really homesick*: to feel unhappy because you miss being with your friends and family at home

---

4 ▶ Ss discuss the questions in small groups.

EXTEND THE LEAD-IN
Write on the board: *independent traveller* and *package holiday tourist*. Ss list the advantages and disadvantages of these approaches to travel.

2.1 The jungle bug

In this lesson, Ss read an article about a journalist who spent 19 weeks making a documentary TV programme in the jungle. Ss describe unusual/interesting travel experiences they have had.

Reading

Dr Charlotte Uhlenbroek was born in England but grew up mostly in Ghana in Africa and Kathmandu in Nepal. After doing a PhD in Zoology, she went to Tanzania to study chimpanzees with the world-famous Jane Goodall. She has been part of several programmes for the BBC, including *Cousins* (about chimps), *Talking with Animals* (about animal communication), *Secret Gorillas of Mondika* (about gorillas) and *Safari School* (a reality TV programme about game rangers). In 2003, she made *Jungle*, in which she explored the rainforests of South-East Asia, the Amazon and Africa. For more information, go to: www.bbc.co.uk/nature/programmes/who/charlotte_uhlenbroek.shtml

OPTIONAL WARMER

Play a quick game of word association. Write the word *jungle* on the board. Ask Ss to work in pairs and to write down as many words/phrases associated with the jungle as they can. You could give them examples to get them going (e.g. *snakes*, *rainforest*, *sweat*). Group the words together as a mindmap.

1a ▶ Ss focus on the photos and title of the article. Elicit from Ss what they think the article will be about.

▶ Ss discuss the questions. Get feedback from the whole class and ask: *What would be the hardest thing for you in the jungle – insects or snakes?*

2 ▶ Tell Ss that the woman in the photo is Charlotte Uhlenbroek and that she spent over four months in the jungle. Ss read the article and check their answers to the questions in exercise 1.

Answers
1 the jungle (in the Amazon, the Congo or Borneo). Charlotte says the jungle is 'extraordinary' and 'like a city'.
2 things she found difficult: climbing high trees; sand fly bites; sweat bees on her face; being bitten by leeches
3 things she wanted to do: have long, hot showers; see her family; enjoy her favourite meal

3 ▶ Ss read the article again and decide if the statements are true, false or the information is not given. They compare their answers with a partner, giving their reasons.

Answers
1 F
2 F (she was worried the ropes would break)
3 F (the sand flies were the itchiest)
4 NG (it mentions 'tears' but we don't know if she cried)
5 NG (they might have done, but they also wanted to film the leeches)
6 T
7 NG (there wasn't much water, but we don't know if it was dirty or not)
8 NG (she enjoys eating with her family, but the article doesn't mention cooking)

4 ▶ Write the following headings on the board *positive things* and *unpleasant things*. Elicit from the whole class things about a jungle expedition (e.g. positive things: adventure, seeing rare plants and animals, sense of achievement; unpleasant things: insects, the heat).

▶ Ss then discuss the question in pairs, describing what they would like/not like about a jungle expedition. Encourage them to give reasons for their answers.

Grammar | Present Perfect Simple and Continuous

OPTIONAL LEAD-IN

Write the following sentences on the board: *She's made TV programmes about the jungle during her career* and *She made TV programmes about the jungle during her career*. Ask Ss to choose which of these sentences probably refers to a woman who is retired from her job. (the second sentence – the use of the Past Simple indicates that her career is finished now, so she won't be going to the jungle again as part of her job. The use of the Present Perfect Simple in the first sentence shows us that she may return to the jungle as part of her job, so she is not retired yet). Ask Ss to think about the sentences and the questions, but you may prefer to delay giving feedback until after Ss have read the Active grammar box in exercise 5.

Then, write the following gapped sentences on the board: *She's worked _____.* and *She's been working _____.* Ask Ss to choose which of these phrases best completes them: *in three different jungles* or *in the jungle for four months*, and to give reasons (*She's worked in three different jungles.* – the focus here is on the number of times she has done this. *She's been working in the jungle for four months.* – the focus here is on the activity itself; the use of the Present Continuous suggests that she is in fact still in the jungle). Ask Ss: *Which sentence suggests she is still in the jungle and has not finished her trip there yet?* (*She's been working in the jungle for four months.* – the continuous form suggests that the action is not finished yet).

Again, Ss think about the sentences and the questions. However, you may not want to give feedback yet but to return to the sentences after they have completed exercise 5.

5a ▶ Ss read the examples given to illustrate the first two rules in the Active grammar box and then choose the correct verb forms in order to complete rules A and B. Ss compare their answers with a partner.

Active grammar

A   Past Simple; Past Continuous
B   Present Perfect Simple; Present Perfect Continuous

---

b ▶ Ss read rules C and D in the Active grammar box and then complete the examples using the correct form of the verb *to live*. Ss compare their answers with a partner.

Active grammar

1   has lived
2   have been living

▶ Focus Ss' attention on the Reference section on page 33.

▶ Point out the difference between *for* (duration/length of time) and *since* (when an activity/state started).

▶ Highlight the difference in meaning between *already* (happened sooner than expected), *just* (happened a very short time ago) and *yet* (hasn't happened as soon as expected).

6 ▶ Ss choose the correct form of the verb. Ss compare their answers with a partner.

Answers

1   went
2   has bought
3   have visited
4   have you been doing
5   Have you seen (if it is still morning time) / Did you see (if it is afternoon or evening of the same day)
6   started
7   have been going
8   was waiting

---

7 ▶ Ss identify the two correct sentences and delete the extra word from the remaining sentences. Let them compare their answers with a partner.

Answers

1   going
2   been
3   correct
4   been
5   having
6   did
7   correct
8   lived

Pronunciation | connected speech (2)

8a ▶ Ss look at the sentences and mark the weak forms, vowel–consonant and consonant–consonant connections.

Answers

2   I've always wanted to travel as much as possible.
3   What time did you get to the airport?
4   I've been learning English for three years.
5   A: Has she been working here for long?
    B: Yes, she has.
6   I was walking in the mountains when I fell and broke my leg.

---

b ▶ ● 1.11 Play the recording. Ss listen and check their answers. Then they practise taking turns to say the sentences.

▶ Focus Ss' attention on the section on Connected speech in the Pronunciation Bank on page 161.

9 ▶ Ss ask and answer the questions from exercise 7. Encourage Ss to ask their partner for more details about the events. Get feedback from various Ss on the most interesting thing they found out about their partner.

OPTIONAL EXTENSION

Ask Ss to write one or two paragraphs about an experience of their own or their partner's experiences based on the questions in exercise 7.

Vocabulary | describing situations and feelings

10a ▶ Ss work in pairs. They find the adjectives in the article on page 22 and discuss what they think they mean. Encourage them not to use dictionaries for this exercise but to use the context around the words to help work out the meaning. Get feedback from the whole class.

Answers

1   *fascinating* = extremely interesting
2   *daunting* = making you feel concerned that you might not be able to do/achieve what you want
3   *challenging* = difficult in an interesting or enjoyable way
4   *petrifying* = extremely scary/frightening, especially so that you cannot move or think
5   *annoying* = making you feel slightly angry
6   *disgusting* = extremely unpleasant and making you feel sick
7   *inspiring* = giving people a feeling of excitement and a desire to do something great
8   *worrying* = making you feel concerned/unhappy because you keep thinking about a problem or something bad in the future

---

b ▶ Ss discuss the question in pairs.

▶ Ask Ss to compare: *He was fascinated.* and
He was fascinating. (The first sentence describes how he
felt about something – he really enjoyed the story/film/
book. The second sentence describes how he behaved – he
made other people feel this way.)

> **Answers**
> adjectives with -*ed* endings describe feelings
>   (*interested*; *amused*; *bored*)
> adjectives with -*ing* endings describe situations/states
>   (*interesting*; *amusing*; *boring*)

11a ▶ Ask Ss to read each dialogue and then complete
them with the most appropriate form of the adjectives from
exercise 10a. Then they compare with a partner.

> **Answers**
> 1 petrified
> 2 daunting
> 3 worried
> 4 inspiring
> 5 annoyed
> 6 disgusting
> 7 fascinating
> 8 challenging

b ▶ Ss work with a partner. They take turns to ask each
other the questions in the mini-dialogues from exercise
11a. Encourage them to use adjectives from exercise 10a
and exercise 10b. Get feedback from the whole class.

> **OPTIONAL VARIATION**
>
> Ss stand up and mingle with the whole class, asking
> different Ss one question from exercise 11a before moving
> on to another student.

12 ▶ Ask Ss: *What is the weather like today? What
about in Alaska/the Sahara desert?* Elicit stronger words
to describe how cold/hot it is (cold – freezing; hot –
scorching).

▶ Focus Ss' attention on the pairs of words from the box.
Ss read the Lifelong learning box and the example given
for *fall/plummet*. In pairs, they decide which of the four
categories might apply to the choice of word to use for the
other three pairs of words.

> **Answers**
> *interesting/fascinating*: *fascinating* is a stronger feeling than
>   *interesting*
> *difficult/daunting*: *daunting* is used to describe difficult jobs
>   and tasks which have to be done, describing a situation
>   where you feel you might not be able to finish/achieve
>   something; *difficult* is more general in meaning and can
>   apply to all situations which are not easy
> *get used to/become accustomed to*: *become accustomed to*
>   is a more formal expression than *get used to*

Speaking

13a ▶ 🔘 1.12 Ss read through the situations. Teach the
meaning of *sanctuary* (a safe place). Play the recording. Ss
listen and identify the situation which applies to Oliver.

> **Answer**
> 3

b ▶ Ss read through the questions. Play the recording
again. Ss listen and answer the questions. Let them
compare with a partner.

> **Answers**
> 1 in a village in Kenya
> 2 teaching mostly Maths in the village school on a
>   voluntary basis
> 3 He has mixed feelings about leaving
> 4 seeing his family
> 5 the children in the village

14a ▶ Ss work with a partner. They choose one of
the situations and use the questions in exercise 13b to
prepare what they might say about their experiences there.
Encourage them to be inventive and imaginative about
what happened or how they felt.

b ▶ Ss work with a new partner. They take turns to ask
each other about their experiences using the questions in
exercise 13b. Remind Ss of ways of sounding interested
which were covered in Lesson 1.1.

> **OPTIONAL EXTENSION**
>
> Write the following on the board: *most relaxing/
> most romantic/most exciting/most interesting/most
> challenging/most boring*. Ss work in small groups and
> take turns to tell each other about places they have been/
> would like to go to, which fit these categories (e.g. *Paris is
> the most romantic place I've been to*.), giving reasons for
> their choices. Get feedback from the whole class.

2.2 A magical kingdom

In this lesson, Ss read a short text about Bhutan and then listen to people asking for more information about the culture, the weather and what you can do there. Ss ask and answer questions about other interesting holidays.

Reading

Bhutan is a country of about 750,000 people in the eastern Himalayas, between India and China. It is a very private country where culture, tradition and nature are all flourishing. The Bhutanese people believe that all forms of life, human and non-human, are precious and sacred. People live in harmony with each other and with nature, creating a clean country with a huge variety of plant and animal life and virtually no discrimination at all. In order to safeguard this rich natural environment and peaceful culture, Bhutan has adopted a cautious and controlled approach to tourism. In 2010, the number of foreign tourists to Bhutan was limited to 30,000. However, it has been reported that the government is planning to dramatically raise the number of tourists permitted in Bhutan. So far, no independent travellers have been permitted in Bhutan; all tourists must go on a pre-planned, prepaid, guided, package tour.

OPTIONAL WARMER

Write these words on the board: *Africa, Colombia, Europe, Austria, Asia, Australasia, New Zealand, Tanzania, South America, China*. Ask Ss to work together and to divide them into two groups: *Continents* and *Countries*. Ask Ss: *Which country is in which continent?* Ask Ss to add two more countries to each continent group. Then get feedback from the whole class. (Tanzania is in Africa; Austria is in Europe; China is in Asia; New Zealand is in Australasia; Colombia is in South America.) Ss work in pairs to discuss these questions: *How many continents have you been to? If you could go anywhere in the world for two weeks, where would you go? Why?*

1a ▶ Ss focus on the photo and discuss the questions in pairs. Get feedback from the whole class but do not accept or reject any ideas at this stage.

b ▶ Ss read the website extract and check their ideas. Get feedback from the whole class.

2 ▶ Direct Ss to the three points about Bhutan which they have to summarise. Ask Ss to read the website extract again and make notes.

▶ Write the three points on the board. Get feedback from the whole class, adding Ss' ideas under the different headings on the board.

Possible answers

important beliefs of the Bhutanese people: all forms of life are sacred and precious; live in harmony with each other and with nature

nature in Bhutan: pristine environment; flourishing natural environment; a very wide range of flora and wild-life

tourism in Bhutan: a cautious and controlled approach to tourism; no independent travellers allowed; only organised trips; few tourists; worth the effort of getting visa and arranging the trip

Vocabulary | weather

OPTIONAL LEAD-IN

Ss speculate about the weather in Bhutan. Ask them to look again at the photo and compare their ideas. Remind them of Bhutan's location in the eastern Himalayas. Do not accept or reject any of their ideas at this stage but encourage Ss to give reasons for their ideas. You may want to tell Ss that they will come back to the topic of Bhutan (and its weather) later in the lesson.

3 ▶ 🔘 1.13 Focus Ss' attention on the two questions. Play the recording. Ss listen and decide which of the questions each of the three people is talking about. Get feedback from the whole class and ask Ss to say which words and phrases helped them decide.

Answers

1   question 1
2   question 2
3   question 1

4a ▶ Draw a table with six columns on the board. Give each column one of these headings: cold, sky, windy, rain, warm, weather in general. Using the audioscript on page 163, Ss categorise the underlined words. Do not explain the meanings at this stage.

Answers

cold: cool, chilly, sub-zero temperatures
sky: clear, bright, overcast
windy: breeze
rain: pours, showery, drizzle
warm/hot: mild, humid, scorching
weather in general: changeable

4b ▶ Ask Ss to write definitions for each word. Encourage them to use dictionaries.

> **Answers**
> *cool* (adj) = low in temperature but not cold, often in a way that feels pleasant
> *chilly* (adj) = cold enough to make you feel uncomfortable
> *sub-zero temperatures* (n) = below zero or freezing
> *clear* (adj) = no clouds
> *bright* (adj) = sunny and light
> *overcast* (adj) = when the sky is dark with clouds
> *breeze* (n) = gentle wind
> *pour* (v) = to rain very hard
> *showery* (adj) = when the weather has short periods of rain
> *drizzle* (v) = light rain
> *mild* (adj) = fairly warm
> *humid* (adj) = if the weather is humid, you feel uncomfortable because the air is wet and it is usually hot
> *scorching* (adj) = extremely hot
> *changeable* (adj) = when the weather is likely to change, or changes often

5 ▶ Get feedback from various Ss.

Pronunciation | connected speech: linking sounds

> **OPTIONAL LEAD-IN**
> Write the phonetic symbol /j/ on the board and demonstrate the sound. Elicit one or two words which contain this sound (e.g. *year, used, flying*). Now write the following sentence on the board: *He is very hot.* First, enunciate each word individually (not in connected speech). Ask Ss: *Do you hear a* /j/ *sound?* Next, say the sentence normally. Ask: *Do you hear the* /j/ *sound now? Where is it in the sentence?* (between *He* and *is*).
> Next, say: *Tom is very hot.* Ask: *Do you hear the* /j/ *sound now?* (no). Explain that we insert the /j/ sound between *He* and *is* in order to make a smooth link between the two vowel sounds. It is not necessary between *Tom* and *is* because there are not two vowel sounds together.

6a ▶ Focus Ss' attention on the three examples in exercise 6. Enunciate the individual words in each sentence. Remind Ss of the word ending for summer (the fact that the letter 'r' is in the spelling of the word might be confusing).

b ▶ 🌐 1.14 Ss listen and check their answers. Then they take turns to practise saying the sentences in pairs.

> **Answers**
> 1 /r/   2 /w/   3 /j/

Listening

> **OPTIONAL LEAD-IN**
> Ss write a list of everything they can remember about Bhutan and compare their list with a partner. Get feedback from the whole class.

7a ▶ Ss discuss the question in pairs. Get feedback from the whole class.

b ▶ 🌐 1.15 Explain to Ss that they are going to listen to an expert on Bhutan and some people who are considering a trip there. Ss read through the items in the box. Play the recording. Ss listen and number the items in the order they hear them. Let them compare with a partner.

> **Answers**
> 1 b   3 e   5 c
> 2 d   4 f   6 a

8 ▶ Ss read through the notes quickly. Play the recording again. Ss listen in order to complete the notes. Let them compare with a partner.

> **Answers**
> 1   it's cold and snow makes travelling difficult
> 2   it's very hot and often wet
> 3   plants
> 4   walking boots
> 5   sunglasses
> 6   food
> 7   camping equipment
> 8   chilli
> 9   offer thanks to their gods
> 10 communicate with the heavens

9 ▶ Ss discuss the questions in small groups. Get feedback from various Ss.

> **OPTIONAL EXTENSION**
> Ss prepare a leaflet similar to the one in exercise 8 about an area they know well. They can replace the section on 'FLAGS' with another heading more appropriate to the destination they have chosen. If Ss have chosen a variety of different locations for this activity, you might like to put their leaflets around the room. Ss can then mingle, looking at the different leaflets and deciding which place they would most like to visit.

Grammar | questions

OPTIONAL LEAD-IN

Ask Ss to think back to the listening in exercise 7b. In pairs, Ss try to remember the questions that the Bhutan expert was asked. Elicit answers from the whole class. Then, write the following two questions on the board: *When is the best time to go? Can you tell me when the best time to go is?*. Ask: *Which is more direct?* (the first question) and *Which sounds more polite?* (the second).

10 ▶ Ss work in pairs and complete the questions in the Active grammar box. Then direct Ss to the audioscript on page 163 to check their answers.

▶ Check that Ss understand the difference between object and subject questions. Ask Ss to identify the subject in the following two questions: *Who wants to go to Bhutan?* (who) *Who do you want to go to Bhutan with?* (you)

Active grammar

1 Would we need
2 Do they
3 do you recommend
4 is
5 goes
6 they are
7 the food is
8 if there are
9 whether we need

▶ Focus Ss' attention on the Reference section on page 33.

11a ▶ Before starting the exercise, ask: *Are these direct or indirect questions?* (direct questions). Ask Ss to correct the mistake in each question. They then compare with a partner.

Answers

1 Where are you living at the moment?
2 Has he ever been trekking before?
3 Who gave you those lovely flowers?
4 What time will you be here tomorrow?
5 Are you having a holiday soon?
6 When was this company started?

b ▶ Ss change the direct questions in exercise 11a into indirect questions using the prompts given. Encourage Ss to think about word order. They then compare with a partner.

Answers

1 where you are living at the moment
2 if/whether he has ever been trekking before
3 who gave you those lovely flowers
4 what time you will be here tomorrow
5 if/whether you will be having a holiday soon
6 when this company was started

Speaking

12 ▶ Ss look at the six extracts in the How to... box. Ask them to choose a heading for each pair of sentences. They then compare with a partner.

Answers

A Add extra information to illustrate further what you mean
B Use different words to make your description more precise
C Give details of personal experience

13a ▶ Put the Ss in groups (A and B) and tell them that they are going to find out about two other types of holiday: camel trips and bird-watching in exotic locations. Ss A work in pairs to prepare questions to ask about camel trips in Egypt. Ss B work in pairs to prepare questions to ask about bird-watching in Mexico. Focus Ss' attention on the list of prompts to help them think of questions to ask. Encourage them to prepare indirect as well as direct questions.

b ▶ Explain to Ss that they are now going to prepare answers to their partner's questions. Ss A read the text about bird-watching in Mexico on page 147; Ss B read the text about camel trips in Egypt on page 149. Encourage Ss to use the tips from the How to... box when preparing what they will say.

14a ▶ Put the Ss in pairs (A and B). They take turns to ask and answer questions about the holidays.

b ▶ Ss tell each other which holiday they would prefer when they have finished asking and answering questions about the two locations. They should give reasons for their preferences. Get feedback from the whole class. Ask: *Who would prefer a camel trip in Egypt/bird-watching in Mexico?*

OPTIONAL VARIATION

Organise a mingling activity. Explain to Ss that they are representatives for different travel agents. They imagine they are at an exhibition where they have to promote a particular holiday and choose two holiday destinations to include in their new brochure. Prepare a card containing one type of holiday for each student (e.g. hill-walking in Ireland; wine-tasting in California; a tai-chi course in China; spa treatments in Thailand; a wildlife safari in Kenya; tango lessons in Argentina, etc.). Give Ss a few minutes to prepare what they will say to promote their holiday. Then Ss mingle, asking and answering questions about each others' holiday. Ss then decide which holidays they will choose for their brochure.

2.3 On the move

In this lesson, Ss read an article about emigration, including facts about what kinds of people emigrate and their reasons. Ss practise comparing places and discuss issues relating to emigration and integrating into a new culture.

> Emigration is not a modern phenomenon. Over the last few centuries, many thousands of people from many different countries have gone to find a better life abroad. Emigration by British people to North America started as long ago as 1585 and the first successful settlement there was in Jamestown in 1607. Since then, British people have principally emigrated to places such as the US, Canada, Australia and New Zealand and more recently to Spain. Their reasons are many and varied: some were sent to work, some were sent as convicts (mainly to Australia), some were escaping hardship, famine and persecution and some were just seeking a better life. The trend to move abroad continues today.

OPTIONAL WARMER

Ss work in small groups. They discuss their personal experiences on the following topics: *longest time in one home*; *longest time away from home*; *longest flight/train journey*; *longest holiday*.

Vocabulary | verb phrases about moving/travelling

1 ▶ Ss match the underlined verb phrases with the correct definitions a–h. Encourage them to use dictionaries.

Answers
1 c
2 a
3 b
4 g
5 d
6 f
7 h
8 e

2 ▶ Ss complete the questions with the correct form of a phrase from exercise 1. Let them compare with a partner.

Answers
1 leave home
2 see you off
3 set off
4 abroad
5 emigrated
6 moved house
7 are you off
8 roamed around

3a ▶ Prepare the following table as a handout for Ss (or draw it on the board for the Ss to copy).

	You	What you think your partner will say	Your partner's answers
1			
2			
3			
4			
5			
6			
7			
8			

▶ Ss look again at the questions from exercise 2. They think about their own answers and also make a note in the table about what they think their partner's answers to the questions might be under the appropriate headings.

b ▶ Now Ss ask and answer the questions from exercise 2. They give their own answers and complete the table by noting their partner's actual answers to the questions.

Then, Ss compare answers and discuss whether their predictions were right or not.

Get feedback from the whole class. Ask Ss: *How many of their predictions did you get right? How well does your partner know you?*

Reading

OPTIONAL LEAD-IN

Ask Ss why people emigrate to another country. Get feedback from the whole class and write any suggestions on the board. Ss then sort these reasons into the following categories: *personal choice* and *external influences*.

4a ▶ Ss look at the photos on page 29 and discuss the questions as a whole class.

b ▶ Focus Ss' attention on the statements. In pairs, they discuss whether they think the statements are true or false. Get feedback from various Ss but do not accept or reject any of the ideas at this stage.

c ▶ Ss read the article quickly and check their answers. Encourage them to correct the ones that are false. Remind them to read only to check their answers and not to worry about other details at this stage. Let Ss compare with a partner.

Answers
1 false (towards the end of the 19th century)
2 false (over 400,000 British people emigrate every year)
3 true
4 false (after three years)

5 ▶ Ss read the summary sentences. They then read the article again in order to match each paragraph with the most appropriate summary a–g. Tell them that three of the summary sentences cannot be used. Ss check answers in pairs, then as a whole class.

Answers
1   d
2   g
3   a
4   c

6 ▶ Ss discuss the questions in small groups. Encourage Ss to ask lots of questions and to give as much detail as they can in their answers.

▶ Get feedback from the whole class. Ask each group to report back on one interesting aspect of their discussion.

OPTIONAL EXTENSION

You might like to do some further work on vocabulary from the article. Write the following words/phrases on the board: *prestigious*; *funding*; *recognition*; *appealing*; *fed up of*; *romanticise about*; *take for granted*. Ask Ss to find them in the article. Ask them the following questions for each word/phrase:
1   *What part of speech is it (noun, adjective or verb)?*
2   *What does it mean?*
3   *How do you pronounce it?*
4   *Can you make a sentence using it that is relevant to you?*
Encourage Ss to use the surrounding words to help them.

Grammar | modifying comparatives

OPTIONAL LEAD-IN

Prepare a handout with the following sentences, or write them on the board. Ask Ss to use the sentences to review the rules for forming comparative and superlative adjectives.
It is sunnier in Spain than in England.
It can be cheaper to buy a house in another country.
Home is the nicest place to be.
His new job was more interesting than his job at home.
Emigrating was the worst decision I've ever made.
She has a much better quality of life in her new home.
It is much hotter in this country.

The rules are as follows: add *-er* and *-est* to one-syllable adjectives (*cheaper/cheapest*); add *-r* and *-st* to one-syllable adjectives which end in *-e* (*nicer/nicest*); add *-er* and *-est* to two-syllable adjectives which end in *-y* (*sunnier/sunniest*); use *more* and *most* for other adjectives with two or more syllables (*more interesting/most interesting*); *good* and *bad* are irregular adjectives (*better/best*; *worse/worst*).
If Ss find this difficult to do, write the rules on another set of cards and ask pairs to match them to the example sentences.

7a ▶ Ask Ss to look at the Active grammar box. Ss ignore the blanks A, B, and C for now. Focus Ss' attention on the language in the box and find examples of this language in the article on page 29. Get feedback from the whole class and write one example of each phrase on the board.

Answers
1   the numbers are much bigger; people take work much more seriously here; I've got a far nicer life than before; the weather is sunnier and a lot warmer
2   By far the most popular reason for emigrating is …; Places with a more laid-back lifestyle were easily the most popular
3   opportunities were not nearly as good
4   they think life is going to be a little better; the cost of living is a bit lower than in Britain; salaries are slightly higher
5   living overseas is not quite as attractive as it first seems
6   they think it will be nearly as good as this all the time
7   getting work abroad can be just as difficult as it is at home

b ▶ Ss now match the headings with the correct section in the Active grammar box. Let them compare with a partner.

Active grammar
A   2
B   3
C   1

▶ Focus Ss' attention on the Reference section on page 33.

8 ▶ Ss read the example. They then complete the sentences. Ss compare their answers in pairs.

Answers
1   much more easily
2   quite as wet as
3   easily the most expensive
4   slightly less adventurous than
5   by far the best
6   just as good as

OPTIONAL EXTENSION

Ask Ss to make comparisons between the country/city they are in now and another country/city (e.g. *Coffee tastes much better in Italy. There are far more buses in London*). Write the following headings on the board as suggestions: *weather*; *food*; *nightlife*; *work*; *shopping*; *public transport*; *people*; *things to do*. If Ss are from a variety of different countries, they can compare where they are now to their own country. If Ss are from the same area, they should all compare where they are now to another city/country in the area. Encourage Ss to modify the comparatives using the language from the Active grammar box.

Speaking

9a ▶ 🔵 1.16 Explain to Ss that they are going to listen to two people talking about living abroad. Ss read through the statements before they listen. Play the recording.

> **Answers**
> 5 and 4

b ▶ Play the recording again. Ss listen and identify the phrases they hear in the conversation.

> **Answers**
> The more time you spend abroad, the easier you'll find
>   integrating ...
> The more you explore a country, the more you find out
>   about it ...

▶ Focus Ss' attention on the How to... box. Demonstrate the rising-falling intonation pattern typically used with this language. Ss practise saying these sentences in pairs.

▶ Use the following examples to illustrate how a noun, an adjective or a verb phrase can follow *the more* ... and *the less* ....

The more you prepare for the new culture, the more enjoyable it will be.

The more prepared you are for the new culture, the more enjoyment you will gain from the experience.

The more preparation you do about the new culture, the more you will enjoy the experience.

▶ Explain that the normal rules for single-syllable comparatives apply (e.g. *the bigger the problem*).

10 ▶ Put Ss in groups and ask them to look at the topics in exercise 9a again. They choose one to discuss. Ss take turns to exchange views on the statement they have chosen. If one group finishes quickly, they can move on to another statement to discuss.

> **OPTIONAL EXTENSION**
>
> Ask Ss to choose a destination where they might consider moving to (either in their own country or in another country). They then use the following questions to make notes about moving there.
> *Where is the place you might consider moving to?*
> *How similar to/different is it to where you live now?*
> *What are the positive things about moving there?*
> *What are the negative things about moving there?*
> Ss compare their notes with a partner, then write a short essay outlining the advantages and disadvantages of emigrating to this place.

2 Vocabulary | Expressions with *go*

1 ▶ Elicit expressions and phrasal verbs with *go* (e.g. *go for a walk*; *go on with your work*; *It's your go*; *red and blue go together*). Ss will know many expressions containing *go*. Focus Ss' attention on exercise 1. Ss check if they had thought of any of the underlined expressions. Ss then match the underlined expressions with *go* with the correct definitions a–j. Let them compare with a partner.

> **Answers**
> 1 e   6 b
> 2 j   7 i
> 3 a   8 g
> 4 d   9 f
> 5 h   10 c

2 ▶ Ask Ss to look at the example. They take turns to describe an expression from a–j in exercise 1. Their partner then guesses which expression is being described.

3 ▶ Ss choose the correct word. Encourage them not to look at exercise 1 while they are doing this.

> **Answers**
> 1 have   6 on
> 2 away   7 on
> 3 saying   8 down
> 4 on   9 for
> 5 make   10 great

4a ▶ Read through the three example sentences with the class. Tell Ss that they are going to describe an experience. Their story can be true or false but it must include one of the sentences and five of the expressions from exercise 1. Give Ss time to prepare their story, and encourage them to make brief notes.

b ▶ Ss take turns to tell each other their stories. The student listening must guess whether the experience being described is true or not. Get feedback from the whole class. Ask: *Who told a true story?*

> **OPTIONAL EXTENSION**
>
> Ss write about the experience they described in exercise 4b. Remind them to include the sentence and the five expressions they chose and to organise their story into paragraphs.

2 Communication

In this lesson, Ss talk about types of holidays they like. Then they do a quiz to find a good travelling companion who likes/dislikes the same things as they do on holiday.

OPTIONAL WARMER

Write the following words/phrases from the quiz on the board: *a package holiday, a travelling companion from hell, a penknife, a tent, an intrepid adventurer, arts and crafts, the locals, scuba diving, open-ended, mosquitoes, dread, a souvenir.* Ss work in pairs to explain the meanings of the words/phrases.

---

1 ▶ Ask Ss to look at the photos and discuss the questions in small groups. Get feedback from the whole class: conduct a quick survey to establish which photo appealed to Ss in the class.

2a ▶ Tell Ss that they are going to try to find someone in the class who would make a good travelling companion. Read through the introduction paragraph of the quiz with the whole class. Ss match the questions with the possible answers. Elicit the meaning of dread in question 5 (to feel anxious or worried about something that is going to happen or may happen). Ss compare their answers with a partner.

Answers

1	c	3	e	5	d
2	b	4	f	6	a

---

b ▶ Ss now think about their own answers to the questions. Point out that they can also add their own ideas to the different boxes.

c ▶ Ask Ss to mingle, conducting the quiz with as many Ss as possible in the time given. Try to ensure each student speaks to four or five other Ss. They will need to have paper to write notes on. Ss compare answers, explaining the order of importance they chose and any additional ideas. Ss should make notes for each student they speak to.

3a ▶ Ss read the descriptions on page 147. Explain who Stanley and Livingstone are (two explorers, famous for their expeditions into parts of Africa previously unknown to the British public). Elicit the meaning of *creature comforts* (a pleasant living environment).

b ▶ Ss discuss their ideas with a partner. They decide who would make a good travelling companion for each other. Get feedback from the whole class. Ask: *Who is a 'love your creature comforts' traveller? Who falls into the 'love a touch of adventure' category?*, etc.

OPTIONAL EXTENSION

Put Ss in small groups. Try to ensure that the groups are made up of Ss with different approaches to travelling. Ask Ss to plan a holiday together which will provide something for everyone in the group. They must decide on the following categories: *where*; *when*; *how long*; *activities*; and *accommodation*. Get feedback from the whole class.

---

2 Review and practice

1 ▶

Answers

1	've been writing	5	ever
2	saw	6	've lived
3	for	7	's been working
4	visited	8	just

2 ▶

Answers

1 He's already phoned me three times this morning.
2 We went to India for three weeks last summer.
3 I've just seen a really fantastic musical.
4 Have you heard the news yet?
5 I've been decorating the living room all day.
6 I've known my best friend since primary school.
7 Have you ever read the *Lord of the Rings* books?
8 How long have you been living abroad?

3 ▶

Answers

1 How long have you had your motorbike?
2 What's she going to study at university?
3 How tall are you?
4 Can you reach that box on the top shelf for me?

4 ▶

Answers

1 Can you tell me / Can I ask you what time this shop closes?
2 I'd like to know if I can buy theatre tickets here.
3 Would you tell me what time you'll finish your homework?
4 Can you tell me what the most interesting country you've ever visited is?

5 ▶

Answers

1	much	5	louder
2	worst	6	friendly
3	as	7	a
4	easily	8	as

6 ▶

Answers

1 ~~putting~~ → setting
2 ~~scratchy~~ → itchy
3 ~~make~~ → have
4 ~~of~~ → with
5 ~~speaking~~ → saying
6 ~~country~~ → culture
7 ~~to~~ → on
8 ~~away~~ → off

2 Writing bank

1 ▶ Ss read the blog and answer the questions.

Answers
1   in India; to do voluntary work with elephants
2   the family he is staying with and Alex, another volunteer on the project
3   his blog readers

2 ▶ Ss read the blog again and answer the questions.

Answers
1   T
2   T
3   F
4   T
5   F

3a ▶ Ss complete the How to... box with words from the blog.

Answers

Difficult		Nice	
1	challenging	1	friendly
2	exhausting	2	fun
3	demanding	3	rewarding
4	hard	4	amazing
5	tough	5	fascinating
6	tricky	6	fantastic

b ▶ Ss work alone to rewrite the blog.

Suggested answers
travelling on my own was daunting/hard
travelling on buses was exciting but daunting/
    challenging/hard
finding my way to the village was tricky/hard/tough
an amazing/fantastic/fascinating
everyone I've met has been so friendly
quite an exhausting/demanding/tough
seems like an amazing/fascinating/fantastic

c ▶ Ss compare answers.

4a/b ▶ Ss write a blog or diary entry.

3 Old or new

Overview

Lead-in	**Vocabulary:** Describing old things/ buildings, etc.
3.1	**Can do:** Tell a clear and engaging story **Grammar:** Past Perfect Simple and Continuous **Vocabulary:** Time expressions **Speaking and Pronunciation:** How to... engage your listener **Reading:** Film heroes
3.2	**Can do:** Talk about inventions and reach an agreement **Grammar:** Articles **Vocabulary:** Materials **Speaking and Pronunciation:** Connected speech: elision **How to...** reach an agreement **Listening:** China
3.3	**Can do:** Give a clear, well-prepared talk expressing personal opinions **Grammar:** Adjectives and adverbs **Vocabulary:** Verb phrases with *take* **Speaking and Pronunciation:** Speech units **Reading:** The good old days? **Listening:** A prepared talk
Vocabulary	Making nouns
Communication	**Can do:** Tell a short anecdote
Writing bank	Write a clear, engaging narrative **How to...** engage your reader
Extra resources	ActiveBook and ActiveTeach

CEFR Can do objectives
3.1 Tell a clear and engaging story
3.2 Talk about inventions and reach an agreement
3.3 Give a clear, well-prepared talk expressing personal opinions
Communication Tell a short anecdote
Writing bank Write a clear, engaging narrative

CEFR Portfolio ideas
a) You have been asked to participate in a TV programme entitled *The Greatest Heroes of the Past*. Choose a historical figure and prepare a short presentation explaining why you think this person is a hero using the language in the How to... box on page 38. The class can vote on the greatest hero.
b) Think of a new invention (e.g. a machine for choosing which programmes to watch on TV). Make an advert, promoting this new product. Include the name, key features and benefits of the product.
c) Look at the photos on page 43. Imagine you work for a research company and are conducting a survey on people's shopping habits. Write a questionnaire on when, where and how people like to shop.
d) Write a short essay about a hero, explaining why the person is a hero and why you chose him/her.

Lead-in

OPTIONAL WARMER
Introduce the topic of *old and new*. Ask Ss to think about a place they know well and discuss what they know about the following topics: *one of the oldest buildings*; and *one of the newest buildings*. Prompt Ss by asking questions (e.g. *Where is it? When was it built? What's it for? Who built it? Is it open to the public? What do you like about it?*).

1 ▶ Focus Ss' attention on the photos and ask them to discuss the questions in pairs. If Ss do not know the places, give the information below.

Suggested answers
Main photo: the Glass Pyramid serves as the entrance to the Louvre museum, Paris. Built entirely of glass and metal, it is surrounded by three smaller pyramids. It was designed by the architect I. M. Pei and has become a landmark symbol of Paris. It was built about 1989.
Top photo: the Temple of Kukulkan, Mexico, is often referred to as *El Castillo* (the castle) and is located in Yucatán state in the ancient Mayan city of Chichen Itza. It is a step pyramid built over an earlier pyramid. It was built about 1200.
Middle photo: Sydney Opera House in Sydney, Australia has become an Australian icon. In the late 1950s, a competition was held for its design. The winner was Danish architect, Jorn Utzon whose evocative design of a ship at full sail creates a dramatic view. It was built about 1973.
Bottom photo: the Taj Mahal in Agra, India is often seen as a symbol of eternal love. Shah Jahan fell in love with Arjumand Banu Begum at first sight, when he was in his teens. Five years later he married her. From that time onwards, she became his inseparable companion. After she died while giving birth to their 14th child, Shah Jahan constructed this beautiful monument in her memory. Both of them are entombed there. It was built about 1653.

2a ▶ Ask Ss: *What is the opposite of 'old'?* If Ss say *'young'*, ask: *What about a pair of jeans?* If Ss say *'new'*, ask: *What about a child?* Point out that different adjectives collocate with different things. Focus Ss' attention on the table. Ss find the three incorrect underlined adjectives.

Answers
1 ~~ancient~~ → antique
4 ~~elderly~~ → old
6 ~~antique~~ → ancient

b ▶ Ss work in pairs to ask and answer the questions. Get feedback from various Ss.

3.1 Heroes

In this lesson, Ss read a blog entry about the film *Avatar*. They discuss what it means to be a hero in today's world and choose a hero to describe to a partner.

Reading

> **OPTIONAL WARMER**
>
> Teach the meaning of these words: *blockbuster* (a book or film that is very popular, especially because of its exciting content) and *ingredients* (what you use to make a dish, e.g. flour, water, salt). Put Ss in pairs. Ask them to write a list of ingredients for a blockbuster film (e.g. a handsome hero, a villain, a beautiful girl in danger, a chase of some kind, a fight between the hero and the villain, etc.). Get feedback from the whole class by writing Ss' suggestions on the board.

1a ▶ Ss discuss the first two questions in pairs. Get feedback from various Ss and write up on the board the adjectives they use to describe their heroes.

b ▶ Ss look at the film poster and discuss the film. Get feedback on whether the majority of Ss have seen/liked this film.

2 ▶ Read through the list of topics with the class. Ss then read the blog entry quickly to find out which topics are mentioned. Give a two-minute time-limit for this. Explain to Ss that they will have an opportunity to read in more detail later.

> **Answers**
> 1, 2, 4, 6

3 ▶ Ss read again, this time more slowly. They decide whether the statements are true or false. Encourage them to correct the false statements. Let them compare with a partner.

> **Answers**
> 1 T
> 2 F (The old story of heroes and villains is brought into the 21st century by the vision and technological skill of the director)
> 3 F (He worked on the script in 1994 but not for several years)
> 4 T
> 5 F (*Avatar* was the first film to do this.)
> 6 F (We do not know that the writer is irritated by this)
> 7 T (Sully decides to do the right thing, even though this puts him in danger)

4 ▶ Ss discuss the questions in small groups. Get feedback from the whole class.

> **OPTIONAL EXTENSION**
>
> Write the following words on the board: *a hero*, *a celebrity*, *a champion*, *an idol*. Ask Ss to discuss what they think the difference is between these words and elicit adjectives to describe each one (*hero* = a person who is admired for doing something extremely brave; *a celebrity* = a living person who is famous and often in the news; *a champion* = a person who has won a competition, especially in sport; *an idol* = a person who is loved and admired by many people). Ss then write a definition for each term and give three examples of people in each category. Get feedback from the whole class.

Vocabulary | time expressions

5 ▶ Write the following sentences on the board.
As I was watching the film, people behind me were talking.
Then, I decided to leave the cinema.

Ask Ss if the underlined words refer to: a time before; a time after; a specific time; or actions at the same time. (*As* = actions at the same time; *Then* = a time after) Elicit that these are time expressions.

▶ Ss find the time expressions in the blog. They look at the surrounding words and decide what category each refers to.

> **Answers**
> a time before: *until I actually saw it*; *for the previous 12 years*
> a time after: *after that*; *he decided*; *since he saw the epic film*; *from that point on*
> a specific time: *in December 2009*; *at that time the technology wasn't available*
> actions at the same time: *throughout the whole film*; *during its release*; *while I was watching*

6 ▶ Ss choose the correct option in each sentence.

> **Answers**
> | | | | |
> |---|---|---|---|
> | 1 | During | 6 | After that |
> | 2 | From that point on | 7 | Since then |
> | 3 | For | 8 | until |
> | 4 | in | 9 | At that time |
> | 5 | throughout | 10 | While |

Grammar | Past Perfect Simple and Continuous

7a ▶ Focus Ss' attention on the four examples in the Active grammar box. Without looking back at the blog, ask them to complete the sentences with the correct form of one of the verbs. Don't ask for feedback at this point.

> **Active grammar**
>
> | | | | |
> |---|---|---|---|
> | 1 | had heard | 3 | had been looking |
> | 2 | had started | 4 | had been thinking |

b ▶ Ss check their answers in the blog.

c ▶ Ss now complete the rules in the Active grammar box.

> **Active grammar**
> A Past Perfect Simple
> B Past Perfect Continuous

d ▶ Ss discuss the questions about the four sentences in the Active grammar box with a partner. Deal with any difficulties during feedback.

> **Answers**
> Question 1
> 1 seeing the film *Avatar* (before I saw it)
> 2 2009
> 3 the release of the film *Avatar* (before it came out)
> 4 the point when Cameron began to work on the script for the film (before he started writing the script)
>
> Question 2
> sentence 4

> **OPTIONAL EXTENSION**
> Write the following sentences on the board.
> 1 When he <u>arrived</u> at the cinema, the film <u>started</u>.
> 2 When he <u>arrived</u> at the cinema, the film <u>was starting</u>.
> 3 When he <u>arrived</u> at the cinema, the film <u>had started</u>.
> Elicit the sequence of events in the three sentences
> (1 first he arrived and then the film started; 2 he arrived during the opening scene of the film; 3 first the film started, then he arrived).
> Write the following on the board: *When he arrived at the cinema …* Ask Ss to think of a suitable ending using the Past Perfect Continuous (e.g. … *the film had been running for 10 minutes/he was disappointed because he had been hoping the others would wait for him.*).
> Ask Ss to suggest other example sentences and finish them in suitable ways to illustrate the time reference.

▶ Focus Ss' attention on the Reference section on page 47.

8 ▶ Ss choose the best option in each sentence.

> **Answers**
> 1 had read
> 2 had been looking
> 3 had used
> 4 had been working
> 5 hadn't seen
> 6 had been watching
> 7 had been wondering
> 8 hadn't thought

9a ▶ Ss complete the sentences about themselves. Give one or two examples about yourself before they start to encourage them to write interesting information.

b ▶ Ss compare their sentences with a partner. They ask each other questions and give further detail about their answers. Get feedback from various students.

Speaking

> **OPTIONAL LEAD-IN**
> Write the following jobs on the board: *fire-fighter, nurse, heart surgeon, musician, teacher, TV presenter, soldier, actor, cleaner in a hospital, top model, mountaineer, ambulance driver, bus driver, taxi driver.* Put Ss in small groups. First, they decide which of these jobs has the highest/lowest earning potential. Then, they rank the jobs in order of who they think should earn the most money. Get feedback from the class and encourage Ss to give reasons.

10 ▶ Focus Ss' attention on the photos. They discuss the two questions in pairs. Get feedback from the class and elicit three or four examples of 'modern-day heroes'.

11a ▶ ● 1.17 Ask Ss to read the questions. Play the recording. Ss listen and answer the questions. Let them compare with a partner.

> **Answers**
> 1 someone from 'real life' – his father
> 2 Ss' own answers

b ▶ Direct Ss to the extracts in the How to... box and explain that these are ways to keep your listeners interested in what you are saying. Teach the phrase rhetorical question (a question used for stylistic purposes, no answer is expected). Play the recording again. Ss listen and put the extracts in the order in which they hear them. Ss compare answers with a partner.

> **Answers**
> 1 … many people have different definitions of what a hero is
> 2 … I would think of people who do things that we can learn from.
> 3 … he was born in a mud-brick house in the Kalahari.
> 4 … he told me that his father had once explained to him that …
> 5 Now, what did he do?

12a ▶ Elicit the names of famous heroes from the whole class. These can be heroes from the past, books or films, modern times, etc. Accept all suggestions. Ask Ss: *Can you think of heroes who are not famous?* Elicit one or two examples of this. Ss choose a hero that they will talk about. It does not have to be someone famous.

▶ Give Ss time to prepare what they will say. Explain that they should think about why this person is a hero, what heroic deeds they have been involved in; what they know about the background and life of this person and why they chose this person as their hero. Alternatively, ask Ss to prepare for homework so that they can research particular details about their chosen hero before continuing with exercise 12b in the next lesson.

b ▶ Ss tell their partner about the hero they have chosen. Encourage Ss to ask questions as they listen.

3.2 Land of invention

In this lesson, Ss listen to a radio programme about China, including facts about life in both ancient and modern times and with a particular focus on Chinese inventions. Ss describe various objects and inventions and the materials they are made of. They discuss the most important inventions of all time.

Listening

China is a huge country with an incredibly long and rich history. One of the things ancient China is famous for is being a 'land of invention', credited with inventing many important things, from paper and umbrellas to gunpowder. Modern China is a fascinating place too, with 1.3 billion people – a staggering one fifth of the world's population. Agriculture has always been important but now there are many booming industries too, including the production of such things as toys, clothes, cars and electronic goods.

OPTIONAL WARMER

Introduce the topic of China by asking Ss to answer the following questions with a partner. Encourage them to guess even if they don't know.
Which 14 countries share a land border with China?
(Mongolia, Russia, North Korea, Vietnam, Laos, Myanmar, Bhutan, Nepal, India, Pakistan, Afghanistan, Tajikistan, Kyrgyzstan, Kazakhstan)
What's the population of China? (1.3 billion)
What percentage of the world's population lives in China? (20%)
What's the capital of China? (Beijing)
What are the official languages? (Mandarin and Cantonese – there are also many dialects)
What famous Chinese people do you know?

1a ▶ Write the following headings on the board: *buildings, people, food, cities, transport*. Ss work in pairs and discuss the questions in relation to modern-day and ancient China. Get feedback from the whole class, writing Ss' ideas on the board. Elicit a list of things Ss think were invented in China. Accept all suggestions at this stage and write them on the board.

b ▶ ⬤ 1.18 Play the recording. Ss listen to see if the speakers mention any of the things they talked about. Get feedback from the whole class, writing Ss' ideas on the board.

2 ▶ Ss read through the statements. Then, play the recording again. Ss check answers with a partner, giving their reasons.

Answers
1 T
2 NG (it is now the third-biggest economy in the world but how important it was before is not mentioned)
3 F (around 105 AD)
4 T
5 NG (loads could be carried by one person but who invented it is not mentioned)
6 T
7 T
8 F (15% of the economy is based on agriculture)
9 NG (these things are produced but we don't know if they are exported)
10 T
11 NG (it is growing but we don't know by how much)
12 T

3 ▶ Ss discuss the questions in pairs. Get feedback from various Ss.

4 ▶ Ask Ss: *Did you find the listening easy or difficult? Which questions were the most difficult/easiest to answer?* Direct Ss to the listening strategies in the Lifelong learning box. Ss read through these, then discuss the questions in pairs.

Grammar | articles

OPTIONAL LEAD-IN

Write these groups of sentences on the board.
A 1 *China is huge country.*
   2 *China is a huge country.*
   3 *China is the huge country.*
B 1 *Iron is an important export.*
   2 *An iron is an important export.*
   3 *The iron is an important export.*
Ask: *Which sentence in each group is correct?* (Group A: 2; Group B: 1). Don't ask for feedback at this stage – you might like to return to these sentences later in the lesson. Elicit what the grammar focus of this lesson will be (articles). Check that Ss know specific terms (*the* = definite article; *a/an* = indefinite article; no article = zero article).

5 ▶ Ss look at the list of nouns in the box and then use them to complete the Active grammar box.

Active grammar

B the Chinese
C the story I told you before
D the simplest invention
E the moon
F the Himalayas
G the Republic of China
H the Yangtze River
I an inventor
J a machine for making cast iron
K China
L cars
M rice
N wealth

▶ Focus Ss' attention on the Reference section on page 47.

6 ▶ Ss complete the sentences using the, *a/an* or the zero article. Ss compare their with a partner.

Answers

1	The/–	5	a/the
2	The/the	6	a/a/The
3	–/an/the	7	The/–
4	The/the	8	a/–

Pronunciation | connected speech: elision

7a ▶ Write the following on the board: *fish and chips* and *comfortable*. Ask Ss: *How do you say these?* Ss should be familiar with how we pronounce /fɪʃəntʃɪps/ and /kəmftəbl/. Explain what we mean by elision (when vowel sounds, consonant sounds or whole syllables are swallowed into the surrounding sounds so that they are omitted, particularly in connected speech).

▶ 🔵 1.19 Focus Ss' attention on the three sentences. Play the recording. Ss listen and identify the sounds which have almost or completely disappeared when these sentences are spoken in connected speech.

Answers

the words *a, the, I, for, of, that, and* are understressed and almost disappear

---

b ▶ Ss listen again and repeat the sentences.

8 ▶ Write the following topics on the board: *cuisines of the world*; *wild animals*; *countries to visit*. Ss read the three statements in exercise 7a again and then think about their own preferences in relation to the three headings. Ss then compare their ideas with a partner. Get feedback from various Ss.

Vocabulary | materials

9a ▶ Focus Ss' attention on the photos. In pairs, they describe the objects using the words from the box. Get feedback from the whole class, checking Ss understand all the words.

Answers

A metal, plastic, rubber
B metal, leather, rubber, plastic, glass
C paper
D metal, plastic, rubber
E gunpowder; plastic
F metal, rubber, wood
G glass, metal

---

b ▶ Ss decide whether the words from the box are types of fabric or metal. They check answers in pairs, then as a whole class.

Answers

fabric: cotton, denim, lycra, silk, wool
metal: bronze, gold, iron, silver

---

10 ▶ Ask Ss to think of five things they own. In pairs, they describe each thing to each other using the words from exercise 9.

OPTIONAL VARIATION

Put Ss in pairs. They take turns to ask each other about five of their possessions (e.g. *bag, watch, jacket, hat, pen, iPod*). Ss have one minute to ask questions about each object without their partner saying what the object is. Then they guess what it is. You might want to give an example first. Use one student and ask about one of his/her possessions: *How long have you had it? Was it a present? Who gave it to you? Why? Where did you buy it? What do you like about it? What is it made of?*
Get feedback from various Ss.

---

11 ▶ Ss match the underlined adjectives with the correct definitions. Ss check answers in pairs, then as a whole class.

Answers

1	a	5	f
2	d	6	h
3	g	7	b
4	c	8	e

---

12 ▶ Elicit important inventions and write them on the board (e.g. the computer, the TV, the airplane, the elastic band, money, the washing machine, etc.) Accept all suggestions. Ss think of an invention. In pairs, they take turns to guess each other's invention by asking yes/no questions. Encourage them to use the materials and adjectives in the previous exercises in their questions and to ask about where it was first invented (e.g. *Is it made of leather? Is it stretchy? Was it invented in Japan?*).

Speaking

13a ▶ 🔊 1.20 Play the recording. Ss listen and answer the questions. Then they compare with a partner.

> **Answers**
> 1 which is the most important invention
> 2 paper

> **OPTIONAL EXTENSION**
>
> Ask Ss: *Apart from paper, which other inventions do they discuss?* (gunpowder; the computer; the lightbulb; the wheel; the telephone). Write these on the board. Play the recording again. Ss make notes about what the two people say about each invention. (Gunpowder: a negative influence but very significant because it changed the power relations in global communities. Didn't have equal importance in every country; not influential from a positive perspective. Paper: changed how we communicate and document things; without paper, we wouldn't have other things, like computers; we still use paper. Computers: changed our lives fundamentally. The lightbulb, the wheel, paper: have become normalised, all invented a long time ago so we don't notice them. The computer, the telephone: we notice them.)

b ▶ Focus Ss' attention on on the How to... box. Play the recording again. Ss identify the phrases they hear. Ss compare answers in pairs, then in the audioscript on page 164. Get feedback, demonstrating typical intonation and stress patterns for this language. Remind Ss how to use intonation in order to sound tentative/confident in their opinions (Lesson 1.2).

> **Answers**
> If you take into account what a negative influence it's had ...
> But then again, so is the lightbulb.
> Communication, yes as you say, ...
> Birthday cards, yeah you're right.
> OK, paper it is.

14a ▶ Make a list of all the inventions which have been mentioned in the lesson and write them on the board (*gunpowder, the umbrella, the wheelbarrow, paper,* fireworks, *machine for making cast iron, the computer, the lightlbulb, the telephone, the wheel,* etc.). Ss choose one invention (it doesn't have to be on the list) which they consider to be the most important invention of all time. Give Ss time to prepare notes about their reasons for choosing this invention.

b ▶ Put Ss in small groups. They each put forward the invention they chose and explain their reasons. Ss must discuss the different inventions and try to agree on which one is most important. Remind them to use the language from the How to... box. Get feedback from each group.

> **OPTIONAL EXTENSION**
>
> Put Ss in groups. Ask them to try to come up with an idea for a new invention (e.g. a machine for peeling oranges; a machine for turning pages of your book while you are lying on a beach). Elicit one or two ideas first, then Ss prepare to give a presentation about their invention. They must include the following points: the name; the key features (e.g. what it is made of, how it works, what it is used for, etc.); and the benefits of the invention. Ss present their ideas to the whole class. Then they vote for the best invention.

3.3 The good old days?

In this lesson, Ss read several blog entries on the topic of globalisation and the so-called 'good old days' of the past. Ss give their own views about the positive and negative effects of these changes on our lives. They also prepare and deliver a short oral presentation.

Over the last few decades, the phenomenon of globalisation has changed the world. Many people now complain that 'every high street is the same' with the same shops appearing in high streets in London, Tokyo, Moscow and Buenos Aires. Some people fear that the individual character and culture of different countries is being eroded and that the world is becoming too uniform. Others view it differently, however, seeing globalisation as a positive thing, with increased choice and diversity available to a much larger number of people.

Reading

OPTIONAL WARMER

Focus Ss' attention on the photos. Ask: *Which photo depicts modern shops? How do you know?* Put Ss in pairs. They discuss how shopping has changed in the past 40 years. Write the following headings on the board to help focus their discussion: *types of shops*; *the Internet*; *opening hours*; *locations*; *money*; *price*.

1a ▶ Ss discuss the question in pairs. Get feedback from the whole class.

b ▶ Ss read the blog and discuss the questions.

2a ▶ Tell Ss that they are going to read two different responses to Oliver's blog. Put Ss in pairs (A and B). Ask Ss A to read the text on **page 148** and answer the questions; B to read the text on **page 149** and answer the questions. Ss then compare their answers with a partner who read the same text. Go round the class monitoring. Don't ask for feedback at this point.

b ▶ Ss regroup into pairs so that Ss A work with Ss B. Ss tell each other about what they read.

Answers

Student A's text
1. mostly disagrees
2. 'the tyranny of geography' – when people had restricted choice according to where they lived
3. There is a huge amount of choice in his high street.
4. to show that there are shops from many different countries in one high street
5. He says we can now choose much more how we want to be and what we want to do (not defined by our nationality/place we live)

Student B's text
1. mostly disagrees
2. She says that different variations of food are being created and that is good.
3. no
4. a type of English which is used for people to communicate with other non-native speakers
5. A single language is when everyone speaks one language (e.g. English) and a common language is when people speak their own language but can also speak English, so can communicate with each other.

3 ▶ Explain that people often refer to this period as the good old days. Ask: *Why do you think is this?* Ss discuss the three questions, giving their reasons.

OPTIONAL EXTENSION

Ask Ss to think about their grandparents' generation. Ask: *Would you like to have lived in that period? Why/Why not?* Put Ss in small groups. They make a list of five advantages and five disadvantages of living in the 'good old days' when their grandparents were young.

Grammar | adjectives and adverbs

OPTIONAL LEAD-IN

Write the following sentences on the board and ask Ss what the difference is between the underlined words and why.
I have strong opinions about this.
I disagree strongly with what he's saying.
(*strong* = an adjective, describing the noun 'opinions'; *strongly* = an adverb describing the verb 'disagree')
Then, write the following words on the board: *differently*, *good*, *ugly*, *well*, *different*, *never*, *hard*.
Ask Ss to put them into two groups: **adjectives** and **adverbs** (*differently*: adv.; *good*: adj.; *ugly*: adj.; *well*: adv.; *different*: adj.; *never*: adv.; *hard*: adj./adv.).

4a ▶ Ss read the example and then choose the correct options in the Active grammar box.

Active grammar

A nouns   B before

b ▶ Read through rule C with the whole class. Remind Ss that we can use adverbial phrases as well as adverbs (e.g. *in the corner, last year*).

▶ Explain that there are different positions for adverbs (and adverbial phrases) in a sentence. Ss look at the sentences (1–10). They match the adverbs and adverbial phrases with the categories given in the Active grammar box. There are 10 sentences and 9 categories.

> **Active grammar**
>
> | | |
> |---|---|
> | 1 b) | 6 g) |
> | 2 c) | 7 e) |
> | 3 d) | 8 h) |
> | 4 f) | 9 a) |
> | 5 c) | 10 i) |

▶ Remind Ss that when an adverb goes before the main verb in the middle of a sentence, this means after an auxiliary verb (e.g. *I have frequently shopped on Sunday; I frequently shop on Sundays*).

▶ Explain that the *-ly* suffix in adverbs is generally unstressed. Model the sentence stress in sentences 2, 4, and 7 to demonstrate how we usually stress adverbs of certainty, comment and manner in sentences in order to give effect. Ss practise saying these sentences.

▶ Focus Ss' attention on the Reference section on page 47.

5 ▶ Ss decide if the underlined words are adjectives or adverbs. Refer them back to rules A and C in the Active grammar box if necessary. Ss compare their answers with a partner.

> **Answers**
> 1 *lovely* = adjective; *lonely* = adjective
> 2 *lively* = adjective; *silly* = adjective
> 3 *fine* = adjective/adverb
> 4 *deadly* = adjective
> 5 *high* = adverb; *well* = adverb
> 6 *(got up) early* = adverb; *early* (train) = adjective
> 7 *friendly* = adjective; *ugly* = adjective

6 ▶ Ss write the missing adverb or adverbial phrase in the correct place. Remind them that sometimes two different places may be possible and refer them back to rule D in the Active grammar box. Get feedback from the whole class.

> **Answers**
> 1 I definitely want to try the local food when I'm in Thailand.
> 2 I accidentally spilt my coffee all over my new jacket. / I spilt my coffee all over my new jacket accidentally.
> 3 I work in a really modern building on the 19th floor.
> 4 I went on a tour of the six capital cities in Europe last month. / Last month I went on a tour of the six capital cities in Europe.
> 5 I'm quite shy about practising my English in shops. However, I'm going to try.
> 6 My grandmother has never been on a plane in her whole life.
> 7 The new building is expertly designed to be both attractive and practical.
> 8 I learned Spanish quickly before I went travelling to Spain.

7a/b ▶ Ss choose the correct option in order to complete the pairs of sentences. Get feedback from the whole class, then ask SS to practise asking and answering the questions with a partner.

> **Answers**
> 1 a completely
> b complete
> 2 a late
> b lately
> 3 a definitely
> b definite

Vocabulary | verb phrases with *take*

8 ▶ Put Ss in pairs. They read through the sentences and try to work out the meaning of the underlined verb phrases. Ask Ss which words and phrases in the sentence helped them deduce the meaning.

> **Answers**
> 1 taking control or responsibility for something
> 2 to be very surprised because something is very beautiful or exciting
> 3 to cope calmly with things without making a fuss
> 4 to believe that something is true without thinking about it or making sure
> 5 like something or someone
> 6 to participate in something, usually a group game or activity
> 7 to understand what you read, hear or see
> 8 to start to increase/improve/become more popular

9 ▶ Ss complete the sentences with the correct form of the phrases in exercise 8. Ss compare answers with a partner.

> **Answers**
> 1 take it for granted
> 2 took part in
> 3 taken over
> 4 took my breath away
> 5 took off
> 6 took (it) in her stride
> 7 take in
> 8 take to

10a ▶ Ss choose the correct option for each question. Ss compare answers with a partner.

> **Answers**
> 1 taking over
> 2 take it in your stride
> 3 taken off
> 4 take in
> 5 took to

10b ▶ Ss discuss the questions in pairs. Get feedback from various Ss.

Pronunciation | speech units

11 ▶ Write the following sentence on the board and say it: *Ladies and gentlemen let me introduce you to Mary Smith who is going to talk to you today about shopping.* Ask: *What kind of language is this? How do you know?* (a speech/talk) Elicit how and why the way that we speak during a speech is different to normal conversation (we are slower, clearer, pause more to make it easier for the audience to follow what we're saying and to highlight key information). Say the sentence again naturally. Ask: *How many pauses are there?* (three, after *gentlemen, Smith* and *today*).

▶ 🔵 1.21 Focus Ss' attention on the topics from the box. Play the recording. Ask Ss to close their books and to listen and identify the topics mentioned in the talk.

> **Answers**
> small, local shops; large supermarkets; good service; fresh food

12a ▶ Focus Ss' attention on the audioscript on page 44. Explain the // symbol, which indicates where the speaker paused. Play the recording again. Ss listen and mark the places where they hear a distinct pause. Ss compare answers, then listen again to check answers.

> **Suggested answers**
> I really like the town where I live // and I think one of the main reasons is that,// in terms of shopping,// there is a lot of variety.// The main street has many different types of shops.// Some of them are run by local people// and they have been there for a long time.// I like going into these shops// because you get very good service.// They are always very helpful and friendly.// Also, if you're buying food,// like vegetables, meat or fish, for example,// the food is always fresher, tastier and cheaper than in the large supermarkets.// There is one large supermarket in the main street// which is very convenient for lots of the basic things you need to buy.// I'd say that I'm very lucky // because there is such a good variety of shops in walking distance of where I live. // I have a mixture of local shops and large supermarkets // and therefore I have the best of both worlds.

b ▶ Ss look at the pauses they have marked. Ask: *Is there any pattern to these pauses*? Elicit/explain that the pauses often occur in the following places: at the end of sentences; between clauses linked by words like *and, therefore, because, also*; and before and after a phrase which gives additional information.

▶ Explain that we also sometimes pause for effect, to highlight key information for the listener. Compare: *The food is fresher, tastier and cheaper.* and *The food is fresher,// tastier // and cheaper.*

▶ Focus Ss' on the pronunciation bank on Speech units on page 161.

Speaking

13a ▶ Tell Ss that they are going to give a short presentation. They choose one of the topics given. Ss prepare notes about what they will say for their presentation.

b ▶ Ss practise giving their presentation with a partner. Encourage Ss to give each other feedback. They should focus on the following points: clear organisation of ideas; presentation style – speaking in a slow, clear way, making frequent pauses; maintaining good eye contact. Give Ss some time to make any necessary changes or improvements to their presentations.

▶ Ask one or two Ss to volunteer to give their presentations to the whole class. Do not spend too long on this.

> **OPTIONAL EXTENSION**
> Ss work in groups of three, so that each student is working with others who have prepared presentations on different topics. Ss give their finalised presentation to the others in their group. Get feedback from the whole class. Ask: *Was it easier/more difficult doing it a second time?*

3 Vocabulary | Making nouns

OPTIONAL WARMER

Write the following words on the board: *neighbourhood, happiness, journalist*. Ask Ss what kind of words they are and how they know (nouns/they have noun endings). In pairs, Ss write a list of as many noun endings as they can, and an example for each. Get feedback from the whole class.

Then, put Ss into small groups and give a name to each (team 1, team 2, team 3, etc.). Team 1 starts. They provide a noun ending (e.g. *-ion, -ist, -ity*). Each member of team 2 must think of a noun with that ending. Team 2 then thinks of a new noun ending and each member of team 3 must think of a noun with that ending. Each team gets one point for each correct noun they think of. The team with the most points at the end wins. You may find it more useful to wait until after exercise 2 to do the second part of this activity.

1a ▶ If you did the optional warmer, ask Ss to look through the rules and see which ones they thought of and which they did not.

▶ Put Ss in pairs. They read the rules and examples given and think of more examples for each category. Get feedback from the whole class.

b ▶ Ss take turns to test each other on correct noun endings.

2 ▶ Ss complete the sentences with the correct noun form of the word in brackets. Encourage Ss to use dictionaries if necessary. Ss compare answers with a partner.

Answers
1 employer
2 childhood
3 happiness
4 supervisor
5 flexibility
6 communication
7 violinist
8 reduction
9 development
10 excitement

3 ▶ Ss work with a partner to find the incorrect noun in the list and correct it.

Answers
1 production
2 enjoyment
3 employment
4 typist
5 modernity
6 development

4a ▶ Put Ss in small groups. Elicit one or two examples of an opening sentence in a story (e.g. *Mary looked with pleasure at her new invention ...; The writer stared out of the window, lost in thought ...; It was with an air of inevitability that Peter opened the door and walked into the office ...*). Each student writes the opening sentence of a story on a page. The sentence must contain one of the nouns from exercise 1a. Ss then pass on their page to another student in the group. The next student continues the story by writing one more sentence, again containing a noun from exercise 1a. They pass their page on to the next

student who continues the story in the same way. Continue in this way until everyone has written approximately three sentences for each story. Tell Ss when there is only one minute left, so that each student can write a final sentence for the story on the page they have in front of them.

b ▶ Each student should have a different story in front of them. They prepare to read the story aloud to the others in their group. Give Ss time to decide on how they will read the story and where they will pause while reading aloud. Remind Ss of the exercises which they did on speech units in Lesson 3.3.

c ▶ Ss read their stories aloud to the others in the group. Ss decide which story was the best in their group.

OPTIONAL EXTENSION

Ss choose one of the stories from their group. They prepare a good draft of this story, proofing and re-drafting until they are happy with the language and style of the story. Collect the stories and either photocopy these to make a collection of class stories or display them around the room for Ss to read at their leisure over the next few lessons.

3 Communication

In this lesson, Ss talk about and listen to someone talking about school subjects. Ss prepare and tell each other short anecdotes about their school days.

OPTIONAL WARMER

Ss compare the education system in England with that in their own country. Ask Ss: *At what age do children start leave/school/take public exams?* (children in England have to go to school aged 5–16, but some stay until 18. At 16, they take an average of eight public exams known as 'GCSEs' (General Certificate in Secondary Education), in a variety of subjects. Students can stay at school or go to a Sixth-Form College to do an average of three 'A-levels' (advanced-level exams). They need A-levels in order to go to university.

1 ▶ Ss discuss the questions in pairs. Get feedback from the whole class.

2a ▶ ◉ 1.22 Ss read through the questions with the class. Play the recording. Ss listen and answer the questions. Ss compare answers with a partner.

Answers
1 No, he has good memories of school but his life has been much more interesting and rewarding since he left school.
2 Learning a language – it opens opportunities for work and travel.
3 He has a career in marketing; he finds it interesting and enjoyable (but he is not passionate about it and regrets that he did not pursue his passion for drama while he was at school).
4 If you have a passion for something, you should follow it in order to lead a more fulfilling and happier life.

b ▶ Read through the half sentences with the class, checking they understand the phrases. Ensure Ss understand the structure of *I wish I had (I'd)...* (used to express past regrets). Ss reflect on their schooldays and complete the sentences to make them true about themselves.

c ▶ Ss compare their answers with a partner. Encourage them to ask questions and give more detailed explanations in their answers.

3a ▶ Ss look again at the questions in exercise 1. They choose one to focus on. Explain that they are going to write a short anecdote about their school days. Tell them that it can be something funny or sad, something they regret or enjoyed, something that had a big influence on their lives, etc. Give Ss time to think of an anecdote and write about it.

b ▶ Ss practise how they will read their anecdote aloud to the others. Remind them of the focus on speech units and pausing from Lesson 3.3.

4 ▶ Ss take turns to tell each other their anecdotes in small groups. Get feedback from various Ss. Ask: *Who had a positive/sad/funny memory?*

3 Review and practice

1 ▶

Answers
1 We had **been** walking for twenty minutes when it started to rain.
2 Today I bought that leather bag that I **had** seen online.
3 When I got to the party, Jack **had** already gone home.
4 ✓
5 While Cristina **was** sitting on the bus, someone stole her gold watch.
6 ✓
7 Someone finally answered the phone after I'd **been** waiting for ten minutes.
8 As soon as I saw her at the party, I realised I **had** met her before.

2 ▶

Answers
1	had been working	5	had wrapped up
2	had you been doing	6	Had you been learning
3	had stolen	7	had been running
4	had been thinking	8	Had you read

3 ▶

Answers
1 She lives in Alexandra Road. It's not far from **the** antiques shop.
2 People say that **the** British are reserved.
3 I'm not sure but I think I'd like to be **an** architect when I grow up.
4 Don't forget your sun cream. The sun is very strong today.
5 ✓
6 We stayed at a very nice hotel in Barcelona.
7 That was one of the best books I've read for ages.
8 Shall we sit in the garden for a while?

4 ▶

Answers
1	a badly b bad	3 a perfect b perfectly
2	a careful b carefully	4 a well b good

5 ▶

Answers
1	enormous	3	quickly	5	surprisingly
2	incredibly	4	completely	6	certain

6 ▶

Answers
1 ~~stretchy~~ → itchy
2 ~~head~~ → breath
3 ~~fashion~~ → trendy / fashionable
4 ~~of~~ → in
5 ~~while~~ → during
6 ~~time~~ → hand
7 ~~on~~ → in
8 ~~While~~ → Since

3 Writing bank

1 ▶

> **Answers**
> 1 an entry for a short story competition in an
>   International English magazine
> 2 c
> 3 b

2 ▶

> **Answers**
> 1 to going back
> 2 moved since/hadn't been
> 3 slowly/rough; took my breath away
> 4 I felt disappointed/I was expecting

3 ▶

> **Answers**
> 1 the shock of getting off the bus and seeing the huge
>   shopping centre in the village; images of the peaceful
>   village where he grew up
> 2 mainly past tenses: Past Simple to narrate the story
>   and describe feelings (e.g. *I went*; *I walked*; *I saw*; *I felt
>   disappointed*; *I felt worried*; *It mattered to me*); Past
>   Perfect Simple to describe things that had happened
>   before he got off the bus (*had lived there*; *I had
>   remembered*; *had changed*; *had moved with the times*,
>   etc.); Past Perfect Continuous to describe feelings that
>   continued up to the point of getting off the bus (*had
>   been looking forward to*); Past Continuous to set the
>   scene (*was shining*; *was expecting*)
> 3 time expressions: *for a long time*; *15 years ago*; *since
>   then*; *in the days before I went*; *for years before that*; *on
>   the day I went*; *as I got nearer*; *immediately*; *from that
>   point on*
>   linkers: *as*; *also*; *however*; *but*; *so*; *in fact* (to keep the
>   story moving along; to create immediacy; to identify
>   which period of time (before or after arriving in the
>   village) to link sentences and ideas in the text)
> 4 adjectives: *excited, special, worried, peaceful,
>   traditional, rough, large, modern, trendy, new, beautiful,
>   busy, thriving*
>   adverbs/adverbial phrases: *beyond recognition, at the
>   edge of the village, slowly, right in front of my eyes,
>   immediately, under the trees in the main square*
>   verb phrases: *looking forward to, took my breath away,
>   expecting the worst, moved with the times*
> 5 paragraph 1: to introduce the idea of going back to the
>   village where the writer had grown up and how the
>   writer felt about this
>   paragraph 2: immediate reactions on getting off the bus
>   in the village
>   paragraph 3: further feelings as the writer walks through
>   the village

4a ▶ Ss choose one of the ideas from exercise 1 and plan their writing.

b ▶ Ss write short stories. Ss can swap and read each other's stories when they have finished.

4 Work

Overview

Lead-in	**Vocabulary:** Qualities needed for work
4.1	**Can do:** Talk about certain and uncertain future plans
	Grammar: Futures (1)
	Vocabulary: Work
	Speaking and Pronunciation: How to... talk about future plans
	Reading: WORK – the daily grind we just can't do without
4.2	**Can do:** Discuss how you spend your time
	Grammar: Future Perfect and Future Continuous
	Vocabulary: Verb phrases about time
	Speaking and Pronunciation: Stress: sounding sure
	How to ... make your point in a confident way
	Listening: The Rock Gardens of Chandigarh
4.3	**Can do:** Discuss attitudes to clothes and the workplace
	Grammar: Verb patterns: *-ing* forms and infinitives
	Reading: Dressed for business
Vocabulary	Collocations with prepositions
Communication	**Can do:** Take part in an interview for a job or course
Writing bank	Write a CV for a job/course application
	How to... write a successful CV
Extra activities	ActiveTeach and ActiveBook

CEFR Can do objectives
4.1 Talk about certain and uncertain future plans
4.2 Discuss how you spend your time
4.3 Discuss attitudes to clothes and the workplace
Communication Take part in an interview for a job or course
Writing bank Write a CV for a job/course application

CEFR Portfolio ideas
a) Choose a job from exercise 1 page 49. You want to apply for a training course in one of these areas. Write a letter explaining why you are interested, outlining the qualities you possess. You can invent details.
b) Choose one of the following jobs: tour guide for the Chandigarh Rock Gardens; or advisor for a recruitment agency. Decide on the qualities which are necessary and the questions which might be asked at a job interview. Take turns to interview each other for the job. You can invent details.
c) You are running for president of the Student Union where you are learning English. Prepare a leaflet for potential voters, explaining your plans for the next two years. Think about school facilities, classes, course materials, extra-curricular activities.

Lead-in

1 ▶ Ss work in pairs to match the jobs to the photos. One job is not depicted in the photos. Give feedback on Q 1 and 2 and Ss then discuss whether they would like these jobs or not.

Answers
1 Main photo: firefighter(s)
   Top photo: journalist
   Middle photo: nursery nurse
   Bottom photo: surgeon(s)
2 journalist = someone who writes news reports for newspapers, magazines, television or radio
   firefighter = someone who rushes to the scene of a fire in order to put it out and save lives
   nursery nurse = someone who looks after young children
   surgeon = a doctor who does operations

2a ▶ ● 1.23 Play the recording. Ss listen and match each speaker with the correct job in exercise 1. Students compare their answers with a partner.

Answers
1	journalist		4	firefighter
2	nursery nurse		5	social worker
3	surgeon			

2b ▶ Read through the phrases with the class but do not explain them at this stage. Play the recording again. Ss listen out for the phrases and the context each one is in. After listening, Ss to discuss what they think each phrase means with a partner.

Answers
a change of career = when someone stops the career that they have been doing and retrains to do something different
a labour of love = when someone does a job not for the money but because they really love it
a career path = the different steps that someone takes to progress in a certain career
to take a year out = to stop working for a year and do something completely different (e.g. travel)
job satisfaction = the feeling of happiness someone gets from doing their job

3 ▶ Ss work in pairs and think of a job which fits each of the qualities in the box. Get feedback from the whole class.

4a ▶ Ss look at the phrases from exercise 2b and exercise 3 and underline the ones which apply to themselves. Ss write a short paragraph in which they describe the qualities which they feel apply to them.

b ▶ Put Ss in pairs. They take turns to read their paragraphs to each other. Encourage Ss to ask questions and give details about their choice of phrases.

4.1 The daily grind

In this lesson, Ss read an article about attitudes to work and how work has changed over the years. They discuss their own opinions about different ways of working (e.g. working at home, voluntary work) and discuss their future plans in relation to work and study.

> The nature of work has changed radically over the last 1,000 years. Ways of working are very different and more varied now, mostly due to changes to production methods, especially during the Industrial Revolution and more recently due to huge advancements in technology. Despite these changes, however, some things remain constant, especially our apparent psychological need to work.

Reading

> **OPTIONAL WARMER**
> Write the following two sentences on the board:
> 1 *I work to live.*
> 2 *I live to work.*
> Check Ss understand what they mean (1 = my main reason for work is to earn money to enjoy things in life; 2 = I love my work so much that it is one of the most important thing in my life). Ask Ss to discuss which of the two sentences is closest to their own feelings about work. Ask Ss to suggest what qualities they associate with people who advocate either of the two ideas (e.g. *I live to work = conscientious, ambitious,* etc).

1 ▶ Ss discuss the questions in pairs. Get feedback from the whole class but don't confirm any answers at this point on questions 1 or 2.

> **Answers**
> 3 The word *grind* is used to mean something that is hard work, tiring and boring. People often refer to their jobs as their daily grind; to do without something is a phrasal verb which means to manage without something. It is usually used in the negative (I can't do without it) and means we can't manage/survive without something.

2 ▶ Ss read the article quickly and check their ideas about question 2 in exercise 1. Ss compare their answers with a partner.

> **Answers**
> According to the article, work has changed a lot over the last 1,000 years.
> Pre-industrial age: people worked for food and goods necessary for survival; work structured by seasons; whole communities worked together; less division between 'work' and 'free time'; people worked for money; work was structured by the clock; there is a clear division between 'work' and 'free time'.
> Now: the workplace has become a social community; many people work flexible hours; now we often work from home.
> Similarities: the overall attitude to work – we work because we have to but we miss it if we don't (as implied by the title).

3 ▶ Ss read the article again, this time more slowly, and decide if the statements are true or false. Encourage Ss to underline the parts which help them with the answers and to say why the false statements are false. Ss compare their answers with a partner.

> **Answers**
> 1 T
> 2 F (self-esteem increases if you're paid to work)
> 3 F (even doing things which are not enjoyable at work increases self-esteem)
> 4 T
> 5 T
> 6 F (people who don't have work become irritable)
> 7 T
> 8 T
> 9 T
> 10 F (the writer thinks that working remotely may become more common)

4 ▶ Ss summarise the main argument of the article by completing the sentence. Encourage them to be concise and focus only on the main argument. Ss compare their sentences in pairs. Get feedback from various Ss.

> **Suggested answer**
> Although the nature of work has changed over the years, people's attitudes towards it remain the same.

5 ▶ Ss discuss the questions in pairs. Encourage them to use examples from their own experience or from people they know to justify their opinions. Get feedback from different pairs on the most interesting part of their discussions.

Vocabulary | work

6 ▶ Ss work in pairs and help each other to find the meaning of the underlined phrases. Encourage them to use the surrounding context to guess the meanings where possible and to use dictionaries to check the meaning. Remind them that dictionaries can help with the pronunciation and collocations of new words/phrases as well as the meaning.

Answers
1   travelling to and from work
2   to do the majority of your work at home
3   earning money for the work you do
4   working for a charity or for the community without being paid for it
5   someone who finds it difficult to stop working during their free time
6   the building or room where people do their jobs
7   the regular pattern of work
8   a culture where people are given respect and status according to their jobs and how much they earn
9   when people have a fixed starting and routine in their job which is the same as most other people, usually starting at 9:00 a.m. and finishing at 5:00 p.m. with an hour free at lunch time
10   when individual workers have some control over when they start and finish work

---

7a ▶ Ss find the three correct sentences and correct the mistakes in the others. Students compare their answers with a partner.

Answers
1   ~~make~~ → do
2   ~~flexibility~~ → flexible
3   ✓
4   working from ~~the~~ home
5   work-~~centred~~ rhythm
6   ✓
7   ~~cultural~~ → culture
8   ✓
9   ~~employer~~ → employment

---

b ▶ Ss can choose six or all of the questions to discuss with their partner. Encourage them to ask follow-up questions. Get feedback from various Ss on a few of the questions.

OPTIONAL EXTENSION

Give Ss the following ideas and get them to write three or four more themselves.
Find someone who ...
1 ... has flexible hours.
2 ... has had a part-time job in a shop.
3 ... would like to work at home but doesn't.
4 ... has gone on strike.
5 ....has a nine-to-five job.
Ask Ss to walk around the room and ask the questions to different Ss. Explain that the aim is to get a different name for each topic. Get feedback from the whole class.

Grammar | futures (1)

8a ▶ 🔊 1.24–1.27 Focus Ss on the questions. Play the recordings. Ss listen and answer the questions. Ss compare their answers with a partner.

Answers
1   feeling fed up with work, working longer and longer hours and feeling exhausted; no definite plans but might do some voluntary work abroad
2   wants to go back to college and retrain as a vet; has definite plans; taking an exam in three weeks' time and if successful will start the course probably in September
3   feels isolated working from home and misses having colleagues; has definite plans (has a job interview tomorrow afternoon)
4   wants a more senior position with more responsibility at work; no definite plans

---

b ▶ Ss talk about whether they have had similar experiences to the people in the recording with a partner, giving their reasons. Get feedback from various Ss.

9a ▶ Focus Ss' attention on the extracts in the Active grammar box. Explain that these are all ways of referring to the future. Play the recordings again. Ss listen and complete the first five sentences. Ss compare their answers with a partner.

Active grammar
1   they'll offer   4   I'm going to leave
2   Dominic's going to be   5   I'm meeting
3   I'll go

▶ Demonstrate the contractions commonly used in these future forms, especially the contracted *'ll* sound which Ss often neglect to use (e.g. *I think it' ll rain later*).

b ▶ Focus Ss' attention on the four categories of sentences. Ss match the missing headings to the correct category. Ss compare their answers with a partner.

Active grammar
C   2   D   1

---

c ▶ Ss look at the examples under headings C and D and decide which form of the verb is used in each.

Active grammar
1   the infinitive   2   the *-ing* form

▶ Remind Ss that the choice of which future form to use often depends largely on the attitude of the speaker. For example, if the speaker feels confident that everything has been arranged, they may choose to use the Present Continuous. However, if there is a tiny doubt in the speaker's mind, other future forms may also be appropriate and grammatically correct.

▶ Focus Ss' attention on the Reference section on page 61.

10 ▶ Ss choose the best alternative for each sentence. Remind them to look for clues in the sentences as regards the attitude of the speaker (e.g. how sure they are or if they feel they have any evidence). Ss compare their answers with a partner.

Answers
1 going to apply
2 's bound to get
3 're meeting
4 'm on the verge of asking
5 're certain to get
6 'll talk
7 'm about to have
8 's sure to be

11 ▶ ⏺ 1.28 Explain that there are particular expressions we use when we want to indicate vagueness or a degree of uncertainly about future plans. Ss look at the How to… box. Play the first two dialogues again. Ss listen and complete the sentences with words in the box. Ss compare their answers with a partner.

Answers
I'm **thinking** about leaving.
I'm not **sure** yet …
One **idea** is to …
It **depends** on being …
I think I'll leave in the next month or **so**.
I'm doing the exam in about three **week's time**.
I'll probably start the course this **coming September**.

▶ Remind Ss of Lesson 1.2 and how to use intonation to sound tentative. Ss practise saying these expressions.

12a ▶ Ss make notes about their work/study/life plans for the future.

b ▶ Ss work in pairs and tell each other about their future plans. Remind Ss to use the language in the Active grammar and How to… boxes as appropriate. Get feedback from the whole class, eliciting to what extent Ss' plans are similar/different to each other.

OPTIONAL VARIATION
Ss work in small groups. They discuss their New Year's resolutions in relation to the following topics.
1 *Things I want to change this year.*
2 *A new hobby I'm interested in starting.*
3 *My English studies in the next year.*
4 *Places I will visit.*
5 *My 'three-year-plan'.*

4.2 A work of art

In this lesson, Ss listen to a radio programme about Nek Chand and how he created his Rock Gardens in Chandigarh. They also listen to two people discussing their work/life balance. Ss discuss the role that work plays in their lives.

Listening

Nek Chand is an artist and the creator of the extraordinary Rock Gardens of Chandigarh. He was inspired to recycle waste materials and spend every spare moment creating thousands of sculptures and landscaping his gardens. He worked privately for 18 years until finally his work was discovered and became India's second most popular tourist attraction (after the Taj Mahal) with 5,000 visitors every day. For more information, go to: www.nekchand.com

OPTIONAL WARMER
Write the following famous parks and gardens on the board: *Parc Guell, Barcelona; Central Park, New York; Kew Gardens, London; Shinjuku Gyoen, Tokyo.* Ask Ss to discuss the following questions.
What do you know about any of these parks or gardens? Have you ever visited any of them? When? Who with? What is the attraction of visiting parks and gardens?

1a ▶ Ss look at the photos. Explain that they are the Rock Gardens of Chandigarh in India and that the man's name is Nek Chand. Do not give Ss any more details at this point but ask them to write two questions they would like to ask about what they can see, in pairs.

b ▶ ⏺ 1.29 Play the recording. Ss listen to check if their questions are answered. They think of an appropriate title for the story.

2 ▶ Read through the notes with the class. Then play the recording. Ss listen and complete the notes. Ss compare their answers with a partner.

Answers
1 modest, creative and hard-working
2 farmer
3 Government road inspector
4 the design and construction of his city, Chandigarh
5 building on government-owned land
6 all kinds of recycled material
7 the government discovered his gardens
8 the gardens were opened to the public
9 5,000
10 happy

3 ▶ Ss discuss the questions in pairs.

Ss discuss question 1 in pairs. Elicit feedback on their views during whole class feedback.

Next, set up questions 2 and 3 as a more lengthy group discussion, starting in small groups for question 2 and then expanding to a larger group for question 3. Ss work with different Ss for question 3. Get feedback from various Ss.

Grammar | Future Perfect and Future Continuous

OPTIONAL LEAD-IN

Write the following sentences (from the Active grammar box) on the board and ask Ss to complete them using the verbs in brackets.

Tomorrow morning, he'____ the same as he's doing today. (do)
Soon, he ____ half a century working on this garden. (spend)
He ____ the garden by the time he retires. (not finish)

Ss compare their answers with a partner and then look at the Active grammar box on page 54 to check.

4 ▶ Ss match the examples in the Active grammar box with the correct future form.

Active grammar

A   2, 3
B   1

▶ Write the following sentences on the board: *This time tomorrow, Tom will have visited the Gardens.* and *This time tomorrow, Tom will be visiting the Gardens.* Ask: *Where is Tom in each sentence – in the gardens or back in his hotel room?* (first sentence: back in his hotel room – his visit to the Gardens is over; second sentence: still in the Gardens – his visit to the Gardens is not over yet, he is still there).

▶ Focus Ss' attention on the Reference section on page 61.

5 ▶ Ss complete the sentences. Then they compare their answers with a partner. As an extra check you could ask if the action will be in progress (Future Continuous) or if it will be finished (Future Perfect) for each question. Ask Ss to practise saying each correct sentence using the contracted forms.

Answers

1   will have finished
2   will be playing
3   will have gone
4   will be having
5   will have finished
6   will be lying
7   will have spent
8   will be having

OPTIONAL EXTENSION

For intensive pronunciation work, focus on the auxiliary verbs in these two verb tenses, particularly the Future Perfect. The auxiliary verbs are unstressed weak forms and often run together (e.g. *He will have* = /hiːləv/; *he will be* = /hiːlbiː/). Use the sentences in exercise 5 to model the contracted forms (e.g. *He'll 've finished*; *You'll 've spent*, etc.). Ss listen and practise saying the sentences in pairs.

6 ▶ Ss ask and answer the questions in pairs. Remind them about pronunciation. Get feedback from various Ss.

Vocabulary | verb phrases about time

7 ▶ Elicit expressions which contain the word *time*. Ss will probably be familiar with *waste time*, *spend time*, *full/part-time*. Focus Ss' attention on the 10 underlined verb phrases in exercise 7. Ask Ss to read the sentences and work out the meanings of the phrases with a partner. Don't ask for feedback at this point. The sentences are self-explanatory and should provide Ss with enough information to complete exercise 8.

8a ▶ Ss complete the sentences using the correct form of the verb phrases covered in exercise 7. Ss compare their answers with a partner.

Answers

1   save time
2   wasting time
3   spend a lot of time
4   have time to spare
5   work full-time
6   pass the time/kill time
7   run out of time
8   take my time
9   make time
10 kill time/pass the time

▶ Elicit the difference between these phrases: *kill time* (doing something while you are waiting for something/someone to start/arrive, when you have nothing else to do); *pass the time* (doing something to make the hours seem to go by more quickly); *waste time* (spend time in a way that is not productive or useful); *have time to spare* (have extra time to do something different before you start a new task). These verb phrases are quite similar in meaning, particularly *kill time* and *pass the time*.

b ▶ Ss discuss how true the sentences are for them with a partner. Encourage them to ask for and give further details.

Listening

9 ▶ 🔵 1.30 Tell Ss that they are going to listen to two people talking about their working lives. Read through the questions with Ss. Play the recording. Ss listen and tick the questions the people talk about. Ss compare their answers with a partner.

Answers
They talk about all the questions except for 5 and 7.

10 ▶ Ss look at How to... box and discuss with a partner what the missing words might be. Play the recording again. Ss listen and complete the sentences.

> **Answers**
> The fact is ...
> I really do.
> Believe me, I know ...
> Without a doubt ...
> Family and friends are the most important, for sure.

Pronunciation | stress: sounding sure

11a ▶ ⬤ 1.31 Play the recording. Ss listen and identify the stressed words. Ask: *Why are these words stressed?* (to give emphasis to what the person is saying) Ask: *Do we speak more slowly or quickly when we want to sound sure about something?* (more slowly).

> **Answers**
> The **fact is**, I have a **really busy** work schedule. I **really do**.
> **Believe me**, I **know**, it's not easy, but I **do** think it's possible to improve it.
> **Without a doubt**, I'd say that I 'work to live' and not the **other** way round.
> **Family** and **friends** are the **most important**, for sure.

b ▶ Play the recording again. Ss listen and repeat the sentences.

12a ▶ Elicit what Ss consider the most interesting questions from exercise 9. Put Ss in groups according to their preferred topics so that each student is working with two or three others who are interested in similar things. Then, give each student time to prepare a response to the questions they have chosen. Ss should make notes, not write out exactly what they will say. They identify the points they feel very sure about.

b ▶ Ss discuss the three questions in their groups. Get feedback from the whole class. Ask a student from each group to report back on similarities/differences among them.

> **OPTIONAL EXTENSION**
> Ask Ss to conduct a survey on attitudes to work/life balance. Put Ss in groups of five or six Prepare a heading for each student (e.g. *working at weekends/on holiday*; *leaving work late/working through lunch time*; *checking work emails/ taking work-related calls at home*; *making time for family/ friends*; *stress/sleeping difficulties because of work*; *getting through your workload/inbox*; *job satisfaction*). Ss prepare questions to ask others in relation to their heading. Ss then mingle and speak to as many Ss as possible. Remind Ss to take notes as they do this. Ss then gather their responses and discuss them in their groups. Each group prepares a short report for the class on the results of their survey. They should identify results which they found surprising.

4.3 Dressed for business

In this lesson, Ss read a website about dress codes at work and give their views on what to wear in the workplace. They listen to two people talking about learning English and discuss strategies and goals for improving their English and for other work-related topics.

Reading

> **OPTIONAL WARMER**
> In pairs, Ss discuss what they might wear in the following situations.
> *an interview for a job in a bank*
> *an audition for a part in a theatre company*
> *an interview for a job in an advertising company*
> *an interview for a job in a fashion magazine*

1 ▶ Ss look at the photos and discuss the questions with a partner.

> **Answers**
> A suit, tie
> B neat hairstyle, piercings
> C baggy T-shirt, large logo

2 ▶ Ss look at the four ideas, then read the website quickly to decide which one best summarises the advice given. Give Ss a two-minute time limit and explain that they will have an opportunity to read the text more slowly in the next exercise.

> **Answer**
> 2

3 ▶ Ss read the website again, this time more slowly and use two words to complete each sentence. Ss compare answers with a partner.

> **Answers**
> 1 more casual
> 2 the season
> 3 dark colour
> 4 loud colours
> 5 loose, baggy
> 6 your boss
> 7 details
> 8 smart outfit

4 ▶ Ss discuss the questions in small groups. Get feedback from the whole class. Elicit which tip the majority of Ss find most useful.

OPTIONAL EXTENSION

Write the following definitions on the board. Ss match them to words in the website.

1 *changed (altered)*
2 *pieces of advice (tips)*
3 *situations which influence the way something is or happens (factors)*
4 *satisfactory or appropriate (acceptable)*
5 *shows (indicates)*
6 *has a sophisticated appearance (chic)*
7 *professionally made/tailored (well-cut)*
8 *things you add to clothing, usually for decoration (accessories)*
9 *stop yourself from doing something (resist)*

As a follow-up exercise, put Ss in pairs. They put the words into sentences which illustrate their meaning (e.g. *Many pop stars alter their image to suit changing tastes in music.*; *The tennis coach gave me some useful tips about how to improve my game.* etc.).

Ss then take turns to read out their sentences in pairs, but replace the key word with "BEEP!". (e.g. *Many pop stars BEEP their image to suit changing tastes in music.*) The other student tries to guess what the missing word is.

Grammar | verb patterns:
-*ing* forms and infinitives

5a ▶ Point out that some verbs are followed by the infinitive form of the verb and some by the -*ing* form of the verb. A few verbs can be followed by both forms of the verb but usually this changes the meaning of the verb.

▶ Ss look at the examples in the Active grammar box and decide whether they should be followed by the infinitive or the -*ing* form of the verb. Ss compare answers with a partner, then check in the website.

Active grammar

1	to dress	5	look
2	keeping	6	wearing
3	to give	7	to resist
4	wearing		

b ▶ Ss look at the verbs in bold and match them to the correct category. Then they compare answers with a partner.

Active grammar

A	suggest	D	see
B	hope	E	try
C	advise		

▶ The difference in meaning for most verbs in category E of the Active grammar box relates to the sequence of events. Ask: *Which event happened first in these two sentences?*

He stopped looking at her.
He stopped to look at her.

(In the first sentence, he looked at her, then he stopped. In the second sentence, he stopped what he was doing, then he looked at her.)

▶ Focus Ss' attention on the Reference section on page 61.

6 ▶ Explain that the sentences in exercise 6 relate to category D in the Active grammar box.

Answers
1a When I saw him, he was already sitting at his desk and already working.
1b The desk was empty and the computer turned off and I saw the entire action. First he arrived, then he sat down at his desk and turned on the computer.
2a I didn't hear the entire conversation but I heard part of it.
2b I heard the entire conversation from beginning to end.
3a He had started his lunch before I noticed him and he had not finished it when I walked past.
3b I watched him peel, eat and throw away the skins of three bananas.

7 ▶ Explain that the sentences in exercise 7 relate to category E in the Active grammar box.

Answers

1a	wearing	3a	to tell
1b	to wear	3b	telling
2a	to go	4a	buying
2b	going	4b	to buy

8 ▶ Ss complete the sentences using the verb given. Let Ss check with a partner.

Answers

1	suggested going	5	remember working
2	persuaded me to buy	6	advised me to speak
3	tried to speak	7	avoid getting
4	agreed to give	8	saw him stealing
		9	encouraged me to get

OPTIONAL EXTENSION

Divide the class into two teams: noughts (Os) and crosses (Xs). Draw a grid on the board with a different verb in each square.

regret	allow	avoid
hear	stop	hope
practise	suggest	notice

Ss try to make a line going up, down or diagonally, using the appropriate team symbol. In order to insert an X or an O into the table, one member of each team must make a correct sentence using the verb in the square. Teams take turns to give a sentence.

9a ▶ Ss complete the sentences so that they are true about themselves.

b ▶ Ss compare their sentences with a partner. Encourage them to ask for and give further details. Get feedback from various Ss.

Speaking

10a ▶ 🌐 1.32 Ss look at the list of topics from the box. Elicit the meanings of these expressions: *morale* (positive feelings among a group of people, usually in the workplace); *punctuality* (being on time); and *to fit in* (to be suitable). Play the recording. Ss listen and identify which topics are mentioned. Ss compare answers with a partner.

Answers
using English for work and study
'fitting in' at work/school/another country

b ▶ Play the recording again. Ss listen and answer the questions. Ss compare answers with a partner.

Answers
1 to study in the UK
2 to sound like a native speaker
3 at first self-conscious about his accent but found that it didn't matter. Now he is happy with his English and with his accent.

11a ▶ Put Ss in pairs. Focus their attention on the Lifelong learning box. Ss discuss the ideas in the box and add their own suggestions.

b ▶ Ask Ss about their personal aims for learning English and write their suggestions on the board.

12a ▶ Ss choose one of the topics in the box in exercise 10a to talk about. Give them time to prepare what they would like to say about their chosen topic. Encourage them to think about the reasons why this topic is important for them and what suggestions they might have to improve.

b ▶ Put Ss in groups with others who have chosen different topics, so that there are at least two or three different topics to discuss in each group. Ss take turns to talk about each other's chosen topic. The student who chose the topic should start and then the others give their opinions. Before moving on to a new topic, Ss should decide whether their views are similar or different. Get feedback from each group.

4 Vocabulary | Collocations with prepositions

1 ▶ Explain to Ss that some adjectives collocate with particular prepositions. (You may need to explain that *collocate* means 'go together for no particular reason' and that Ss just have to learn which words go together). Ss complete the sentences by choosing the correct preposition. Ss check answers in pairs, then as a whole class.

Answers

1	in	6	to
2	about	7	from
3	of	8	at
4	about	9	of
5	on	10	about

2 ▶ Explain that some verbs also collocate with particular prepositions. Ss complete the sentences with the correct preposition from the box. Ss compare answers with a partner.

Answers

1	for	6	about
2	from	7	for
3	on	8	on
4	for	9	in
5	in	10	of

3 ▶ Ss find and correct the eight sentences which contain mistakes. Ss check answers in pairs, then as a whole class.

Answers
1 passionate about salsa dancing
2 insisted on helping me
3 ✓
4 consist of three different sections
5 modest about his success
6 depends on how much sleep
7 ✓
8 succeeded in upsetting everyone
9 keen on coming
10 proud of your exam results

4 ▶ Ss look at the example, then take turns to practise the collocations with a partner. One student chooses one of the adjectives or verbs from exercise 1 and exercise 2 and says the word; the other student gives the correct preposition which collocates with the word.

5a ▶ Ss complete the gaps with the correct preposition.

> **Answers**
> 1 of/about
> 2 on
> 3 about
> 4 to
> 5 from
> 6 at
> 7 for
> 8 about
> 9 of

b ▶ Put Ss in groups. They ask each other about the things in exercise 5a and find someone who matches each point. Once they find a match, encourage them to ask further questions (e.g. *Which is your favourite rock band? Do you often go to rock concerts?*). Get feedback from the whole class.

> **OPTIONAL VARIATION**
> Give each student one of the points in exercise 5a. Ss stand up and mingle, asking as many others as they can about their topic. Encourage them to ask follow-up questions. Get feedback from the whole class.

4 Communication

Ss talk about their experiences of job and/or university interviews. Ss listen to parts of four different interviews and prepare for and roleplay two different interview situations.

> **OPTIONAL WARMER**
> Write the word *interview* on the board. Put Ss in pairs and ask them to write down any words/phrases associated with *interview*. Get feedback from the whole class. Elicit words/phrases from Ss and write them on the board.

1 ▶ Ss discuss the questions in groups. Get feedback from the whole class. Elicit how they feel about interviews. Write the adjectives and expressions they use on the board.

2a ▶ Ss discuss the list of things that can happen in interviews in pairs. Encourage Ss to justify their answers particularly for the more controversial items on the list.

> **Answers**
> The positive ones are: 4, 6, 9, 10

b ▶ Ss talk about their personal experiences.

3 ▶ 🌐 1.33–1.35 Ss read the questions. Play the recordings. Ss listen and answer the questions. Let them compare with a partner.

> **Answers**
> Candidate 1 job interview (7) – she talked about her previous experience in a negative way
> Candidate 2 university interview (1) – she was late
> Candidate 3 job interview (4)

b ▶ Ss try to complete the interviewer's sentences.

c ▶ 🌐 1.36 Play the recording. Ss listen and check their answers.

> **Answers**
> 1 applying
> 2 about
> 3 office
> 4 interviewing
> 5 reasons

4a ▶ Say: *I'm very interested in this job* twice, once in a flat, bored way and once in an interested, enthusiastic way. Ask: *Which time did I sound interested? How did my voice change?* (varied intonation; stress on and pause after *very*).

▶ 🌐 1.35 Play the recording. Ss listen and decide how Karema uses her voice to sound interested and enthusiastic.

> **Answers**
> 1 rising and falling intonation
> 2 pauses

b ▶ Ss look at the audioscript on page 167. Ss take turns to read Karema's part, using their voice to sound interested and enthusiastic.

5a ▶ Put Ss in pairs. Ask them to choose one of the adverts on page 148. They must also decide who will be the interviewer and interviewee (if you have uneven numbers, ask two Ss to act as an interview panel of two). Ss then prepare for the interview by each following the relevant instructions for the interviewees and the interviewers. They make notes about what to ask but should not write out the whole interview. It might be useful to ask two 'interviewees' and two 'interviewers' to form a new pair to work together at this stage to help each other. Ss then return to their original partner for the roleplay itself.

b ▶ Ss roleplay the interview with a partner.

c ▶ Ss change roles and roleplay another interview, following the instructions and making notes as before.

d ▶ 'Interviewers' decide whether their partner would get the job. Get feedback from the whole class. Find out who got the job and why.

OPTIONAL EXTENSION

Write the following jobs on the board: *a food taster for a president*; *a songwriter for advertising jingles*; *an undertaker*; *a court interpreter in murder trials*; *a TV journalist*). Ss work in pairs and decide which qualities might be important for each job.

4 Review and practice

1 ▶

Answers
1 'm going to watch
2 'll have
3 's going to
4 'm meeting
5 'll be
6 'll have finished
7 'll be doing
8 'll have been

2 ▶

Answers
1 She's bound to get the job.
2 I'm about to resign from my job.
3 They're certain to take some photos.
4 I'm on the point of shouting at my neighbours.
5 He's sure to buy the tickets today.
6 She's on the verge of telling him everything.

3 ▶

Answers
1 encourage all students ~~doing~~ to do
2 arranged ~~visiting~~ to visit
3 ✓
4 considered ~~to have~~ having
5 ✓
6 suggested ~~to learn~~ learning
7 ✓
8 He advised us to have ~~us~~

4 ▶

Answers
1 going
2 shout
3 talking
4 drop
5 to negotiate
6 to inform
7 running
8 to become

5 ▶

Answers
1 spare
2 commuting
3 voluntary
4 Take
5 deadlines
6 flexible

6 ▶

Answers
1 about
2 in
3 on
4 for
5 from
6 of

4 Writing bank

1 ▶ Ss read the CV and write the headings in the correct place.

Answers
1 e
2 b
3 d
4 c
5 a

2a ▶ Ss read the CV again and answer the questions.

Answers
1 a job in marketing
2 managing key areas of an organisation; problem-solving; influencing; team-work; customer care; taking responsibility; languages; driving

2b ▶ Ss match the advice with the headings.

Answers
1 d
2 c
3 a
4 b
5 e

3 ▶ Ss complete the How to... box.

Answers
1 excellent
2 quality
3 graduate
4 busy
5 discipline
6 fluent

4a ▶ Ss prepare their CVs.

b ▶ Ss write their CVs.

Overview

Lead-in	**Vocabulary:** Attitudes to risk-taking
5.1	**Can do:** Talk about real and imagined risky activities **Grammar:** Conditional structures (1) **Vocabulary:** Verb phrases about challenge **Reading:** One woman's determination
5.2	**Can do:** Talk about different sports **Grammar:** Advice and permission **Vocabulary:** Sport **Speaking and Pronunciation:** Connected speech (3) **Listening:** Hang-gliding **Reading:** Information leaflets
5.3	**Can do:** Describe and choose films **Grammar:** Emphasis **Vocabulary:** Phrasal verbs with out **Speaking and Pronunciation:** Stress: emphasis (1) **How to...** talk about which film to watch **Listening:** Clint Eastwood
Vocabulary	Distances and dimensions
Communication	**Can do:** Participate actively in a debate **How to...** make sure your point is heard
Writing bank	Write a report **How to...** outline arguments and make recommendations
Extra activities	ActiveTeach and ActiveBook

CEFR Can do objectives
5.1 Talk about real and imagined risky activities
5.2 Talk about different sports
5.3 Describe and choose films
Communication Participate actively in a debate
Writing bank Write a report

CEFR Portfolio ideas
a) Look at a TV guide. You and your partner have decided to watch TV this evening. Discuss what to watch between 8:00 and 12:00 p.m.
b) Work in small groups. Participate in a debate about the creation of a large wind farm where you live. First, decide whether you are for or against. Then, prepare what you will say. Explain your position and make recommendations. Use the language in the How to... boxes on pages 74 and 154 to help you. Record your debate.
c) Look at the texts on page 67. Prepare a similar leaflet for the hang-gliding centre on page 68. Use your notes and the audioscript on page 167 to help you.

Lead-in

OPTIONAL WARMER
Write the following ideas on the board and/or elicit two or three more examples of potentially risky behaviour: *taking flying lessons in a small aircraft; going on an organised expedition to climb Mount Everest; going canoeing alone; exploring the Amazon with a local guide; being a zoo-keeper; eating chicken which is undercooked; getting married after knowing someone for six weeks.* Ss work in groups and rank the items in order of risk. Get feedback from the whole class.

1 ▶ Ss focus on the photos and discuss the questions.

Suggested Answers
Main photo: mountain climbing – you might fall
Top photo: snake-charming – you might be bitten or poisoned
Middle photo: protesting – you might get arrested
Bottom photo: getting married – the relationship might not work out

2 ▶ Ss decide which of the alternatives is not possible in each sentence. Give them dictionaries to help if necessary.

Answers
1	hazard	4	belief	7	hardly
2	luck	5	vast		
3	gamble	6	infatuation		

3 ▶ ⊙ 1.37 Ss read the questions. Play the recording. Ss listen and answer the questions.

Answers
1 away from work
2 jumping out of a plane; rap jumping in New Zealand; swimming with sharks; sea kayaking; abseiling

OPTIONAL EXTENSION
Play the recording again. Ss listen and identify the reasons why she enjoys taking risks (she's an adrenaline junkie – she enjoys the rush of excitement she feels when excited or scared; she likes the challenge of doing things that are a bit scary, that she wouldn't normally do; the thrill of doing something scary; a sense of achievement when she accomplishes something that was scary at first; she likes to be in an environment which isn't controlled by rules and regulations, like at work).

4 ▶ Ss discuss the questions in small groups.

EXTEND THE LEAD-IN
Remind Ss of the previous unit and elicit jobs which require an ability to take risks (e.g. *soldier; astronaut*). Ask: *Which job requires the most bravery? Does risk-taking equal bravery?*

5.1 Going solo

In this lesson, Ss read an article about Ellen MacArthur, who sailed solo around the world. Ss discuss their attitudes to risk-taking in a variety of contexts, including language learning. They talk about what they would do/would have done in different situations.

Reading

Ellen MacArthur was born in 1976 and grew up in England. Her love of sailing developed from a boating trip when she was eight years old. In 2001, after several years of dedicated hard work, she finally got the sponsorship she needed. Impressed by her hard work and determination, a European company called Kingfisher backed her with £2 million to enter the world-renowned Vendée Globe – a three-month solo journey around the world. Against the odds, Ellen came second and broke several records. She was the first female competitor ever to lead the race, the youngest solo sailor to ever finish and the fastest women to circumnavigate the globe. Since then, she has broken several more records and in 2005 she became the fastest person ever to circumnavigate the globe alone, covering over 27,000 miles in 71 days, 14 hours, 18 minutes and 33 seconds. The record had been previously held by Francis Joyon. Ellen MacArthur retired from competitive racing in 2009 in order to concentrate on her charity work with seriously ill teenagers.

OPTIONAL WARMER

Ask Ss to imagine they were going to spend three months alone at sea in a small boat. Write the following headings on the board: *a book*; *a piece of music*; *an item of technology*; *a small luxury item*; *a personal item* (e.g. diary, photo of a loved one). Ss discuss in pairs which item in each category they would bring with them.

1a ▶ Ss discuss the questions in pairs. Get feedback from the whole class.

b ▶ Focus Ss' attention on the photos. Get feedback from the whole class on potential challenges but do not comment on Ss' ideas at this point.

2 ▶ Read the topics with the class. Tell Ss to read the article quickly and tick the topics that are mentioned. Remind Ss not to try to understand everything in the article at this point, they will be given an opportunity to read more slowly later. Let Ss compare with a partner.

Answers
1, 3, 4, 6, and 7

3 ▶ Ss read the article a second time, this time more slowly. They decide whether the statements are True, False or Not Given. Ss compare answers with a partner, giving their reasons.

Answers
1 T
2 F (it was broken the previous year)
3 NG (we know she put up with the discomfort of the facilities but not whether she found it difficult)
4 T
5 T (this is implied because Ellen is just 1.6 m tall and the article refers to the importance of mental strength in sailing single-handed)
6 T
7 F (she says that she chooses to face the challenges at sea but teenagers with cancer do not choose their enormous challenge)
8 T

4 ▶ Ss discuss the questions in small groups. Get feedback from one or two Ss.

OPTIONAL EXTENSION

Explain that Ellen kept a diary during her adventure. Elicit ideas on the board about what it might be like on the boat during very stormy weather under the following headings: *What the weather was like* (e.g. stormy, dark skies, high winds, huge, rolling waves); *How she felt* (e.g. terrified, excited, under pressure, focused on the job of staying alive); *what she did* (e.g. stayed below deck, pulled ropes, tried to stop a leak, tied herself to the mast); *how she felt afterwards* (e.g. relieved, exhausted). Ask Ss to imagine that they are sailing single-handedly around the world and have just been through a terrible storm. They write a diary entry.

Grammar | conditional structures (1)

5a ▶ Ss complete examples 1–5 in the Active grammar box using *will*, *would*, *wouldn't* and *would've*.

Active grammar

1	Would	4	wouldn't
2	would've	5	wouldn't
3	I'll		

b ▶ Ss match rules A–E in the Active grammar box with examples 1–5.

Active grammar

A	3	D	4
B	1	E	5
C	2		

Write the following on the board: *If it …, I … the boat trip.* Ask Ss to construct First, Second and Third Conditional sentences using the verbs *to rain* and *cancel*. Ask Ss to compare their sentences with a partner, encouraging them to explain the difference in meaning in each case.

Then write the following sentences on the board.
1   *If it rains, I'll cancel the boat trip.*
2   *If it rained, I would cancel the boat trip.*
3   *If it had rained, I would have cancelled the boat trip.*
Ask Ss to match the following situations to the sentences: *it is a beautiful sunny morning in summer and the boat trip is planned for this afternoon* (sentence 2); *the boat trip took place yesterday during dry weather* (sentence 3); *it rained all day yesterday and there are black clouds overhead now; the boat trip is planned for this afternoon* (sentence 1).

Then write the following Mixed Conditional sentences on the board.
If it had rained, I would be at home now.
Ask: *Did it rain?* (yes). *Where are you now?* (at home).
If it wasn't raining, I would have gone sailing.
Ask: *What was the weather like earlier?* (it was raining). *What is the weather like now?* (it's still raining). *Did you go sailing?* (no).

▶ Review the contracted forms of *will/will not, would/would not* and *would have/would not have*.

▶ Focus Ss' attention on the Reference section on page 75.

6 ▶ Ss correct the mistake in each sentence. Let them compare answers with a partner.

Answers
1   Before you go tomorrow morning, ~~do~~ will you phone me if you need anything?
2   What **would** you have done if a nearby boat hadn't picked up your distress call?
3   You ~~had~~ **would** feel a lot better about things if you took a risk and left your job.
4   She wouldn't have ~~finish~~ **finished** the race if she wasn't such a determined person.
5   What **would** you like to do if you had some free time and money?
6   If I ~~didn't~~ **hadn't** taken a year off to cycle across Africa, I wouldn't have met my wife.
7   If he ~~didn't have~~ **hadn't had** sailing lessons when he was young, he wouldn't be so confident in the water now.
8   If ~~you'll~~ **you see** John, will you ask him if he wants to come parachuting with us?

7 ▶ Ss choose the correct option in each sentence. Ss compare answers with a partner.

Answers

1	would	5	had
2	was	6	'd
3	'd taken	7	were
4	would be	8	'd have liked

Vocabulary | verb phrases about challenge

8 ▶ Ss work out the meaning of the underlined phrases with a partner. Get feedback with the whole class, dealing with any difficulties and demonstrating the pronunciation of the phrases.

9a ▶ Ss choose the correct option for each sentence.

Answers

1	faces	6	broke
2	put	7	deal
3	campaigns	8	endure
4	puts	9	risk
5	battle	10	focusing

b ▶ Ss work with a partner. Ask them to look at the questions in exercise 9a. The first five questions relate to the article about Ellen MacArthur and the others relate to Ss' own experiences. Ss choose six questions that they would like to focus on. Encourage them to choose three about the article and three about themselves. Ss then discuss the questions in pairs. Get feedback from two or three pairs. Ask them to tell the class which questions they found most interesting and to report on their answers to one of the questions.

10a ▶ Focus Ss' attention on the Lifelong learning box. Ask them to discuss the advantages and disadvantages of each one with a partner. Get feedback from the whole class.

b ▶ Ss discuss the questions with a partner. Get feedback from the whole class.

Speaking

11 ▶ 🔘 1.38 Play the recording. Ss listen and answer the question. Let them compare with a partner.

Answer
leaving his job and starting his own business

Play the recording again. Ss listen and note how each speaker feels about working on their own or working for themselves. (The man likes working on his own; enjoys his own company; can concentrate more easily; feels in control; will feel really good about it if things go well; feels he has the experience and motivation to do it. The woman likes being with other people; gets lonely, miserable and bored working on her own; doesn't have the confidence to do it.)

12a ▶ Read through the sentences with the class. Ss work alone and choose three sentences to re-write so that they are true for them.

b ▶ Put Ss in small groups. Ask them to discuss their sentences. Encourage them to ask for and give more details.

5.2 At your own risk

In this lesson, Ss read short leaflets about various dangerous sports and listen to someone describing going hang-gliding for the first time. They talk about their reactions to similar extreme sports and discuss sport in general.

Reading

> The term 'extreme sport' is used to describe an activity which generates the thrill of danger, often involving very high levels of speed, height and/or physical exertion. Extreme sports differ from traditional sports in a number of ways: they tend not to be sanctioned by schools; they tend to be solitary in nature; the danger is an inherent part of the sport; and athletes tend to be pitted against uncontrollable variables such as difficult weather conditions or terrain. Typical extreme sports are: hang-gliding; sky-diving; bungee jumping; speed biking; cliff diving; mountain boarding, etc.

OPTIONAL WARMER

Introduce the term 'extreme sports'. Elicit different kinds of extreme sports (e.g. *kayaking*; *off-piste snowboarding*; *bungee jumping*, etc.) and write them on the board. Ss work with a partner and categorise the list of sports under the following headings: *I have tried*, *I would like to try* and *I would never try*.

1 ▶ Ss look at the photo and discuss the questions with a partner.

Answer
1   hang-gliding

2 ▶ Ask Ss to read the leaflets quickly in order to match the titles. Give a two-minute time limit and explain that they will have an opportunity to read the leaflets in more detail later.

Answers
1   B
2   C
3   A

3 ▶ Ss read the leaflets again and tick the information contained in each one. Ss compare answers with a partner.

Answers
1   C
2   A, C
3   A, B

4 ▶ Ss discuss the questions with a partner. Get feedback from the whole class. Ask: *Which sport do you think is the most dangerous? Which one would/wouldn't you like to try?*

OPTIONAL EXTENSION

Write the following definitions on the board. Ss find the words in the leaflet which correspond to each one.
A   *a person who searches for something* (*seeker*)
     gives (*provides*)
     extra/additional (*spare*)
     limited (*restricted*)

B   *strong feelings of excitement* (*exhilaration*)
     too much (*excess*)
     necessary/required (*essential*)
     acceptable in normal situations (*standard*)

C   *something that blocks movement or action* (*obstacle*)
     something that exists and can be seen, felt, tasted, etc. (*phenomenon*)
     idea/rule (*principle*)

Vocabulary | sport

5a ▶ Ss identify the sports in the photos.

Answers
A   off-road mountain biking
B   rock climbing
C   rugby
D   open-water swimming

b ▶ Ss categorise the sports. Then they add three sports to each category. Let them compare with a partner.

Answers
play: rugby (+ football, tennis, golf …)
go: white-water rafting, rock climbing, horse riding,
     off-road mountain biking, free running, open-water
     swimming (+ hang-gliding, skiing, jogging …)
do: archery (+ gymnastics, a marathon, yoga …)

c ▶ Ss identify which items from the box they can see in the photos. Elicit additional ideas on the board.

Answers
1   helmet, wetsuit, trainers, goggles, mouth guard,
     gloves
2   (possible answers) shin guard, protective vest, spike,
     boots, water bottle, shorts, swimming hat, oxygen
     tank, flippers

6 ▶ Ss discuss the difference in meaning for each pair of words with a partner. Encourage Ss to use dictionaries if necessary. Get feedback from the whole class, helping with precise definitions and pronunciation of the verb phrases.

> **Answers**
> 1 competitive (want to win); addictive (can't stop doing it/ to be obsessed with it)
> 2 participant (takes part in the sport); spectator (watches the sport)
> 3 to win (to come first); to beat (to do better than someone else or another team, not necessarily to come first)
> 4 to take part in (to join in the sport or the competition); to train for (to prepare for the sport or the competition)
> 5 to be successful (to do well at something; others recognise that you do well in this area); to have a sense of achievement (a feeling inside you that you have finished/done well at something which was challenging)

7a ▶ Ss choose one of the words from exercise 6 to complete the sentences. Let them compare answers with a partner.

> **Answers**
> 2 addictive   7 competitive
> 3 successful   8 win
> 4 part   9 achievement
> 5 beat   10 participant
> 6 train

b ▶ Ss choose four of the sentences to focus on. Ss work with a partner and tell each other why the sentences they have chosen are true/not true about themselves.

> **OPTIONAL EXTENSION**
>
> Write the following headings on the board: *team sports* and *individual sports*. Elicit sports in each category and write them under each heading. Put Ss in small groups. They list three advantages and three disadvantages of team sports and individual sports. Get feedback from the whole class.

Listening

8a ▶ Ask Ss: *Do you like being at the top of very high places? Why/Why not?*

▶ ◉ 1.39 Focus Ss' attention on the questions. Explain that they will hear the recording twice. The first time they will listen to get a general idea and then they will listen for more details. Play the recording. Ss listen to get an overall idea and answer the questions. Get feedback from the whole class.

> **Answers**
> 1 No, he was just given brief, general instructions.
> 2 Most of the time, no, but he felt a bit scared when he was doing the steering and when he was about to land.
> 3 Yes.

b ▶ Ss read through the statements. Play the recording again. Ss listen and decide whether they statements are true or false. Ss compare answers with a partner, giving their reasons.

> **Answers**
> 1 T (he arrived soon after 8:00)
> 2 T
> 3 F (at 2,000 feet, 600 metres)
> 4 F (he leaned too hard)
> 5 T
> 6 T (but he wants to do some training first)

9 ▶ Ss discuss the questions in pairs.

Grammar | advice and permission

10a ▶ Ss match the sentences to the categories.

> **Answers**
> 1 You should come with me next time.; If I were you, I'd just go for it.
> 2 You should have moved a bit more gently.; You shouldn't have leaned so far, then.
> 3 You could arrive any time after 8:00 in the morning.; You can't go up alone on your first time.; You can go alone after doing a few flights with an instructor.; Could you do a really low flight? Are you allowed to go up just a little way above the ground?
> 4 Were you allowed to just start without doing any training? I couldn't go straight up without any training at all.; I wasn't allowed to go up before having some brief general instructions.

b ▶ Ss discuss the questions with a partner.

> **Answer**
> *Can* and *Could* can both be used to talk about permission in the present in sentence 1 but *Could* is a little more tentative.

▶ Focus Ss' attention on the Reference section on page 75.

11a ▶ Ss complete the sentences.

b ▶ Ss compare what they have written with a partner. Get feedback from one or two Ss.

12 ▶ Ss choose the correct word to complete the paragraph about white-water rafting.

> **Answers**
> 1 shouldn't have done
> 2 weren't allowed to do
> 3 could choose
> 4 were allowed to wear
> 5 should go
> 6 would wear
> 7 shouldn't be
> 8 should take
> 9 should have taken

Pronunciation | connected speech (3)

13a ▶ Focus Ss' attention on the underlined sentences in the audioscript again. Ask them to mark the pronunciation as directed.

Answers

You could arrive anytime after /r/ 8.oo in the morning.

Were /j/ you /w/ allowed to just start without do /w/ ing any training?

I couldn't go straight up without any training at all.

You can't go /w/ up alone on your first time.

You can go /w/ alone after doing a few flights with an instructor.

I wasn't allowed to go /w/ up before having some brief general instructions.

You should've moved a bit more gently.

You shouldn't have leaned so far then.

You should come with me next time.

If I were /r/ you /w/ I'd just go for /r/ it.

Could you do /w/ a really low flight?

Are /j/ you /w/ allowed to go /w/ up just a little way /j/ above the ground?

b ▶ 🔘 1.40 Ss listen and check to see if they were right. They practise reading the sentences to each other in pairs.

▶ Focus Ss' attention on the Pronunciation bank on page 161 to review what they have learned in previous lessons about connected speech.

Speaking

14a ▶ Give Ss a minute or so to think of a sport or other activity which they have participated in at some point. Ss then make notes about what they will say using the headings provided. They should not write out in full what they will say.

b ▶ Ss discuss in small groups. Encourage Ss to ask for and give further details.

OPTIONAL EXTENSION

Ss work with a partner. They choose a sport or activity and prepare some sentences about it using the language from the Active Grammar box. Teach *supposed to* for this (when you are expected to do something but it is not a rule or some people do not do this). Ss form larger groups and take turns to read out their sentences. They do not say which sport/activity they are referring to. The other Ss must guess which sport/activity it is.

5.3 Million-dollar risk

In this lesson, Ss read a short text about Clint Eastwood and listen to two people discussing *Million Dollar Baby* and *Gran Torino*, focusing on the theme of risk that runs through both films. They also listen to two people deciding which film to watch on DVD. Ss give their opinions on films and discuss which they would rather watch.

Reading

OPTIONAL WARMER

Ss discuss the following film categories in pairs. Ask: *Which type of film would you rather watch and why?*

1 A western or a science fiction film?
2 A romantic film or an adventure film?
3 A comedy drama or a tear-jerker?
4 A psychological drama or a horror film?

Write the eight categories on the board. Get feedback from the whole class and ask: *Who likes westerns/science fiction/romantic, etc. films?* Write the number of Ss who put their hands up beside each category to find the most popular film genre.

1a ▶ Focus Ss' attention on the photos and establish that they are all of Clint Eastwood. Ss answer the questions in pairs. Don't ask for any feedback at this point.

b ▶ Ss check their answers in the short text about Clint Eastwood.

Answers

1 both
2 55
3 in the 1960s
4 Westerns, thrillers, police dramas, comedies, love stories, dramas.

c ▶ Ss exchange views about Clint Eastwood films.

Listening

2a ▶ 🔘 1.41 Explain that Ss will hear the recording twice. The first time, they will focus on the general idea of what the two people say; the second time they will be asked for more detail. Ss look at the three questions. Play the recording. Ss listen and answer the questions. Let them compare answers with a partner.

Answers

1 Paul
2 She thought it was a really good film
3 Yes

b ▶ Ss read the questions. Play the recording again. Ss listen and answer the questions. Let them compare answers with a partner.

> **Answers**
> 1 risk
> 2 he doesn't put a promising young boxer up for a big championship fight
> 3 his daughter – we don't know exactly why
> 4 quite a bad-tempered, bitter war veteran
> 5 confronting his prejudices and getting close to someone he had felt angry towards before
> 6 a and c

3 ▶ Ss look at question 6 in exercise 2b. Ask: *Which of the four themes would make the more interesting storyline for a new film?* Elicit ideas for plots for films for each of the themes and write them on the board (e.g. a – rich teenager befriends a poor pensioner who lives nearby; b – one person falls in love with their best friend's ex-husband).

▶ Ss work in pairs. They discuss the question in exercise 3 in relation to the different storylines they have outlined. Get feedback from various Ss.

Grammar | emphasis

> **OPTIONAL LEAD-IN**
> Write these sentences on the board:
> *A1: I liked 'Million Dollar Baby'.*
> *A2: I did like 'Million Dollar Baby'.*
> *B1: It was such a good film.*
> *B2: It was a very interesting film.*
> *C1: There are so many great scenes in the film.*
> *C2: There are many great scenes in the film.*
> *D1: I watch that film again and again.*
> *D2: It's the film I watch again and again.*
> Ss work in pairs and decide which sentence in each pair is stronger than the other and why (A2; B1; C1; D2). Elicit some of the methods we can use to give emphasis (using the auxiliary *to do*; using emphasising words like *so/such*; starting sentences with *It's/It was*).

4a ▶ Focus Ss' attention on the Active grammar box. They read the three headings A–C. They then complete the sentences. Don't ask for feedback at this point.

> **Active grammar**
> 1 do
> 2 does
> 3 so
> 4 so
> 5 such
> 6 such
> 7 It's

b ▶ Ss check the audioscript on page 168.

▶ Ask Ss what kinds of word come after the following words: *so* (adjectives and adverbs – *so interesting; so well*); *so many* (plural countable nouns or noun phrases – *so many films*); *so much* (uncountable nouns, noun phrases and comparative adjectives/adverbs – *so much skill; so much more interesting*); *such a* (singular countable nouns or noun phrases – *such a good film*); *such* (uncountable nouns, plural nouns or noun phrases – *such wonderful actors; such beauty*).

▶ Focus Ss' attention on the Reference section on page 75.

5 ▶ Ss make the necessary changes in order to rewrite the sentences. Let them compare with a partner.

> **Answers**
> 1 She does know when the film starts.
> 2 I did send you a message this morning.
> 3 They do like dangerous sports.
> 4 He did apologise for being late.
> 5 She does need some help with her homework.
> 6 I do understand how you are feeling.

6 ▶ Ss complete the sentence using *so*, *such* or *such a*.

> **Answers**
> 1 so   4 so
> 2 such a   5 such
> 3 so   6 so

7 ▶ Ss rewrite the sentences, beginning each one with *It* and giving special emphasis to the underlined parts.

> **Answers**
> 2 It was the new Clint Eastwood film that I went and saw yesterday.
> 3 It was his new Mercedes that I asked if I could borrow.
> 4 It is the words to their new song that she really doesn't like.
> 5 It is sociology or psychology that he wants to study at university.
> 6 It was the window that he broke while he was playing with a ball.

Pronunciation | stress: emphasis (1)

8a ▶ ● 1.42 Ss look at the sentences. Play the recording. Ss listen and identify the words/phrases that they hear emphasised. You might want to do the first one as an example to make sure that Ss have got the idea. Ss take turns to practise saying the sentences in pairs.

> **Answers**
> 1 I <u>do</u> <u>like</u> Clint Eastwood.
> 2 There are <u>so</u> <u>many</u> different themes in the film.
> 3 I thought the whole theme of risk was <u>so</u> <u>interesting</u>.
> 4 She <u>does</u> <u>stay</u> with him in the end.
> 5 They're <u>such</u> <u>great</u> films.
> 6 It sounds like <u>such</u> an <u>interesting</u> film.

b ▶ Play the recording again. Ss listen and decide why the speaker is using emphasis in each extract. Pause the recording after each extract. Ss compare answers, then move on the next extract.

Answers
1 The speaker is stressing that she likes Clint Eastwood films but not films about boxing.
2 The speaker is emphasising the fact that she doesn't leave for another coach but decides to stay.
3 The speaker is stressing the number of themes in the film.
4 The speaker is stressing how interesting the theme of risk was in the film.
5 The speaker is emphasising how much he liked both films.
6 The speaker is emphasising how interesting he thinks the film sounds.

9a ▶ Ss work in pairs. They choose a film, actor or place they both are familiar with. Encourage them to think of something which they do not feel the same way about.

b ▶ Ss think about the points they might make to persuade their partner to change their mind about the topic. Ask them to make notes about what they will emphasise, but point out that they should not write out exactly what they will say.

c ▶ Ss discuss the topic in pairs, taking turns to make points for/against the actor/film/place. Get feedback from the whole class. Ask: *Did anyone change their mind?*

Vocabulary | phrasal verbs with *out*

10 ▶ Point out to Ss that phrasal verbs can be learned either grouped by topic (e.g. phrasal verbs about relationships), or by base verb (e.g. phrasal verbs with *take*) or, as here, by particle (e.g. phrasal verbs with *out*). Ss match the phrasal verbs in italics in the sentences to the meanings a–h.

Answers
1 c
2 e
3 h
4 b
5 a
6 g
7 d
8 f

11a ▶ Ss complete the sentences with the correct form of one of the verbs from exercise 10.

Answers
1 put
2 find
3 run
4 work
5 turned
6 fallen

b ▶ Ss work in pairs and ask and answer the questions. Encourage them to give details in their answers and to ask follow-up questions where appropriate.

Speaking

OPTIONAL WARMER

Ss focus on the two films, both directed by Clint Eastwood. Ss work in pairs. They should discuss what they know about each film and decide which one they would prefer to watch together on DVD. Get feedback from the whole class. Ask: *Which film did you choose to watch?*

12a ▶ ● 1.43 Tell Ss they are going to hear two people deciding which DVD to watch. Play the recording. Ss listen and answer the question. If you did the optional warmer, you could compare their answers with what Ss decided.

Answer
Mystic River

b ▶ Play the recording again. Ss listen and complete the sentences. Let them compare answers with a partner.

Answers
I like the look of …
Judging by the cover …
That sounds a bit tame to me …
Sounds like it could be intense.
They're both such good actors.
I have a hard time seeing him as a romantic lead.
It's based on a book …

13a ▶ Ss turn to page 147. They look at the two DVD covers and think about which one they would like to see and why. Ss think about what they will say about each film.

b ▶ Ss discuss the two films in pairs and choose which one they would rather watch. Get feedback from the whole class. Ask: *Which one did you choose? Why?*

OPTIONAL EXTENSION

Write the following headings on the board: *favourite actors*; *favourite directors*; *favourite films*; *favourite film genre*. Ss work in small groups and discuss the three categories. Get feedback from the whole class.

5 Vocabulary | Distances and dimensions

1a ▶ Ss work in pairs and discuss the difference between the pairs of phrases. Encourage them to use dictionaries to help with unfamiliar words.

> **Answers**
> 1 there is a small/high chance that things will go wrong
> 2 a plan that extends a long time into the future/just for a short period into the future
> 3 a call to somewhere near your home/in another part of the country or abroad
> 4 a quicker, more direct way of going somewhere/a route which takes longer than necessary
> 5 someone who is willing to accept behaviour or opinions that are very different from their own/someone who is not
> 6 too thin (used in a negative way)/thin in an attractive way (used positively)
> 7 someone who is not capable of serious thought/someone who is capable

b ▶ Read the example through with the class. Ss work in pairs, taking turns to describe a situation or a person to illustrate the words/phrases in exercise 1a. The other student decides which word/phrase is being illustrated.

2a ▶ In pairs, Ss check they know the words in the table. Then ask them to complete the table with the missing parts of speech, using dictionaries if necessary. Don't ask for feedback at this point.

b ▶ ◉ 1.44 Play the recording. Ss listen and check their answers. Ask Ss to repeat the words with correct pronunciation.

> **Answers**
> 1 short
> 2 widen
> 3 broaden
> 4 high
> 5 depth
> 6 lower

3 ▶ Ss complete the sentences with a word from the table. Let them check their answers with a partner.

> **Answers**
> 1   width
> 2   depth
> 3   height
> 4   widen
> 5   low
> 6   lengthening
> 7   shortens
> 8   broad
> 9   lowered
> 10 heightened

4 ▶ In pairs, Ss choose the correct alternatives, using dictionaries if necessary. Get feedback from the whole class. Help with pronunciation and word stress.

> **Answers**
> 1 expand
> 2 extended
> 3 stretches
> 4 distance
> 5 spreading
> 6 lengthy
> 7 contracts
> 8 shrunk

5a ▶ Ss work in pairs and prepare a story. The story must involve someone taking a risk and include at least five of the words/phrases from exercises 1, 2a and 4.

b ▶ Ss tell their stories to their partner. Get feedback from the class. Ask Ss which story they think involved the biggest risk.

5 Communication

Ss listen to part of a debate about a proposal to locate a nuclear power plant in the local area. Ss debate this issue in small groups.

1a ▶ Ss identify the words in the photos with a partner.

> **Answers**
> A   wind farm
> B   oil rig
> C   nuclear power station

b ▶ In pairs, Ss list one advantage for the locality and one risk for each type of energy source.

> **Suggested answers**
> oil rig: jobs for the area; accidents on the rig
> wind farm: clean energy; birds sometimes fly into the blades
> solar panels: cheap energy
> hydroelectric dam: creates jobs; displacement of local communities and wildlife
> nuclear power station: can produce enough energy for the whole town or area; problems with waste disposal

> **OPTIONAL EXTENSION**
> Elicit further advantages and disadvantages relating to nuclear power stations. Write *Advantages* and *Disadvantages* on the board and elicit Ss' ideas under these headings. (Possible advantages: creates jobs; can produce a great deal of electricity efficiently; alternative to oil; cheap source of energy. Possible disadvantages: danger of accidents with environmental consequences; pollution; health risks to humans and wildlife.)

2a ▶ 🔘 1.45 Explain that you are going to hear part of a debate about a proposal to build a nuclear power plant in the area. Ss look at the questions. Play the recording. Ss listen and answer the questions. Let Ss compare their answers with a partner.

> **Answers**
> 1   Liam Davidson (local government) and Laura Franks (local people) both speak. Other people are mentioned but do not speak.
> 2   For (cheaper, more efficient energy; an opportunity to regenerate the area; job opportunities for local people).
> 3   Against (Liam wants to imply that local people are for the proposal but most local people are against the idea; concerns about health implications for children; effects on the environment and on wildlife).

3 ▶ Play the recording again. Ss listen and use two words to complete the sentences in the How to... box.

> **Answers**
> Excuse me, If I could just make a point here.
> I'd just like to interrupt you for a minute.
> If you could let me finish my point.
> I'm sorry but I haven't quite finished.
> What I mean is ...
> In other words, you are ...

4a ▶ Put Ss into four groups (A, B, C and D). Explain that it doesn't matter if the category doesn't represent their real opinions. Give each group time to prepare points to make which support their role.

b ▶ Put Ss into new groups of four or five, each containing at least one representative from each of the four categories (A–D). Avoid having smaller groups of less than four if possible. Ss discuss the proposal to locate a nuclear power station in the area, putting forward their views and arguing against the views of the other Ss. Get feedback from the whole class. Ask: *What is the final decision?*

> **OPTIONAL EXTENSION**
> Ss write to their local political representative, arguing for or against a proposal to locate a nuclear power plant in the area.

5 Review and practice

1 ▶

Answers

1	g	5	a
2	d	6	f
3	b	7	h
4	e	8	c

2 ▶

Answers
1 What will we do if the taxi doesn't come on time?
2 If I had been born a year earlier, I would have done military service.
3 What would you do if you were offered a better job?
4 If I am not home by 11 p.m., my dad will be really angry.
5 I wouldn't have hired a car if I had known how expensive it was going to be.
6 If she works really hard between now and the exams, she will probably pass.
7 We would have gone to the cinema if we had been able to find a babysitter.
8 If I were you, I would go on a long holiday.

3 ▶

Answers
1 You shouldn't have waited for me.
2 You are not allowed in without some form of ID.
3 If I were you, I wouldn't have got up so early.
4 You can take photos if you don't use a flash.
5 You shouldn't have spoken to the waiter like that.
6 I was allowed to walk to school when I was a child.

4 ▶

Answers
1 My brother is such a competitive person.
2 The participants did ~~arrived~~ arrive on time ...
3 There were so ~~much~~ many people who ...
4 ✓
5 Rock climbing is ~~such~~ so incredibly addictive ...
6 ✓
7 I do ~~playing~~ play a lot of rugby ...
8 It was ~~so~~ such cold water that I ...

5 ▶

Answers

1	endure	5	shorten
2	expand	6	efforts
3	beaten	7	stretch
4	on	8	in

6 ▶

Answers

1	work	5	running
2	find	6	turned
3	fallen	7	put
4	sort	8	give

5 Writing bank

1 ▶ ▶ Ss read the report and answer the questions.

Answers
1 a student representative
2 school management committee/principal
3 providing bicycles for all students; to improve the school environment

2 ▶ ▶ Ss read the report again and answer the questions.

Answers
1 F (the first paragraph provides the overall aim of the report and identifies what will be described)
2 F (both advantages and disadvantages are outlined in the second paragraph)
3 F (the advantages only are described in the third paragraph)
4 F (the purpose of the last paragraph is to give findings and recommendations
5 T
6 T
7 T

3 ▶ ▶ Ss complete the How to... box.

Answers
1 benefits
2 points
3 difference
4 impact
5 benefit
6 beneficial
7 recommend

4a ▶ ▶ Ss prepare what they will put in the report.

b ▶ ▶ Ss write their report.

Overview

Lead-in	**Vocabulary:** Memories
6.1	**Can do:** Describe past habits and changes
	Grammar: *used to, be used to, get used to, would*
	Vocabulary: Appearance
	Speaking and Pronunciation: Consonant clusters (1)
	Reading: A life without money
6.2	**Can do:** Describe personal memories
	Grammar: Wishes and regrets
	Speaking and Pronunciation: Intonation: wishes and regrets
	How to ... reminisce about the past
	Listening: Travel photos
	Listening: Memories from old photos
6.3	**Can do:** Give a detailed reaction to a book
	Grammar: Preparatory *it*
	Vocabulary: Feelings
	Speaking and Pronunciation: Talking about a book or film
	Reading: *The Memory Box*
Vocabulary	Idioms to describe people
Communication	**Can do:** Give your opinions and justify your choices
	How to... justify your choices
Writing bank	Write a review of a book or film
	How to... convey your opinions clearly
Extra activities	ActiveTeach and ActiveBook

CEFR Can do objectives
6.1 Describe past habits and changes
6.2 Describe personal memories
6.3 Give a detailed reaction to a book
Communication Give opinions and justify your choices
Writing bank Write a review of a book or film

CEFR Portfolio ideas
a) Your local bookshop has a noticeboard. Here, people recommend books to other readers, starting with: 'I enjoyed this book because ...'. Choose three books you have enjoyed and prepare cards for the noticeboard.
b) Work in small groups. Decide on a film to see either in the cinema or on DVD, then have a discussion about it. Talk about your response to the film using the headings from exercise 10a on page 86.
c) Your local council has decided to prepare a time capsule and have invited people to make proposals about what should go into it. Write to the council with your proposals. Give reasons for your suggestions.

Lead-in

OPTIONAL WARMER
Write the following decades on the board: *1940s*, *1950s*, *1960s*, *1970s*, *1980s*, *1990s*. In pairs, Ss discuss which decade they think would have been best to live in as a young person, a parent, an elderly person, a child, a man or a woman.

1 ▶ Focus Ss on the photos and ask them to discuss the questions in pairs. Ask Ss to think of events, famous people, music, etc. associated with each decade.

Answers
Main photo: 1960s-style cars outside an American diner
Top photo: 1940s, black-and-white photo, old style of clothes, people fully clothed on beach
Middle photo: 1980s, punk hairstyle, jewellery and clothes
Bottom photo: 1950s, black-and-white television, old-fashioned hairstyles and décor of room

2a ▶ Ss work in pairs and to decide what the underlined words in each sentence mean. Get feedback from the whole class, helping with word stress and pronunciation.

Answers
nostalgic = feel slightly sad when you remember a particular period in your past
reminisce = to talk or write about past experiences which you remember with pleasure
memorable = likely to be remembered for a long time
take me back = make you remember past events vividly
vivid memories = clear, exact memories
vague memories = unclear, inexact memories
memento = an object you keep in order to remember someone or something
souvenir = something you buy/receive/give to remember an event or visit (e.g. a holiday)
forgetful = someone who forgets things easily
remind = make someone remember something, usually something they have to do
remember = to have in your memory
on the tip of my tongue = when you can almost but not quite remember something
a good/bad/terrible memory for something = find it (e.g. hard) to remember a particular area (e.g. names, new words, faces)
mnemonics = something such as a special word or sentence that you use to help you remember something
jog your memory = help your remember something

b ▶ Ss choose four sentences from exercise 2a and rephrase them so that they are true for them. Ss take turns to say their sentences to each other.

3 ▶ Give Ss a minute or two to think of happy/memorable moments from the past year. Ss share the memory with a partner.

6.1 Life changes

In this lesson, Ss read an article about Mark Boyle who changed his life in a dramatic way. They talk about people's appearance.

Reading

OPTIONAL WARMER

Write the following questions on the board: *What kinds of thing do you worry about?* (e.g. money, family, health, career, etc.) *What single thing would you most like to change about your life?* (e.g. your job, where you live, etc.) Ss discuss the questions in pairs.

1 ▶ Ss focus on the photo and discuss the questions in pairs. Don't ask for any feedback at this point.

2 ▶ Ss look at the four sentences and decide which Mark might say. Explain that they can choose more than one sentence. Don't ask for any feedback at this point. Then, Ss read the article and decide which statements Mark might say. Ss compare answers in pairs, then as a whole class.

Suggested answers
1 and 4

3 ▶ Ss look at the questions, then read the article. Ss compare their answers with a partner.

Answers
1   He was a successful businessman.
2   He worried about money and problems caused by money.
3   Nothing – he got it through Freecycle.
4   He found it difficult at first but grew to love it
5   He boiled nuts on his stove.
6   He feels friendship is more important than money in terms of life security.
7   He decided to continue with his money-free life for good.

4 ▶ Ss discuss the questions in small groups. Get feedback from the whole class.

OPTIONAL EXTENSION

Explain to Ss that they must try to work out the meanings of the following words/phrases in the article from the surrounding context. They cannot use their dictionaries at all. Elicit some of the strategies they can use (looking at the part of speech, examining related words like adjectives, adverbs, etc.).
Paragraph 1: *ridiculous* (foolish or silly); *destruction* (damage); *symptoms* (signs of illness or disease)
Paragraph 2: *chores* (domestic jobs like cooking and cleaning); *foraging* (searching for food and supplies); *rain or shine* (in good and in bad weather)
Paragraph 3: *time-consuming* (takes a long time to do); *repercussions* (consequences); *appealing* (attractive, interesting)
Paragraph 4: *for good* (forever)

Grammar | *used to, be used to, get used to, would*

OPTIONAL LEAD-IN

Write these sentences on the board and ask Ss to work in pairs and decide which are true of Mark Boyle.
He used to wash his clothes in cold water.
He is getting used to washing his clothes in cold water.
He is used to washing his clothes in cold water.
He would wash his clothes in cold water.
Don't ask for feedback at this point. When Ss have finished exercise 5, they can return to these sentences to see if they were right. They decide what the difference in meaning is between the four sentences.

5 ▶ Ss read the examples 1–4 in the Active grammar box and complete the rules A–D. Let them check with a partner.

Active grammar
A   *get used to*
B   *be used to*
C   *used to; would*
D   *used to*

▶ Check that Ss are clear about the difference between actions (something you do) and states (a way of being) in the past. Ask: *Do the verbs in the following sentences describe actions or states? I had a dog when I was young (state); I drank milk with my dinner every evening (action); I liked chocolate (state); I owned a beautiful doll (state); I walked to school every day (action).* Explain that the modal verb *would* can only be used to describe repeated actions in the past.

▶ Focus Ss' attention on to the Reference section on page 89.

6a ▶ Ss choose the correct alternative for each sentence. Ss compare answers with a partner.

Answers
1   didn't use   3   I'm used to   5   used to
2   working   4   would   6   get

b ▶ Ss work in pairs and explain to each other what each correct sentence in exercise 6a means in their own words. Get feedback from the whole class.

7 ▶ Tell Ss that there is one word missing from each of the sentences. Ss decide what the word is and add it in the correct place. Ss compare their answers with a partner. If Ss find the exercise difficult, write the six missing words on the board and ask them to think where they should go.

Answers
1   I used to play a lot of rugby at school.
2   I'm finding it difficult to **get** used to my new boss ...
3   Did you use to be so close to your brother ...?
4   ... we **would** always have barbecues ...
5   We **are** slowly getting used to living ...
6   We **didn't** use to be vegetarian ...

8 ▶ Ss discuss the questions in pairs. Get feedback from various Ss.

> **OPTIONAL EXTENSION**
>
> Ask Ss to think about on how lifestyles have changed over the past century (e.g. being a stay-at-home parent now and in previous generations; being an office worker now and in previous generations). They talk about the differences with a partner (e.g. *My grandmother used to spend all day washing clothes by hand on Mondays*; *We have got used to labour-saving devices in the home now*; *Office workers used to have a long lunch break*, etc.).

Vocabulary | appearance

9a ▶ Ss look at the photo of Mark Boyle and read quickly through the article again. Ask: *What kind of clothes does Mark wear now?* (T-shirts, jeans, etc.). *What kind of clothes do you think Mark used to wear ten years ago?* (suits, tie, shirts). *Do you think he had a beard before?* (no, he was probably clean-shaven). *Does Mark look tidy and neat now?* (no, he's a bit scruffy). *Do you think he looked like this when he was a businessman?* (no) *Do you think he's good-looking?*

b ▶ Ss work in pairs and write the words/phrases from the box in the appropriate columns in the table. Ss can use dictionaries to help if necessary.

> **Answers**
> Hair: straight, curly, wavy, dyed, going a bit bald, mousy, spiky
> Face: clean-shaven, wrinkles, round, beard
> Build: muscular, a bit overweight, fat, slim, chubby, stocky, skinny
> General: good-looking, scruffy, elegant, tanned

c ▶ Ss add two words to each column with a partner. Get feedback from the whole class. Write their suggestions on the board.

> **Suggested answers**
> Hair: a fringe, fair
> Face: oval, dimples
> Build: well-built, plump
> General: stylish, attractive, pretty

10a ▶ Ss choose the correct word in each sentence. Ss compare answers with a partner.

> **Answers**
> 1 dyed
> 2 good-looking
> 3 round
> 4 bald
> 5 clean-shaven
> 6 scruffy
> 7 chubby
> 8 skinny

b ▶ Ss discuss the question with a partner.

> **Answers**
> scruffy: negative
> chubby: positive when speaking of a baby, a little bit negative when referring to an adult
> skinny: negative

11a ▶ Explain to Ss that some words contain consonant clusters, which means a group of consonant sounds coming together without a vowel sound in between. Demonstrate the word *clean* which begins with a two-consonant cluster sound (/kl/). Consonant clusters can occur at the beginning, middle or end of words and can sometimes be difficult to pronounce.

▶ Explain that for this exercise, Ss will focus on clusters containing two consonants which come at the beginning of words.

▶ 🔘 2.2 Focus Ss on the table. Play the recording. Ss listen and identify the word, then write it under the correct heading in the table. Let them compare with a partner.

> **Answers**
> spiky, stocky, slim, swim, smile, snow, sphere

b ▶ 🔘 2.3 Explain that for this exercise, Ss will focus on words beginning with three-consonant clusters. Focus Ss' attention on the table. Play the recording. Ss listen, identify the word and write it under the correct heading in the table. Let them compare with a partner.

> **Answers**
> straight, sprint, splash, squash

12 ▶ Ss listen to the words again and practise saying them. Model and correct as necessary.

> **OPTIONAL EXTENSION**
>
> Ss practise saying these two tongue-twisters with a partner.
> *I scream, you scream, we all scream for ice-cream.*
> *A slimey snake slithered down the sandy Sahara.*

Speaking

13 ▶ 🔘 2.4 Ask Ss to identify the actor in the photos (Brad Pitt). Ask: *Do you think Brad Pitt is good-looking or not? Which photo do you think he looks better in? Why?* Play the recording. Ss listen and decide whether they agree with the woman's opinion.

14a ▶ Elicit the names of several famous people under the various headings, or use photos from magazines. Encourage Ss to focus on people whose appearance has changed a lot over the years. Give Ss a minute to think of how to describe one of them. Each student prepares an oral description to tell to a partner.

b ▶ Ss take turns to describe their famous person to a partner, without saying who it is. The other student tries to guess the person.

OPTIONAL VARIATION

Cut out photos of people from magazines or print them out from the Internet. They do not have to be famous people. Put the photos around the room. Ss circulate in pairs, looking at the photos. They prepare a description of one of the people in the photo. Collect the descriptions and jumble them. Read the descriptions aloud to the class one at a time. Ss must identify which person is being described.

6.2 Lasting memories

In this lesson, Ss listen first to two people describing things they didn't do when they had the chance, and then to various people describing memories triggered by old photos from an earlier period in their lives. Ss share personal memories with each other.

If possible, ask Ss to select an old photo to bring to class with them in preparation for exercise 12 and exercise 13.

Listening

OPTIONAL WARMER

Elicit what Ss do with their photos by asking them the following questions.
Do you have a photo as a screensaver on your computer/ mobile phone? What is it?
What do you do with your photos? Do you frame them and put them on wall? Do you print them and put them in albums? Or do you group them in separate files on the computer?
How often do you look at your old photos?

---

1 ▶ Ss look at the photos and discuss the questions in pairs.

2 ▶ Ss work in pairs. They read through the sentences, and match the sentences to the photos.

Suggested answers
1 B
2 B, D
3 B, D
4 D
5 D
6 B, C

---

3 ▶ 🔘 2.5–2.6 Play the recordings. Ss listen and answer the questions. Explain that they just need to understand the general idea at this stage and that they will have an opportunity to listen again in a moment.

Answers
1 B and D
2 B: Eben grew up in Geneva in Switzerland and this is a photo of his wife and children there
   D: This is a photo of the beautiful Japanese gardens near Kyoto which Jeannette visited when she lived there.

---

4 ▶ Play the recordings again. Ss listen for more detailed information in order to answer the questions. Let them compare with a partner.

> **Answers**
> 1 The natural beauty of Switzerland and the fact that it's like clockwork with so much to do.
> 2 He didn't appreciate it enough.
> 3 He thinks it is an ideal place to raise children.
> 4 To experience life there as part of the community.
> 5 At weekends when she used to live near Kyoto.
> 6 To remind her of different features of the gardens in case she or her parents wanted to make a Japanese garden when she went back to the UK.
> 7 She had children very quickly and the garden filled up with play things for the children.
> 8 She would like to but she does not have definite plans.

5 ▶ Ss discuss the questions in pairs. Get feedback from various Ss.

Grammar | wishes and regrets

6a ▶ Teach the word *regret* (something you did/didn't do in the past that you are sorry about now). Ss read the extracts relating to Eben and Jeanette in the Active grammar box, then match the headings to Parts A and B in the box. Ss compare their answers with a partner.

> **Active grammar**
> A 2
> B 1

▶ Ask Ss: *Do you think Eben would raise his family in Switzerland if he had the chance to go back in time?* (yes) Ask: *Do you think Jeanette would build a Japanese garden if she had the chance to go back in time?* (it isn't clear). Eben clearly regrets his decision to raise his family in the US, but this is not necessarily the case with Jeanette. Having children meant that she changed her plans to build a Japanese garden but we are not sure if she regrets this.

b ▶ Ss read the extracts again and complete the rules. Let them compare answers with a partner.

> **Active grammar**
> 1 I'd
> 2 would've

▶ Check that Ss understand that the use of the past perfect after *I wish …* and *If only …* relates to past regrets. Teach the difference in meaning between the following sentences.

I wish I was rich. and *I wish I lived in a big house.*
(now, in the present)

I wish I had been rich. and *I wish I had lived in a big house.*
(when I was young, in the past)

▶ Focus Ss' attention on the Reference section on page 89.

7 ▶ Ss identify the correct sentences and correct the mistakes in the others. Ss compare their answers with a partner.

> **Answers**
> 1 I wish I ~~took~~ had taken …
> 2 If I'd had different advice, …
> 3 ✓
> 4 I could have bought myself a guitar …
> 5 If only I ~~was thinking~~ had thought more about …
> 6 I decided ~~I'm going~~ I was going to be a doctor …
> 7 ✓
> 8 I regret not ~~to learn~~ learning the piano …

8a ▶ Ss choose five of the sentences to work with. They complete them so that they are true about themselves.

b ▶ Ss compare their sentences. Encourage them to ask for and give further details. Get feedback from various Ss.

> **OPTIONAL EXTENSION**
> Write the following headings on the board: *education*; *friendships*; *boyfriend/girlfriend*; *travel*; *career*; *family*. Give Ss a few minutes to think of decisions they made in their life in relation to some of these areas, especially decisions that affected their subsequent lives in some way (e.g. *deciding what to study in university*, *deciding to apply for a particular job*, etc.). Ss form small groups and tell each other about these decisions and to what extent they regret them. Explain that they do not need to talk about something unless they feel comfortable doing so. Ask the whole class: *Are you more likely to drift into doing things or to think long and hard before making decisions?*

Pronunciation | intonation: wishes and regrets

9 ▶ 🌐 2.7 Explain that Ss are going to hear three people describing a past memory. Ss read the questions. Play the recording. Ss listen and answer the questions. Ss compare answers with a partner.

> **Answers**
> 1 1 holidays by the beach
>   2 when she was about six years old
>   3 as a child, she wished she could live there all the time
> 2 1 playing football with friends
>   2 about five years ago when he was at university
>   3 He regrets losing touch with so many of the others on the team.
> 3 1 having breakfast at a café in Italy with a friend
>   2 nine or ten years ago
>   3 She has some regrets about leaving the town in Italy where she lived.

10a ▶ 🌐 2.8 Ss look at the sentences. Play the recording. Ss listen and decide on the intonation, pace and stress patterns used in each sentence. Ss check answers in pairs, then as a whole class. Explain that this is how we sound nostalgic when reminiscing about the past.

> **Answers**
> Generally the sentences are spoken with a higher intonation and slower with pauses between groups of words.
>
> 1 It makes me feel <u>real</u>ly nos<u>tal</u>gic about my childhood.
> 2 Oh, I would've <u>liked</u> to <u>live</u> there <u>all</u> the time.
> 3 <u>Those</u> were the <u>days</u>!
> 4 I <u>wish</u> I <u>hadn't</u> lost touch with so <u>many</u> of them.
> 5 It reminds me of one of the <u>best</u> times of my life.
> 6 I re<u>gret</u> <u>leaving</u> that place <u>in</u> a <u>way</u>.

b ▶ Play the recording again. Ss listen and repeat the sentences.

Speaking

11a ▶ 🌐 2.7 Ss look at the extracts in the How to... box. Play the recording again. Ss listen and number the extracts in the order in which they hear them. Let them compare with a partner. Ask Ss to practise saying these sentences, using intonation, pauses and stress patterns to sound nostalgic.

> **Answers**
> 1 I can remember that place so clearly.
> 2 It makes me feel nostalgic about my childhood.
> 3 I can picture it so well.
> 4 It feels like last week.
> 5 It brings back so many memories.
> 6 Those were the days!
> 7 It reminds me of one of the best times of my life.
> 8 It doesn't feel that long ago.

b ▶ Focus Ss' attention on the audioscript on page 169. Ss read through the three extracts and choose other expressions which might be used when reminiscing about the past.

> **Suggested answers**
> I can still smell the sand and sea …
> in my mind it was sunny all the time …
> We had such a laugh together …
> it must be about nine or ten years ago …

12a ▶ Focus Ss' attention on the photos and think of similar photos they have of when they were a child or of a happy period in their past. Give Ss a few minutes to think of a personal memory from their past. If they can't think of anything, they can use one of the photos on the page and imagine that it is significant for them. However, encourage Ss to use the photos as a springboard and to think of something from their own past. They can use the ideas given to help them identify something.

b ▶ Ss use the questions to prepare what they will say. They should only make notes, not write down exactly what they will say. Encourage Ss to use expressions from the How to... box and to prepare how they will sound nostalgic.

13 ▶ Put Ss in small groups. They tell each other about the memory they have chosen. Encourage Ss to ask for and give further details during the discussion. Get feedback from the whole class. Ask: *Who chose memories of when you were a child/when you were on holiday/when you were in school/university?*

> **OPTIONAL EXTENSION**
> Ask Ss to write about the memory they described in groups. They should describe the following points: where, when and what happened; how they felt about it at the time; and how they feel about it now.

6.3 Memory box

In this lesson, Ss read an extract from the novel *The Memory Box* by Margaret Forster, and discuss their reactions to the book and how they might feel about making or being given a memory box. They talk about books/films they have read/seen recently and discuss extended reading strategies.

Vocabulary | feelings

> **OPTIONAL WARMER**
>
> Introduce Ss to the topic of feelings. Put Ss in pairs. Give them the following situations one at a time and ask them to think of as many adjectives as they can to describe the feelings associated with each one: *a parent waiting for their teenage child to come home after a late-night party – it is 3:00 a.m.*; *it is your first date with someone you like – you are waiting for him/her to arrive*; *you have just received a fantastic job offer in the post – the interview was last week*; *you have just heard that you didn't get the job you were hoping to get – the interview was last week*. Elicit different adjectives for each situation and write them on the board.

1 ▶ ⬤ 2.9 Ask Ss to read the through the adjectives in the box but not to explain the meaning of unfamiliar words yet. Play the recording. Ss listen and match one of the words from the box with each person they hear. Ss compare answers with a partner. Help with the meaning, pronunciation and word stress for the adjectives, especially the initial /kju:/ sound in curious and adjectives with *-ed* endings.

Answers			
1	optimistic	7	sceptical
2	uninterested	8	excited
3	confused	9	annoyed
4	relieved	10	suspicious
5	uneasy	11	shocked
6	curious		

2 ▶ Ss complete the sentences with the most appropriate word from exercise 1. Let them compare with a partner.

Answers			
1	relieved	7	sceptical
2	excited	8	curious
3	uneasy	9	uninterested
4	optimistic	10	suspicious
5	annoyed	11	shocked
6	confused		

3a ▶ Ask Ss to choose six of the feelings from exercise 1 and to remember the last time they felt like that. Be sensitive to Ss who might not want to talk about personal issues.

b ▶ Put Ss in pairs and ask them to explain to their partner why they felt like that, giving details. Get feedback from various Ss about which adjectives they chose without going into details.

> **OPTIONAL EXTENSION**
>
> Write the following adjectives on the board and ask Ss to work in pairs to match each one with a similar meaning in exercise 1: *apprehensive, astonished, comforted, distrustful, doubtful, hopeful, indifferent, inquisitive, irritated, puzzled, thrilled*.
> Encourage Ss to use dictionaries. Remind them that the pairs of adjectives will have similar, but not exactly the same, meanings (e.g. *suspicious – distrustful*).
> (*confused – puzzled*; *suspicious – distrustful*; *uneasy – apprehensive*; *curious – inquisitive*; *annoyed – irritated*; *excited – thrilled*; *uninterested – indifferent*; *sceptical – doubtful*; *optimistic – hopeful*; *shocked – astonished*; *relieved – comforted*)

Reading

> *The Memory Box* by Margaret Forster is a novel about a young woman who leaves a sealed memory box for her baby daughter before she dies. Years later, as a young woman herself, Catherine finds her mother's box full of strange, unexplained objects, carefully wrapped and numbered, like clues to a puzzle. Finding out what the objects represent is her only chance to find out about the mother she never knew. As she tries to solve the mystery of the box of secrets, she discovers that her mother was far more complex, surprising and dangerous than anyone had ever said. As the story of her mother's past unfolds, Catherine also discovers unexpected truths about herself.

4a ▶ Ss look at the cover of the book *The Memory Box* and discuss in pairs what they think it might be about. Don't ask for feedback at this point.

b ▶ Ss read the extract quickly and decide who Susannah, Charlotte and Catherine are. You might find it useful to give them a two-minute time limit in order to encourage them to read quickly just to answer this question and not focus on other details at this stage. Explain that they will have an opportunity to read more slowly in the next exercise. Ss compare answers with a partner.

> **Answers**
> Catherine is the main character (in the book). Susannah is Catherine's birth mother (who died when Catherine was a baby). Charlotte is Catherine's stepmother (who died recently when Catherine was grown-up).

5 ▶ Give Ss plenty of time to read the extract again and answer the questions. Explain that some of the answers require a subjective response. Ss compare answers with a partner, giving their reasons.

Answers
1 People often idealise the dead (i.e. remember their good points and forget their faults).
2 She was sceptical – she didn't believe her mother was as happy and as optimistic as people said.
3 He possibly felt uneasy about what it might contain and the effect it might have on Catherine.
4 Ss' own answers.
5 Ss' own answers.
6 curious, nervous, excited
7 (suggested answers) Catherine was sceptical about how happy her mother was before she died; her father and stepmother were uneasy about giving her the memory box; Catherine is curious about why they felt so uneasy; Catherine was uninterested in her mother when she was growing up and initially she was uninterested in the box; Catherine used to feel annoyed if people referred to Charlotte as her stepmother.

6 ▶ Ss discuss the questions in pairs. Get feedback from various Ss.

Grammar | preparatory *it*

OPTIONAL LEAD-IN

Ask Ss: *Would you like to read 'The Memory Box'? Why/Why not?* Then write the following sentences on the board:
To read this book would be interesting.
To read this book would be boring.
Ask: *What is the subject of these sentences?* (*To read this book*).
Explain that both sentences are grammatically correct but they do not sound very stylish or fluent in English. Elicit other ways of expressing this (e.g. *I would/wouldn't like to read it because I think it would be interesting/boring*) and introduce the idea of putting preparatory *it* at the beginning of the sentence.
Write on board: *It would be interesting/not be interesting to read this book.* Ask Ss to compare these sentences with the earlier ones.

7a ▶ Ss look at the three pairs of sentences and decide which sentence seems clearer in each pair and why. Ss compare answers in pairs, then as a whole class. Ask: *What is the subject of the b sentences in each pair?* (1b *That they were relieved when I showed little interest*, 2b *To find the box at last*, 3b *Going back into our old house*.)

Answers
Sentence a in each pair because of the use of *It* at the beginning of the sentence.

b ▶ Ss look at the Active grammar box and put the headings in the correct place in the box.

Active grammar
A The subject is a clause
B The subject is an infinitive expression
C The subject is an *-ing* form

8 ▶ Explain that we often use *it* at the beginning of sentences in this way; there are also certain commonly used fixed expressions which use preparatory *it*. Ss match the beginning of each sentence to the most appropriate ending. Let them compare answers with a partner.

Answers
2	c	6	a
3	h	7	d
4	b	8	g
5	e		

▶ Ask Ss to decide whether each expression is followed by the following items: a clause (*it's clear, it seemed*); an infinitive (*it's interesting, it was good of you, it's my intention*); an *-ing* form (*it's no use, it's worth*).

▶ Focus Ss' attention on the Reference section on page 89.

9a ▶ Ss complete the sentences to make them true about themselves.

b ▶ Ss compare sentences. Encourage Ss to ask for and give further details. Get feedback from various Ss.

Speaking

10a ▶ 🔊 2.10 Play the recording. Ss listen and decide if the speaker is generally positive or negative about *The Memory Box*. Ss compare answers with a partner.

Answers
generally positive

OPTIONAL EXTENSION

Play the recording again. Ss identify the positive and the negative points mentioned by the speaker. (Positive points: *an interesting idea for a story*; *very well-written*; *you can relate to events, feelings and thoughts in Catherine's life*; *easy to read*. Negative points: *a bit slow*; *took a long time to work out the significance of the objects in the box*.)

b ▶ Ask Ss: *Do you enjoy reading? How many of you are reading a book at the moment? Is it good?* Elicit the names of one or two books which Ss are reading at the moment.

▶ Ss then think about a book (or film if they cannot think of a book) that they have read/seen recently and which they can remember quite well (in any language). They make notes using the four points given. Remind Ss that they just write notes, not write down exactly what they will say.

c ▶ Put Ss in small groups and ask them to tell each other about the book/film they chose. They should talk about the plot, things they liked, how they felt, and any criticisms they have, referring to their notes if necessary. Get feedback from various Ss.

11a ▶ ⬤ 2.11 Ask Ss: *Do you ever read in English? If so, what kind of things do you read – novels, websites, newspaper/magazine articles?* Focus Ss' attention on the questions in the Lifelong learning box but do not ask them to answer the questions yet. Explain that they are going to hear two people discussing reading in English. Play the recording. Ss listen and note down what the speakers say about the four points in the box. Get feedback from the whole class.

> **Answers**
> 1 improve your reading skills, your vocabulary range and your writing
> 2 because there are so many unfamiliar words and it is slow and boring to look them all up in the dictionary
> 3 by reading in chunks of four or five words rather than one word at a time
> 4 it helps you focus on how much you do understand rather than all the words you don't understand.

b ▶ Ss discuss the questions with a partner. Get feedback from the whole class. Write a list of the strategies Ss use on the board.

> **OPTIONAL EXTENSION**
> Encourage Ss to choose a book or graded reader to read, either through the school library, local bookshop or, if your Ss have access to the Internet, through www.penguinreaders.com. When they have chosen and read a book, Ss give a short presentation about it for the class (similar to exercise 10) at the beginning/end of each lesson on a regular basis. Ss could recommend books to each other. In this way you could start a class 'book club'.

6 Vocabulary | Idioms to describe people

> **OPTIONAL WARMER**
> Ss look at the cartoons. In pairs, they discuss what kind of person is being identified in each one. They do not look at the idioms yet.

1a ▶ Ss match the underlined expressions with the correct meanings. Ss compare answers with a partner.

> **Answers**
> 1 f   5 g
> 2 h   6 c
> 3 b   7 d
> 4 a   8 e

1b ▶ Ss match the cartoons to five of the idioms.

> **Answers**
> A 3   B 6   C 5   D 8   E 7

2 ▶ Ss complete the sentences using one of the idioms from exercise 1a. Tell Ss not to look at the expressions in exercise 1 but to try to remember them. Ss compare answers with a partner.

> **Answers**
> 1 know-all
> 2 loner
> 3 high-flyer
> 4 in the neck
> 5 awkward customer
> 6 in the right place
> 7 as nails
> 8 fish

3a ▶ Ss think about five people they know who they could describe with five of the expressions from exercise 1. Ss should not tell each other which expressions they have chosen at this stage.

b ▶ Put Ss in small groups. They take turns to describe one of the people they have chosen to the others in their group. They should say how they know the person and what he/she is like, but they should not mention the expression they think that person typifies. The other Ss try to decide which expression from exercise 1 is appropriate for the person.

4 ▶ Ss discuss the questions in pairs. Get feedback from the whole class. Ask about how these expressions vary/are similar in the Ss' own language.

6 Communication

In this lesson, Ss listen to people talking about making a time capsule and giving advice about how to do it and what to put in. Ss then discuss what they would put into their own time capsules.

Time capsules have become more popular in recent years as a way of leaving our mark on the future. People choose items which somehow represent their lives or life in the present time. These are then put into a special sealed container and buried for future generations to find. Time capsules preserve relevant facts and features of history and can serve as valuable reminders of one generation for another.

OPTIONAL WARMER
Ss discuss these questions in small groups.
If you could save one object from your house in a fire, what would it be and why?
Which one object of yours would you like your children or grandchildren to keep and why?

1 ▶ Ss look at the photo, read the information and discuss the questions as a whole class.

Answer
They are intended for future generations. People put significant objects from this period of time into them so that future generations will be able to understand us better.

2a ▶ 🔘 2.12 Explain that Ss are going to listen to two people planning a time capsule. Focus Ss' attention on the photos of possible things that could go in the capsule. Elicit the meanings of globe and photo album. Play the recording. Ss listen and answer.

Answers
1 five things
2 a globe and a pair of jeans

b ▶ Ask Ss to look at the How to... box. Explain that these are all different ways of explaining reasons for your choices. Ss look at the sentences and try to predict what the missing words in each gap are. Tell Ss that four of the sentences are included in the recording. Play the recording again. Ss listen and complete the four sentences given and then decide on the missing word in the other two sentences. Ss compare answers with a partner.

Answers
We should include a globe **because**, ...
I think we should include a globe of the world **so that** ...
Jeans would be good **since** ...
How about including a photo album **as** ...
In my opinion, we should include some typical clothes in **order to** ...
Why don't we include a newspaper to show ...

▶ Explain that *because*, *since* and *as* are very similar in meaning. *In order to* and *to* also have the same meaning.

3a ▶ Put Ss in groups of four or five and ask them to choose five things to put in a time capsule. Encourage Ss to use their own ideas and to justify their choices by giving reasons.

b ▶ Each group member moves to another group so that each new group is made up of new Ss who have prepared different time capsules. Ss explain their choices to each other. Get feedback from the whole class. Ask Ss: *Did you have similar/different things in your capsules?*

OPTIONAL EXTENSION
Put Ss in small groups. They should identify three positive and three negative things in relation to how future generations will view the present era. Elicit their ideas on the board under the two headings during whole class feedback.
If Ss find this interesting, ask them to write a short letter about this to include in the time capsule and give future historians an insight into how we view ourselves and our era.

6 Review and practice

1 ▶

> **Answers**
> 2 used to be
> 3 get used to not understanding
> 4 used to finish
> 5 get used to having

2 ▶

> **Answers**
> 1 'd reminded
> 2 dyeing
> 3 was going
> 4 'd have brought
> 5 didn't bring
> 6 could've phoned
> 7 would've liked
> 8 hadn't been

3 ▶

> **Answers**
> 1 It was great to talk to you today.
> 2 It is clear that we need someone to take charge.
> 3 It is worth finding out the name of the person you need to talk to.
> 4 It seems that using mnemonics really helps me remember things.
> 5 It's no use complaining to me about it.
> 6 It was really kind of you to give me your ticket.
> 7 It is my ambition to take part in a marathon for charity.
> 8 It is surprising that you don't want to go skiing.

4 ▶

> **Answers**
> 1 relieved
> 2 clean-shaven
> 3 vivid
> 4 sceptical
> 5 muscular
> 6 nostalgic
> 7 scruffy
> 8 confused

5 ▶

> **Answers**
> 1 tip
> 2 bit
> 3 pain
> 4 takes
> 5 right
> 6 hard
> 7 jog
> 8 customer

6 Writing bank

1a/b ▶ Ss discuss the question and then check their answers by reading the review.

> **Answer**
> a = paragraph 3
> b = paragraph 2
> c = paragraph 1

2 ▶ Ss read the review again and answer the questions.

> **Answers**
> 1 F (it takes place in the future)
> 2 F (He was sceptical about whether he would enjoy it)
> 3 T
> 4 F (the book is a bit frightening sometimes)
> 5 F (he thinks everyone should read it, even if you are not interested in politics)
> 6 T

3 ▶ Ss complete the How to... box.

> **Answers**
> One of the **strengths** of the book ...
> ... I couldn't put it **down**.
> I would highly **recommend** this book.
> The only **negative** thing I would say ...
> It is also a very **gripping** story.
>
> Note: the adjective *fascinating* is also used in the review of *1984* but it is not possible to say *very fascinating*).
> Possible adjectives to describe the characters are: *believable, interesting, well-rounded, colourful.*

4a/b ▶ Ss plan and write a review of a book or film they have read/seen.

Overview

Lead-in	**Vocabulary:** Discussing excessive behaviour
7.1	**Can do:** Describe food and different attitudes to food **Grammar:** Quantifiers with countable and uncountable nouns **Vocabulary:** Food and cooking **Speaking and Pronunciation:** Intonation: questions **How to...** give and check instructions **Reading:** Super Size Me
7.2	**Can do:** Explain a problem and request a solution **Grammar:** Passives **Vocabulary:** Verb phrases about shopping **Speaking and Pronunciation:** Stress: emphasis (2) **How to...** complain about goods and services **Listening:** Top prices at auctions
7.3	**Can do:** Talk about luxuries and necessities **Grammar:** *have/get something done* **Vocabulary:** Excess **Reading:** Pet heaven?
Vocabulary	Prefixes
Communication	**Can do:** Communicate clearly in a restaurant, shop and hairdresser's
Writing bank	Explain a problem and request action **How to...** explain a problem and request action
Extra activities	ActiveTeach and ActiveBook

CEFR Can do objectives
7.1 Describe food and different attitudes to food
7.2 Explain a problem and request a solution
7.3 Talk about luxuries and necessities
Communication Communicate clearly in a restaurant, shop and hairdresser's
Writing bank Explain a problem and request action

CEFR Portfolio ideas
a) Prepare a menu for a restaurant which only serves healthy options. Plan starters, main courses, desserts and drinks. Include details of how each dish is prepared and served.
b) Prepare a catalogue entry for an auction. The entry should be for an imagined piece of memorabilia which belonged/was used by a famous person. Describe the item and give details of who it belonged to.
c) You have an important exam in two weeks. Prepare a study timetable for your wall. Give yourself daily and weekly targets and identify treats/rewards you will give yourself if you meet these targets.

Lead-in

OPTIONAL WARMER

Teach the word *junkie* (an addict, usually a drug addict) and the suffix *-oholic/aholic* (most commonly used in *alcoholic* – someone who is dependent on/addicted to alcohol). Explain that we use both terms to describe addictive behaviour. Elicit commonly used colloquial expressions which use these terms and write them on the board (e.g. *a chocoholic* – someone who loves and eats too much chocolate); *a workaholic* (someone who is obsessed with work); *a shopoholic* (someone who spends lots of time and money shopping, often on things that they don't really need); *an exercise junkie* (someone who spends a great deal of time in the gym and on other forms of exercise); *a diet junkie* (someone who tries out new diets to lose weight on a regular basis); *a coffee junkie* (someone who drinks a lot of coffee), etc. Ss discuss how common/healthy these behaviours are in relation to themselves and society in general.

---

1 ▶ Ss discuss the questions in pairs.

2a ▶ Read the questions through with the class. Ss then work in pairs and discuss the meaning of the underlined words. Encourage them to use dictionaries to help with the meaning, word stress and pronunciation of the words. Get feedback from the whole class.

Answers
1 *extravagant* = spending or costing a lot of money, especially more than is necessary or more than you can actually afford
2 *excessive* = much more than is reasonable or necessary
3 *luxury* = something expensive that you do not need but you buy for pleasure and enjoyment
4 *extra-large* = very large
5 *spoilt* = when someone (usually a child) is rude and behaves badly because they have always been given what they want and been allowed to do what they want
6 *overpriced* = when something is more expensive than it should be
7 *far-fetched* = extremely unlikely to be true or to happen
8 *spending spree* = a short period of time when you do a lot of spending

---

b ▶ Ss ask and answer the questions with a partner. Ss report back on how many/which of their answers were similar to their partner's during whole-class feedback.

EXTEND THE LEAD-IN

Ss discuss how much/many of the following things they would consider excessive: *hours of TV viewing for children*; *baths/showers a day*; *husbands/wives in one lifetime*; *children in one family*; *cars for one person*; *holiday homes for one family*; *the salary for the prime minister of a large country*; *guests at a seated dinner party*; *the price of a wedding dress/suit*. Get feedback from the whole class.

7.1 Food for thought

In this lesson, Ss read an article about the film *Super Size Me* and another similar food experiment. They listen to someone describing how to make their favourite dish and discuss how to prepare a favourite dish of their own.

Reading

> *Super Size Me*, made in 2003, is a film which documents Morgan Spurlock's one-month existence on fast food and its disastrous consequences. In the film, Spurlock eats three McDonald's meals a day, every day, for a month. He only eats food from McDonald's and every time an employee asks if he would like to 'super size' the meal, he agrees. Spurlock knew the experiment was extremely unhealthy but his intention was to show people what this kind of diet can do to you. The film could represent your life: in 30 days you see what could happen to you over 20 or 30 years of over-consumption.

OPTIONAL WARMER

Elicit what we usually mean by *fast food* in English-speaking countries and write suggestions on the board (e.g. takeaway restaurants; American-style fast-food restaurants; sandwich bars; ready-made dinners bought in the supermarket and re-heated in the oven). Add typical fast-food choices in Ss' own countries/cultures to the list. Ss discuss which they consider to be the healthiest/least healthy form of fast food and which they like best/least.

1 ▶ Ss look at the photo and discuss the questions in pairs. Get feedback from the whole class. Elicit in what circumstances and how often Ss have fast-food meals.

2a ▶ Ss look at the two questions, then read the article to find the answers. Ss compare answers with a partner.

Answers
1   There were two experiments. One was where Morgan Spurlock ate three McDonald's meals every day for a month. He also had to agree to 'super size' the meal each time an employee asked if he wanted to. In the second experiment, scientists compared the behaviour of rats who were fed a high-fat diet for ten days with rats who were fed a low-fat diet over the same period.
2   Similar results – in both experiments, the high-fat diets high led to severe health damage.

b ▶ Ss read the article again and work in pairs to explain what each of the phrases means. Remind them to look at the phrases in context and use any clues they can to work out the meaning.

Answers
1   a much larger amount
2   eat/drink a lot of food containing high levels of fat
3   getting fatter and heavier was one bad consequence of the experiment – but there were others too
4   a way of quickly predicting what your future life will be like
5   consequences which will happen quickly as opposed to long-term effects, where it takes much longer to see the consequences
6   bring about more damage

c ▶ Ss discuss the questions in pairs. Get feedback from various Ss.

Grammar | quantifiers

OPTIONAL LEAD-IN

Write these sentences on the board.
1   I had a delicious <u>burger/meat</u> yesterday.
2   I had some delicious <u>burger/meat</u> yesterday.
Ask Ss to work in pairs and to decide which of the alternatives in each sentence is correct and why.
(1 *burger* because it is countable and therefore, we use *a*; 2 *meat* because it is uncountable and therefore, we use *some*)

3 ▶ Ss look at the four sentences and then answer the questions about the underlined nouns. Ss compare answers with a partner.

Answers
1   a   *meals* = countable
     b   *food* = uncountable
     c   *(a black) coffee* = countable
     d   *coffee* = uncountable
2   *Coffee* can be both countable and uncountable. You can say *a coffee* or *two coffees* when you are talking about cups of coffee. You can say *some coffee* when you are talking about coffee in general and are not saying exactly how much.
3   (Suggested answers)
     Countable nouns: *banana*
     Uncountable nouns: *salt, bread, fruit*
     Nouns which can be both: *chocolate, cake, chicken*

▶ Explain to Ss that for nouns which can be both countable and uncountable, the meaning is slightly different in each case.

▶ Ask Ss what the difference is between *I bought some chickens* and *I bought some chicken*. (*Chickens* is countable in the first sentence and means 'whole chickens'. We can count the chickens. You could say *I bought two/three chickens*. *Chicken* in the second sentence is uncountable and means the type of meat in general. We do not necessarily mean a whole chicken, and it cannot be used in the plural form *chickens*.)

OPTIONAL EXTENSION

Put Ss in pairs. They discuss the difference in meaning between the following pairs of sentences.
1a *I like two sugars in my tea. (spoons/cubes of sugar)*
1b *I like sugar in my tea. (sugar in general)*
2a *I ate a chocolate. (a separate chocolate in a box of chocolates)*
2b *I ate some chocolate. (chocolate in general)*
3a *I need a room to study in. (a separate room with four walls in a house)*
3b *I need room to study in. (space in general, not necessarily in a separate room)*
4a *I found some grey hairs this morning. (single grey hairs on your head)*
4b *I have grey hair. (your hair in general)*

4a ▶ Explain that *some* can be used with both countable and uncountable nouns but there are many other quantifiers too. Some quantifiers can be used with both countable and uncountable nouns and some with either countable or uncountable nouns only. Ss look at the underlined quantifiers in the Active grammar box and match them with the rules. Ss compare answers with a partner.

Active grammar

A a large number of, many, a few
B a great deal of, a little, much, a piece of, a bit of

▶ Focus Ss on the Reference section on page 103.

b ▶ Ss look at the quantifiers in the Active grammar box again and categorise them according to the groups given. Ss check answers with a partner, then as a whole class.

Active grammar

a a large number of, a lot of, a great deal of, many, much, lots of
b a little, a few
c some, a bit of, a piece of, any

c ▶ Ss work in pairs. They discuss the use of *few/a few* and *little/a little* in the four examples.

Answers
few and *little* (without *a*) are used in a rather negative way, meaning not as many/much as you expected or wanted
a few and *a little* are used in a more positive way.

5 ▶ Ss complete the sentences with the correct word/phrase. Ss compare answers with a partner.

Answers
1	many	6	lots
2	a little	7	a great deal of
3	much	8	bit
4	piece	9	a few
5	some	10	lot

6a ▶ Ss identify the two correct sentences and find and correct the mistakes in the other six.

Answers
1 a lot of time
2 How much sugar / How many sugars
3 ✓
4 a bit of cake
5 How ~~many~~ much fruit
6 ✓
7 a ~~large number~~ great deal of money / large amount of money
8 ~~a few~~ some new furniture

b ▶ Ss take turns to ask and answer the questions from exercise 6a in pairs.

Vocabulary | food and cooking

OPTIONAL LEAD-IN

Write the following headings on the board: *fish/meat*; *fruit/vegetables*; *dairy*; *carbohydrates*; *drinks*. Ask Ss to list all the things they ate/drank over the previous day according to the headings. Ss then compare their lists in pairs. They tell each other whether they prepared/chose the food themselves. Get feedback from the whole class. Ask: *What type of food did you eat most?*

7a ▶ Ss work in pairs and put the words in the box in the correct place in the mind map. Encourage them to use dictionaries to help if necessary. Get feedback from the whole class. Help with the meaning and pronunciation of these words.

Answers
Food: beef, peach, cabbage, parsley
Ways of cooking: bake, scramble, fry, roast, boil, grill
Kitchen equipment: saucepan, oven, cooker, frying pan, wooden spoon, plate
Taste: sweet, bitter, salty, sour, savoury

b ▶ Ss work with a partner and discuss the difference between the pairs of words.

> **Answers**
> 1. a cook = a person who cooks.
>   a cooker = the machine you use for cooking.
> 2. a vegetable = a food like carrot, potato.
>   a vegetarian = a person who does not eat meat.
> 3. a recipe = instructions about how to cook something.
>   a dish = the thing you make (e.g. beef stroganoff).
> 4. rare = cooked only a little (usually for meat, especially steak).
>   raw = not cooked at all.
> 5. to stir = to mix slowly.
>   to beat = to mix quickly.
> 6. to slice = to cut into thin pieces.
>   to chop = to cut into small squares.
>   to grate = to use a grater to make very small pieces of food (e.g. cheese or carrots).

c ▶ Ss add at least two more words to each group of words in the mind map with a partner. Pool suggestions on the board during whole class feedback, making sure Ss understand all the words.

> **Suggested answers**
> Food: chicken, apple
> Ways of cooking: simmer, peel
> Kitchen equipment: casserole dish, baking tray
> Taste: dry, moist

8 ▶ Ss choose the correct alternatives.

> **Answers**
> 1. raw
> 2. stir
> 3. salty
> 4. chop
> 5. sweet
> 6. boil
> 7. dish
> 8. cooker
> 9. roast
> 10. vegetarian

Pronunciation | intonation: questions

9 ▶ 🔘 2.14 Play the recording. Ss listen and decide whether they would like the meal described or not.

> **OPTIONAL VARIATION**
> Explain that Ss will listen to the recording twice: the first time just to get the general idea and the second time to focus on the language used in more detail. Write the four questions from exercise 10a on the board. Explain that these are asked during the recording. Play the recording. Ss listen and find the answers to the questions.
> (1 her grandma's pancake recipe as a special meal for some friends. 2 pancakes and spinach are layered, covered in sauce and baked in the oven. 3 Yes. 4 Yes.)
> Get feedback from the whole class. Ask: *Would you like to eat this pancake dish? Why/Why not?*

10a ▶ 🔘 2.14 Play the recording. Ss listen to the four questions and identify which of the two question types mentioned they are. Ss compare answers with a partner.

> **Answers**
> Questions 1 and 2 use questions words (*What/How*) and are asking for specific information.
> (Other questions words are *Who, where, when, why, which, whose*).
> Questions 3 and 4 use *Yes/No* questions and are just checking information. Question words are not used in these types of question.

b ▶ Ask Ss to listen to the four questions again and decide whether the intonation goes up or down in each one. Play the recording again. Ss listen and then repeat the questions.

▶ Point out that the intonation rises at the end for questions 1 and 2 which use question words and are asking for specific information; the intonation falls at the end for questions 3 and 4 which are Yes/No questions used to check information.

▶ Focus Ss' attention on the section on Intonation in the Pronunciation bank on page 161.

Speaking

11 ▶ Ask Ss to look at the How to... box. Play the recording again. Ss listen and complete the sentences. Ss compare answers with a partner.

> **Answers**
> First, you make ...
> Then, you fry ...
> Finally, you bake ...
> ... make **sure** it's not too thick.
> ... be **careful** not to put too much ...
> The **important** thing is ...
> Is that **because** there are ...
> So you **mean** you pour ...
> So it **sounds** like there are ...

12a ▶ Give Ss a few minutes to think of their favourite dish under the headings given.

b ▶ Put Ss in small groups and take turns to describe the dish to each other. Encourage Ss to ask for and give further details as they discuss the different dishes.

> **OPTIONAL EXTENSION**
> Ask Ss to write a recipe of the dish they talked about, including a list of ingredients and instructions. Ss collect their recipes together and make a 'Class Recipe Book'.

7.2 Buy, buy, buy

In this lesson, Ss listen to part of a radio programme about the extraordinary things people buy and the very high prices they pay at auctions, both at traditional auction houses and online. Ss listen to a conversation where a customer is complaining about damaged goods and then practise making and responding to complaints themselves.

Listening

Two of the most famous auction houses operating internationally are Sotheby's (established in London in 1744) and Christie's (established in London in 1766). People go to look, to bid and perhaps to buy a range of different items, especially collectable art, furniture and jewellery. Nowadays, however, traditional auctions also need to compete with online auctions like eBay, which was founded by Pierre Omidyar in 1995. It started small, and has now become a massive success with over 125 million users, buying and selling an endless array of different products. Buyers and sellers are brought together quickly and easily: sellers can list items for sale, buyers can bid for items of interest and all eBay users can browse through listed items in a fully automated way.

OPTIONAL WARMER

Elicit different kinds of shops and write them on the board (e.g. *bookshop*; *clothes shop*; *second-hand shop*; *arts and crafts shop*; *record store*; *outdoor market*, etc.). *Ss discuss the following questions in small groups.*
What is your favourite kind of shop to browse in?
Do you prefer to shop alone or with someone else? Why?
Do you like shopping online? Why/Why not?
What do you do if you decide afterwards that you don't like something you've bought?

1 ▶ Ss look at the photos with a partner and discuss the questions. Get feedback from the whole class. Don't confirm any answers at this point.

2 ▶ ⊙ 2.15 Tell Ss that they are going to listen to part of a radio programme. Explain that they will hear the recording twice. The first time, they will listen for the general idea. The second time, they will listen for more detailed information. Play the recording. Ss listen and answer the questions. Then they compare answers with a partner.

Answers
1 the sculpture; the comic; the *Star Wars* figures; Marilyn Monroe's dress; the glove. Each of these things was sold at auction (either traditionally or on eBay).
2 Some of Elvis Presley's hair, leftover toast from Justin Timberlake, a used tissue from Scarlett Johansson.

3 ▶ Ss read through the statements. Play the recording again. Ss listen and choose the correct option for each statement. Then Ss compare answers with a partner.

Answers
1	$104.3 million	6	know
2	don't know	7	1958
3	1938	8	a fan
4	one	9	$5,300
5	one		

4 ▶ Ss discuss the questions in small groups.

OPTIONAL EXTENSION

If your Ss have access to the Internet, they could do some research for a mini-project. Put Ss in pairs. Give each pair a different topic: e.g. *clothes*; *music*; *paintings*; *stamps*; *books*; *furniture*; *cars*, *historical figures*; *the British royal family*; *religious figures*. Each pair must find out some interesting facts relating to collections of items/sales of individual items on their topic and prepare a short presentation for the class.

Vocabulary | verb phrases about shopping

5 ▶ Ss work in pairs and discuss the difference in meaning between the underlined verb phrase in each pair of sentences. Encourage them to look at the context and try to work out the meaning.

Answers
1 a *to bid for something* = to make an offer to buy something at an auction
   b *to haggle for something* = to negotiate with the seller over the price of something especially in a market
2 a *to get a bargain* = to pay a lower than usual price for something
   b *to get a discount* = to pay less than the original price because the seller lowers the price
3 a *to get a refund* = to take something back to a shop and get your money back
   b *to get a receipt* = to get a piece of paper from the shop to prove you bought something
4 a *to be able to afford something* = to have enough money to pay for something
   b *to be worth it* = for something to be the value of what you paid for it

6a ▶ Ss rewrite the sentences using one of the verb phrases from exercise 5. Ss compare answers with a partner.

Answers
1 offer to pay for = bid
2 cheap, good things = bargains
3 money off the real price = a discount
4 haven't got enough money = can't afford it
5 my money back = a refund
6 try and negotiate a lower price = haggle
7 too expensive = not worth it
8 the paper they give you when I buy something = a receipt

b ▶ Ss talk about which of the sentences are true for them. Encourage Ss to ask for and give further details during the discussion.

Grammar | passives

7a ▶ Ss look at the example sentences in the Active grammar box and answer the questions in pairs. Get feedback from the whole class on question 1. Don't ask for any feedback on question 2 at this point.

> **Answers**
> 1   Active: *bought*
>   Passive: *was bought*

b ▶ Ss check their answers to question 2 by reading the rules of meaning A and B in the box. Explain that we would choose the passive voice in 1 because we do not know who performed the action, and in 2 because the focus is on the action of buying Michael Jackson's glove (not who bought it), and so this is put at the beginning of the sentence.

▶ Focus Ss' attention on the Reference section on page 103.

8a ▶ Ask Ss to look at the audioscript on page 170 and find examples of the passive voice. Ss compare answers with a partner.

> **Answers**
> the sculpture **was sold** at auction
> the winning bid **was made** ...
> one of the helmets ... **was found** ... and **bought** ...
> huge sums of money **have been paid** ...
> $1,300,000 **was paid** ...
> one of Michael Jackson's gloves ... **was bought** ...
> it **will** now **be displayed** ...
> a clump of Elvis Presley's hair ... **was cut**
> it **was sold**
> it **was bought** by a fan

b ▶ Remind Ss how to form the passive voice by using a particular form of the verb to be followed by the past participle. Ss read the rule about forming the passive in the Active grammar box and complete the sentences with the correct passive form of the verb in brackets. Ss compare answers with a partner.

> **Answers**
> 1   is being cleaned
> 2   was found
> 3   was being displayed
> 4   have been bought
> 5   had been published
> 6   will be paid
> 7   is going to be opened
> 8   can be bought

9 ▶ Ss look at the spoken sentences, then rewrite them to make them more formal, written sentences. They must begin each sentence as indicated and use the passive as required. Ss look at the example given so that they are clear about what to do. Ss compare answers with a partner.

> **Suggested answers**
> 1   ... are going to get higher bids at next month's auction.
> 2   ... has been bought by an anonymous buyer.
> 3   ... was bought for over $104 million in an auction.
> 4   ... will be sold for even higher prices.
> 5   ... was worn by Ursula Andress in the James Bond film *Dr No* was sold in 2001.
> 6   ... was bought for $61,000 by the American, Robert Earl, co-founder of Planet Hollywood.
> 7   ... was composed, was bought by the singer George Michael.

Speaking

10 ▶ Read through the four situations with the class. Ss discuss with a partner what they would do in each situation and why. Get feedback from the whole class. Find out how many Ss feel similarly about the situations. Encourage them to give reasons.

11 ▶ ● 2.16 Ask Ss to read through the questions. Play the recording. Ss listen and answer the questions. Ss compare answers with a partner.

> **Answers**
> 1   situation 2
> 2   irritated but resigned
> 3   to collect the damaged TV the following Thursday and send a replacement as soon as possible

12 ▶ Ss focus on the sentences in the How to... box. Play the recording again. Ss listen and complete the gaps. Ss compare answers with a partner.

> **Answers**
> I'd just like to **complain** ...
> You **promised** that delivery ...
> Oh, I'm **terribly sorry** ...
> I can only give my **apologies** ...
> I do **apologise** for that
> I'm not prepared to accept **damaged** goods.
> I'd be **grateful** if you could ...
> We'll send someone to pick up the **faulty** TV ...
> I'll send out a **replacement**
> I can **assure** you ...

Pronunciation | stress: emphasis (2)

13 ▶ ● 2.17 Explain to Ss that they are going to hear two versions of the same conversation. Focus Ss' attention on the underlined part of the audioscript on page 170. Play the recording. Ss listen to the two versions. Ask: *Which is the more effective way to complain? Why?*

> **Answers**
> The speakers in version 2 stress key words
> (e.g. Woman: *complain, promised, two weeks,*
> *acceptable*; Man: *terribly sorry, little later, apologies*) to
> give emphasis to what they are saying. There is also a
> higher range of intonation in version 2. This has the effect
> of making the speaker sound confident, assertive and
> sure of themselves. Version 1 is spoken in a rather flat,
> emotionless way.

▶ Focus Ss' attention on the Pronunciation bank on page 161.

14 ▶ Put Ss in pairs (A and B). They choose one of the situations in exercise 10. Ss A take on the role of customer making a complaint; Ss B take on the role of employee, responding to the complaint. Encourage Ss to use the language from the How to... box. When they have finished the roleplay, Ss choose a second situation and change roles. Ask some of the pairs to perform their role plays for the class.

> **OPTIONAL EXTENSION**
> Put Ss in small groups. Ask them the following questions.
> *What kind of things are you most likely to complain*
> *about?*
> *What kind of things (if any) do you tend not to complain*
> *about, even when you are dissatisfied with goods or*
> *services you have received?*
> *Do you prefer to complain in writing, by phone or in*
> *person? Why?*
> *Who do you complain to?*

7.3 It's a dog's life

In this lesson, Ss read a magazine article about how some people overindulge their pets and they discuss their own reactions and attitudes to pets. They also discuss the necessities and luxuries of life.

Reading

> **OPTIONAL WARMER**
> Elicit different breeds of dog (e.g. *poodle, terrier, spaniel,*
> *German shepherd, Irish wolfhound, labrador*). Teach the
> word *mongrel* (mixed breed). If possible, show pictures of
> different types of dog, especially a Yorkshire terrier, which
> is mentioned in the article.
> Ss work in pairs and tell each other which breeds of dog
> are popular in their country and which type of dog they
> like best and why.

1 ▶ Ss look at the photos and discuss the questions in pairs. Get feedback from the whole class. Ask: *What would you say about the owners of the dogs in the photos?*

2 ▶ Ss read the article quickly (you might like to give Ss a two-minute time limit) and answer the question. Remind them not to try to understand everything at this stage but just to focus on the one question. Explain that they will have an opportunity to read the article more slowly afterwards. Ss compare answers with a partner.

> **Answers**
> The dog in the bed, the dog with the necklace and the
> terrier (in the coat) are mentioned in the text. The poodle
> in the hair salon is not mentioned.

3a ▶ Read the four statements through with the class. Ss then read the first paragraph again and decide if the statements are true, false or not given. Ask Ss to correct the false statements. Ss compare answers with a partner.

> **Answers**
> 1 T   3 NG
> 2 F (40%)   4 T

b ▶ Ss read the rest of the article and decide whether the descriptions apply to one of the pets mentioned and, if so, to which ones. Explain that some of the descriptions apply to more than one of the pets. Encourage Ss to highlight the part of the article which tells them the answers. Ss compare answers with a partner.

▶ Useful vocabulary from the article will be dealt with in exercise 8.

> **Answers**
> 1 Pixie   5 Pixie/Beauty
> 2 Beauty/Mignon   6 Mignon
> 3 Pixie   7 none
> 4 none   8 Beauty

4 ▶ Ss discuss the questions in pairs. Get feedback from the whole class. Compare different attitudes to pets in different countries.

OPTIONAL EXTENSION

Put Ss in small groups. They make a list of five advantages (e.g. guard-dog; company for an older person) and five disadvantages (e.g. taking it on holidays; barking at night) of having a dog. Get feedback from the whole class and pool all the suggestions on the board. Put Ss in pairs (A and B) and ask them to roleplay the following situation: *A and B are flatmates/family members. A wants to get a dog; B does not want to get a dog.* They try to find a solution in the roleplay.

Grammar | *have/get something done*

OPTIONAL LEAD-IN

Write these sentences on the board.
1 Claudette washed Mignon's hair.
2 Claudette had Mignon's hair washed.
Ask Ss to discuss this question in pairs: *What is the difference in meaning (if any) between them?*
(1: Claudette washed Mignon's hair herself;
2: Claudette arranged/paid for Mignon's hair to be washed by someone else)

5a ▶ Ss complete the examples in the Active grammar box using *had*, *have* and *gets*. Then ask them to check their answers in the text on page 98. Ss compare answers with a partner.

Active grammar

1 have
2 had
3 gets

---

b ▶ Ss complete the rule.

Active grammar

Form: *have* (or *get*) + object + past participle

---

c ▶ Ss look at the rule and answer the question. Ss compare answers with a partner.

Active grammar

by the hairdresser

---

d ▶ Ss to work in pairs again and to look at rules B and C in the box. Ss match each rule (B and C) with the correct example 4–6. Ss compare answers with a partner.

Active grammar

B 4 and 5   C 6

▶ Explain that Rule B usually applies when something bad happens to someone or to their possessions, something they didn't want to happen, which was done by someone or something else. It is used in informal English (*I got my leg broken playing football; They had their roof damaged by a falling tree*) to describe unpleasant things, caused by someone or something else. When used to talk about something unpleasant or unwanted, this use is quite similar to the passive. However, when we are talking about pleasant things or things that you arranged to happen, Rule A usually applies (*I had flowers delivered to my house*).

▶ Focus Ss' attention on the Reference section on page 103.

6 ▶ Ss identify the two correct sentences and find and correct the mistakes in the other six sentences. Ss compare answers with a partner.

Answers
1 I've never had my hair ~~dye~~ dyed.
2 ✓
3 I never **have my house** decorated – I do it myself.
4 I haven't had my eyes ~~testing~~ tested for ages.
5 I've got a lot of things to get ~~doing~~ done by this weekend.
6 I have **some of my clothes dry-cleaned** every month.
7 ✓
8 I'd like to get my photo ~~took~~ taken by a professional photographer.

---

7 ▶ Read through the questions and the examples with the class. Then Ss discuss the questions in groups. Get feedback from various Ss.

Vocabulary | excess

8a ▶ Ss look at the example and compare the meaning of the underlined words.

Answer
a necessity = something you need
a luxury = something pleasant that you like but do not need

---

b ▶ Explain that they are going to focus on some of the vocabulary from the article on page 98 which relates to excess. First, Ss find the underlined word, then they look at the second example and discuss the meaning with a partner. Get feedback from the whole class. Model pronunciation and word stress, especially the *-ed* and *-t* endings and consonant clusters in *indulge*, *pampered* and *treated*.

Answers
1 completely extravagant
2 high-quality food
3 very expensive, luxurious
4 allowed to behave exactly as he or she wants and given everything he or she asks for
5 allow yourself (or someone else) to do something for pleasure
6 treat yourself well
7 to be very generous and kind towards someone
8 paid for something nice/special for somebody else

9a ▶ Ss choose the correct option in each sentence. Ss compare answers with a partner.

Answers			
1	indulge	6	treated
2	necessity	7	pamper
3	spoil	8	lavish
4	gourmet	9	luxury
5	over-the-top	10	spoilt

b ▶ Ss discuss which of the sentences are true about themselves with a partner. Get feedback from one or two Ss. Ask them to say a sentence that they completely agreed/disagreed with and elicit whether other Ss feel the same way.

Speaking

10a ▶ Focus Ss' attention on the Lifelong learning box. Ss look at the three ways of keeping yourself motivated and focused when studying. They think of an example for each with a partner.

Suggested answers
1 a plan of what to study each day for next week
2 'I will read an article from an English newspaper over the weekend.'
3 'I will take a break when I finish and have a bar of chocolate and a coffee.'

b ▶ Ss discuss the questions in pairs. Get feedback from the whole class.

OPTIONAL EXTENSION

Write the following headings on the board.
Where (library, kitchen table, bedroom)?
When (morning, late at night, before class)?
Noise (radio in background, complete silence)
How long (regular short bursts or long periods of study)?
Interruptions (phone, TV programmes)
Deadlines (in advance, at the last minute, ask for extensions)
Put Ss in small groups and ask them to compare their personal study habits and preferences.

11 ▶ Ss take turns to answer the questions in the quiz with a partner. Get feedback from the whole class. Find out how different/similar Ss are to each other.

OPTIONAL EXTENSION

Put Ss in small groups. Ask them whether the following topics related to animals are necessities or luxuries for humans: *zoos*; *testing products on animals*; *eating meat*; *pets*; *trained dogs and other animals*.

7 Vocabulary | Prefixes

OPTIONAL WARMER

Write the items a–c from exercise 1 on the board. Ask Ss, in pairs, to think of one example for each situation (e.g. a = someone talking loudly on a mobile on a bus).

1a ▶ ⬤ 2.18 Play the recording. Ss listen and match the people with the correct item. Ss compare answers with a partner.

Answers	
a	1
b	3
c	2

b ▶ Play the recording again. Ss listen and make brief notes about each story.

c ▶ Ss take turns to retell each story, using their notes from exercise 1b.

2a ▶ Ask Ss to look at definitions and at the audioscript on page 170. Explain that they are going to focus on prefixes. They find a word in the audioscript to match each definition. Ss compare answers with a partner.

Answers		
1	a	unusual
	b	extra-large
	c	monotonous
2	a	oversleep (overslept)
	b	underestimate(d)
	c	ex-boss
3	a	retrain
	b	bilingual
	c	multinational

b ▶ Ss look at the words from exercise 2a again and write the appropriate prefixes in the table. Ss compare answers with a partner.

Answers		
Prefixes	**Meanings**	**Examples**
mono	none/single	monotonous
bi	twice/two/every two	bilingual
multi	many	multinational
over	more than	oversleep
under	less than	underestimate
ex	former	ex-boss
re	again	retrain
extra	very	extra-large
un	not	unusual

c ▶ Focus Ss' attention on the hyphens in *ex-boss* and *extra-large*. Read the rule about hyphens through with the class. Ss write one more example for each prefix. Ss compare with a partner, then as a whole class

Possible answers
1 monocycle/monopoly
2 bimonthly/bilateral
3 multicoloured/multimedia
4 overspend/overripe
5 underage/underperform
6 ex-wife/ex-employer
7 redo/reboot
8 extrasensitive/extra-light
9 undecided/unfair

3a ▶ Ss complete the sentences with a word from the box. Not all the words can be used. Don't ask for feedback at this point.

b ▶ Ss compare their answers with a partner.

Answers
1 biannual
2 multi-purpose
3 extra-strong
4 undercooked
5 overworked
6 monolingual
7 rewrite
8 ex-girlfriend

4a ▶ Ss choose an item in exercise 1a to tell a story about. Ss prepare their stories, using as many words from exercises 2a and 3a as they can.

b ▶ Ss practise telling their stories in pairs.

7 Communication

In this lesson, Ss listen to dialogues about goods and services provided in a restaurant, a shop and a hairdresser. Ss then practise their own dialogues.

OPTIONAL WARMER

Ask Ss to discuss these questions in pairs.
When did you last go to a restaurant/clothes or shoe shop? Who did you go with? Where did you go? What did you eat/ buy? Was it overpriced or not? Did you get a bargain? When did you last go to the hairdresser? What did you have done? What did you do while you were waiting/having your hair done? Did you get value for money?

1a ▶ Ss look at the photos. They complete the word maps in pairs, including as many words as possible related to each place.

b ▶ Ss compare their word maps with a partner. Get feedback from the whole class. Pool ideas on the board, helping with unfamiliar words.

2 ▶ Ss look at the sentences and answer the question. Ss compare answers with a partner.

Answers
a 1, 4, 8
b 3, 6, 9, 10
c 2, 5, 7, 11

3a ▶ Divide the class into As (customer) and Bs (waiter/assistant). Ss A think of two problems for each situation and what action they would like done about it; Ss B think of problems which might cause complaints in each situation and what action they might take to solve the problem.

b ▶ Put Ss in pairs (A and B). They do the roleplay for the situations they chose in exercise 3a. Get feedback from the whole class. Ask: *Did you find a solution? What was it?*

OPTIONAL EXTENSION

Put Ss in pairs and ask them to prepare a leaflet about how to make complaints about goods or services. Write the following headings on the board to help Ss think or what to write: *who to speak to*; *tone of voice*; *gestures*; *how to behave*; *what to say*. Ss decide on six tips to include in the leaflet (e.g. *Try not to get angry, It is better to keep calm and polite.*)

7 Review and practice

1 ▶

Answers
1 some
2 a piece of
3 much
4 is
5 a little
6 a few
7 a bit of
8 some

2 ▶

Answers
1 She had new tyres fitted to her car yesterday.
2 She had a new cooker delivered yesterday.
3 She had her hair cut and had highlights done this morning.
4 She's having a carpet fitted in the living room at the moment.
5 She's going to have her watch repaired this afternoon.
6 She's going to have her eyes tested tomorrow.
7 She's going to have her windows cleaned tomorrow.
8 She's going to have her coat dry-cleaned tomorrow.

3 ▶

Answers
1 is included
2 was sent
3 will be delivered/are going to be delivered
4 is being repaired
5 has been opened
6 will be caught
7 were charged
8 had been employed

4 ▶

Answers
1 raw
2 for
3 worth
4 treat
5 lavish
6 refund
7 boil
8 sweet

5 ▶

Answers
1 over
2 under
3 mono
4 re
5 bi
6 multi
7 re
8 un

7 Writing bank

1 ▶

Answers
1 She didn't receive food and accommodation costs and was given misleading information after her flight from Malaga to London was cancelled due to an airline strike. This resulted in her rebooking a flight for four days later at double the standard price, even though there were cheaper flights available the following day.
2 Immediate compensation for the price of the rebooked ticket and for the accommodation and food costs she incurred.
3 state the problem; give details; request action

2 ▶ Ss' own answers.

3 ▶

Answers
explain a problem
was told
compensate me

4a/b ▶ Ss prepare and write an email about one of the situations.

8 Success

Overview

Lead-in	**Vocabulary:** Discussing excessive behaviour
8.1	**Can do:** Describe how you behave in different situations **Grammar:** *It's time, I'd rather, I'd better* **Vocabulary:** Describing personality **Speaking and Pronunciation: How to...** introduce general and specific points **Reading:** Are YOU a successful leader?
8.2	**Can do:** Report and describe what people say to you **Grammar:** Reported speech **Vocabulary:** Adjectives and intensifiers **Speaking and Pronunciation:** Intonation: reporting **Listening:** Sports psychology
8.3	**Can do:** Report the results of a survey **Grammar:** Reporting verbs **Speaking and Pronunciation: How to...** report the results of a survey **Reading:** Technology for toddlers **Listening:** A survey
Vocabulary	Phrasal verbs with three parts
Communication	**Can do:** Take an active part in a discussion
Writing bank	Write a positive description of someone **How to...** use appropriate language
Extra activities	ActiveTeach and ActiveBook

CEFR Can do objectives
8.1 Describe how you behave in different situations
8.2 Report and describe what people say to you
8.3 Report the results of a survey
Communication Take an active part in a discussion
Writing bank Write a positive description of someone

CEFR Portfolio ideas
a) Read the article on page 112. Imagine you have two children under five. Both are bright but one seems particularly so. A teacher has recommended the school in the article and you are considering sending both children there. In pairs, discuss how best to help your children reach their potential and succeed in school.
b) Conduct a survey among six people you know. Find out who they think is the greatest political leader of the past 100 years and which qualities they consider to be important in a leader. Write a report of your findings.
c) Write a magazine article. The title is 'Who am I now?' and it should describe how different situations can affect people's behaviour and bring out different sides to their personalities. Give examples and include personal experiences.

Lead-in

OPTIONAL WARMER
Write these seven verbs on the board and ask Ss to say which is the odd one out and why: *succeed*, *triumph*, *flourish*, *thrive*, *fail*, *achieve*, *accomplish*
(all the verbs have a similar meaning to *succeed* except *fail*, which means the opposite).
Then put Ss in pairs (A and B). Ask Ss A to look at the verbs *succeed*, *flourish* and *thrive*, and the Ss B to look at *achieve*, *accomplish* and *triumph*. Ss use dictionaries and write a definition and an example sentence for each of their three verbs. Ss then tell each other the definitions and examples for the verbs they looked at.

1 ▶ Ss look at the photos and discuss the questions in pairs. Get feedback from the whole class.

2a ▶ Ss complete the sentences with the words/phrases from the box. Encourage them to guess the meaning by using the context of the sentence and then to check their answers in a dictionary.

▶ Ss compare answers with a partner. Model correct pronunciation, especially for *boasting* and *proud*.

Answers	
1	succeed
2	give it a go
3	managed
4	give up
5	proud
6	achievement
7	boasting
8	high-achiever

3 ▶ Ask Ss to work in pairs and to tell each other about the last time they achieved something special. Encourage them to think about smaller achievements as well as big things. Get feedback from various Ss.

EXTEND THE LEAD-IN
Continue the theme of success/achievement. Ask Ss to complete these sentences about themselves.
1   *Recently, I managed to ...*
2   *I'm quite proud of myself for ...*
3   *The last time I won something was when ...*
4   *One of my main ambitions in life is to ...*
5   *My definition of success is ...*
Then ask Ss to compare and discuss their sentences in small groups. Encourage them to ask for and give further details about their sentences. Get feedback from the whole class. Find out to what extent Ss had similar/different views and experiences.

8.1 Lead or follow?

In this lesson, Ss read part of a brochure and discuss their ideas about the qualities of a successful leader. They listen to part of a work appraisal interview and also to two people describing different sides to their personalities. Ss talk about how people behave differently in different situations.

Leadership and management training is an important part of most companies nowadays. People generally now accept that almost anyone can be a successful leader or manager as long as they get the appropriate training and support. There are many courses available in leadership training.

Reading

OPTIONAL WARMER

Put the following headings on the board: *hospital*; *building site*; *football team*; *restaurant*. Elicit different jobs associated with each heading and write them on the board (e.g. *Hospital: nurse, surgeon, receptionist*, etc.). Ask Ss to work in pairs. They must decide which of the jobs require good leadership skills and why. Get feedback from the whole class. Encourage Ss to give reasons for their answers.

1 ▶ Ss discuss the questions in pairs. Get feedback from the whole class.

2 ▶ Ss to read the text quickly and to match the questions in exercise 1 to the correct paragraphs. Explain that Ss will have another opportunity to read the text in more detail but now, they must read quickly just to get the general idea. (You may find it useful to give Ss a time limit of two minutes for this.) Ss compare answers with a partner.

Answers
A   3
B   4
C   1
D   2

3 ▶ Ss read the text again and decide if the statements are true, false or not given. Encourage Ss to highlight the relevant parts of the text and to correct the false statements. Ss compare answers with a partner.

Answers
1   T
2   F (all kinds of groups, including social groups, need leaders)
3   T
4   NG (he says that true leaders are born but he doesn't specifically include himself)
5   NG (leaders should overcome their fears)
6   NG (leaders should allow all group members to contribute but it does not say if they contribute equally)

4 ▶ Ss discuss the questions in pairs. Get feedback from the whole class, particularly about whether Ss prefer to work in pairs, groups or alone in their English lessons and why.

Grammar | *It's time, I'd rather, I'd better*

5 ▶ Explain to Ss that they are going to listen to part of a work appraisal interview. Elicit the meaning of a work appraisal interview is (a formal discussion between an employee and his/her boss to assess positive and negative aspects of the employee's work and specific goals for their future work).

▶ ⬤ 2.19 Read through the three summary sentences with the class. Play the recording. Ss listen and decide which of the sentences best summarises the main points. Ss compare answers with a partner.

Answer
Sentence 3

OPTIONAL EXTENSION

Ss listen to the recording again and answer the following questions.
1   How long has Will worked for this company? (three years)
2   What work does he do? (he tests computer games)
3   Does he like it? (he loves it)
4   Why does he want to change? (he'd like more responsibility)
5   What choices are given to him? (becoming a team leader in the same department or changing to the marketing department)
6   When will Will do his training course? (next week)

6a ▶ Ss complete sentences 1–4 in the Active grammar box. Ss compare answers with a partner.

Active grammar
1   time
2   'd rather
3   'd rather
4   'd better

b ▶ Ss complete the rules of form in the Active grammar box by writing *past tense* or *infinitive*.

▶ Ask what the difference is between the *'d* in *I'd rather* and *I'd better* (the *'d* in *I'd rather = I would* and the *'d* in *I'd better = I had*).

Active grammar
A   past tense
B   past tense
C   infinitive
D   infinitive

c ► Ss look at sentences 1–4 in the Active grammar box again and discuss the meanings with a partner. Remind them to read the rules about meaning (in the box) to help them. Get feedback from various to explain what each one means and help with any difficulties. Demonstrate the sentence stress for this language, stressing the words *time*, *rather* and *better*.

d ► Ss find another example of each structure in the audioscript on page 171. Ss compare answers with a partner.

> **Answers**
> It's time I moved on now
> I'd rather we didn't waste any more time
> I'd rather stay in the same department
> I'd better not promise anything

► Focus Ss' attention on the Reference section on page 117.

7a ► Ss complete the dialogue using *It's time*, *'d rather* or *'d better* and the correct form of the verb in brackets. Don't ask for feedback at this point.

b ► 🔘 2.20 Play the recording. Ss listen and check their answers. Get feedback from the whole class.

> **Answers**
> 1 it's time I had   3 I'd rather you were
> 2 I'd rather stay   4 I'd better go

8a ► Ss write three sentences about themselves starting with *It's time … .* Read the examples through with the class to get them started and remind Ss that their sentences can be about small, more trivial things or larger, more important things.

b ► Ss compare their sentences with a partner. Encourage them to include details in their answers and to use *I'd better* and *I'd rather* where appropriate (e.g. *It's time I tidied up the house but I'd rather watch TV tonight.*).

Vocabulary | describing personality

> **OPTIONAL WARMER**
> Ask Ss if they can remember any of the adjectives/qualities used to describe successful leaders in the text they read in exercise 2. Ss look back at the text (especially paragraph 4) to check their ideas (*self-confidence*; *overcoming fears*; *calm*; *intelligent*; *able to work out good strategies*; *able to make sound judgements under pressure*; *sensitive*; *sociable*; *able to influence people*; *allows all members to contribute*).
> Then ask Ss the following questions.
> *Which of the qualities from paragraph 4 of the text do you think are the most important to be a successful leader? Can you add two more adjectives to describe a successful leader?*
> Get feedback from the whole class.

9a ► Divide the class into Ss A and Ss B. Ss A work in small groups and Ss Bs work in small groups. Ss use dictionaries to find out the meanings of the adjectives in the relevant box. Remind them to use the dictionary to help with pronunciation and word stress too. Be available to help where necessary.

b ► Put Ss in pairs (A and B) and ask them explain to each other about the meaning and pronunciation of the six words in their group.

> **Answers**
> *outgoing* = someone who likes social occasions and meeting new people
> *open* = honest and not wanting to hide things from people
> *proactive* = someone who causes things to happen rather than just reacts to them
> *aggressive* = very assertive spoken or physical behaviour which can be perceived as threatening by others
> *opinionated* = someone who expresses very strong opinions about things in a way that can be irritating
> *single-minded* = being very focussed on one goal
>
> *easy-going* = someone who stays calm and unworried about things
> *selfish* = caring only about yourself rather than other people
> *witty* = using words in a funny, interesting and intelligent way
> *manipulative* = good at controlling people to their advantage
> *introverted* = someone shy, quiet and unable to make friends easily
> *headstrong* = very determined to do what you want

10 ► Ss look at the questions and sample answers given. Ss then and discuss the questions in pairs. Encourage them to give examples of the ways in which people with these qualities behave. Get feedback from the whole class.

11a ► Ask Ss: *Do you know a very confident person? Do you think they are confident in every situation they are in? Why/why not?* Elicit from Ss that we all have different sides to our personality and that we behave differently in different situations. Read through the situations in the list with the class.

► 🔘 2.21 Explain to Ss that they are going to listen to two people talking about how they behave in different situations. Play the recording. Ss listen and say which situations are discussed.

> **Answers**
> leading a discussion at work
> giving a presentation at work
> being in a crowd of people at a party
> making a complaint in a shop

b ▶ Ss discuss whether they think the two speakers are similar or different to each other.

> **Suggested answer**
> Mostly similar to each other. Both say that they behave differently in different situations. Both say they are calm/confident about making presentations in work when they can prepare what they are going to say. The first speaker seems to agree with the other that it is harder when they are talking to people they don't know in social situations.

c ▶ Play the recording again. Ss listen and tick the expressions from the How to... box they hear. Ss compare answers with a partner. Then they practise saying the expression.

> **Answers**
> Most of the time, I'm quite a calm person.
> Generally, at work I think that I'm fairly confident.
> I actually became quite aggressive with the person.
> Suddenly, I changed into this aggressive person.
> If I don't know people, then I find that I'm a lot less confident.

▶ *Actually* is a false friend for many Ss and it might be useful to give some other examples of this adverb in use. Explain that it is similar in meaning to *In fact* and is often used to indicate information which is somehow surprising or not what you would expect (e.g. *I intended to stay for a week but I actually ended up staying for a month*; *I thought Peter would like the play but actually he didn't*; *I'm one of the few people who doesn't actually like chocolate*.)

12a ▶ Ss think about how they themselves and other people behave in different situations using the ideas in exercise 11a as well as their own ideas. They make notes but do not write complete sentences at this point.

b ▶ Ss work in pairs and discuss how people behave differently in different situations. Encourage them to use the adjectives and expressions from exercises 9 and 11. Get feedback from two or three Ss about whether they tend to behave similarly or differently to their partner during the situation.

8.2 Winners

In this lesson, Ss listen to a radio programme about winners in sport and the use of sports psychologists to help athletes succeed. Ss discuss their own attitudes to winning and success.

> Sports psychology is a huge industry. Most athletes use a psychologist to help with motivation and mental preparation. The radio programme in this lesson talks about some famous sportspeople who are naturally focussed on winning and don't seem to need any help with motivation including the boxer Mohamed Ali. It also talks about runner Kelly Holmes, who struggled with injury and a negative mental attitude. She used a sports psychologist to help her go on to win two gold medals at the Athens Olympics in 2004. Also mentioned are the New Zealand All Blacks rugby team who start every game with their famous Haka war dance. This is a traditional Maori chant with hand gestures and foot-stamping originally performed by warriors before battle to show their strength and to intimidate the opposition.

> **OPTIONAL WARMER**
> Ask Ss to discuss these questions.
> *Are there any sportspeople that you particularly admire? Why?*
> *What kind of people do you think make successful athletes?*

Listening

1 ▶ Ss answer the question in pairs. Get feedback from the whole class. Ask: *Do you recognise anything in the photos?*

> **Answers**
> A completely ecstatic (Kelly Holmes winning the 1500m race at the Athens Olympics in 2004)
> B absolutely devastated (Ryan Giggs playing for Manchester United against Bayer Leverkus in UEFA Champions League 2002)
> C totally single-minded (the New Zealand All Blacks rugby team doing the Haka war dance before a game)

2 ▶ ● 2.22 Ss read the questions. Play the recording. Ss listen and answer the questions. Then they compare answers with a partner.

> **Answers**
> 1 'almost all' sportspeople
> 2 to focus themselves on winning and intimidate the other team

3 ► Play the recording again. Ss listen and write one sentence summarising the speaker's main points about each thing in the list. Remind Ss of the main strategies we use when summarising. Get feedback from the whole class.

> **Possible answers**
> 1 There are some famous athletes like Mohamed Ali and Michael Schumacher who have succeeded because they have complete self-belief in their ability to win.
> 2 Sports psychologists can work with sportspeople to help change their negative thoughts about failing into positive ones about winning.
> 3 Some athletes and teams have personal lucky 'routines' that they do in order to focus on their goal or to bring players together as a team.

4 ► Ss discuss the question in small groups.

Vocabulary | adjectives and intensifiers

5a ► Ss look at the underlined adjectives in the table and discuss the question in pairs.

> **Answers**
> Gradable adjectives: the meaning is relative
> (e.g. *extremely big*, *very big*, *quite big*).
> Non-gradable adjectives: the meaning is extreme.

b ► Ss match the gradable adjectives 1–4 with the correct non-gradable adjectives a–d.

> **Answers**
> 1 b
> 2 d
> 3 a
> 4 c

> **OPTIONAL EXTENSION**
> Write the following adjectives on the board: *hot, boiling, clean, filthy, fascinating, freezing, small, spotless, dirty, tiny, cold, interesting.* Ask Ss to work in pairs and divide the list into *gradable* and *non-gradable* adjectives (gradable adjectives are *hot*; *cold*; *small*; *dirty*; *clean*; *interesting*).

6 ► Ss read the rule. They then look at the sentences and decide if one or both of the intensifiers is correct.

> **Answers**
> 1 really/absolutely
> 2 extremely/very
> 3 really
> 4 really/absolutely
> 5 absolutely
> 6 really

7 ► Ss think of a true story about themselves when they experienced one of the emotions listed in the box in exercise 1. Ss take turns to tell their story to a partner. Encourage Ss to ask for and give further details as they tell their story.

Grammar | reported speech

> **OPTIONAL LEAD-IN**
> Ss think back to exercise 7 and try to remember the story that their partner told them. Ask them to write down two sentences from their partner's story. Then ask them to rewrite the two sentences in reported speech.
> (e.g. *I worked hard for my exams.* → *He said that he had worked hard for his exams.*)

8a ► ● 2.23 Play the recording. Ss listen and complete the sentences and questions. Ss compare answers with a partner.

> **Answers**
> 1 are talking
> 2 help me
> 3 How do
> 4 is to
> 5 can help
> 6 improved dramatically

b ► Ss look at the reported speech in the Active grammar box and compare it with the direct speech in exercise 8a. Ss find examples of the changes/differences between the examples of direct and reported speech and write them in the Active grammar box. Ss compare answers with a partner.

► Ask: *How is the punctuation different in direct questions and reported questions?* (there is no question mark in reported questions).

> **Active grammar**
> 2 could
> 3 we → they; you → he
> 4 me → her
> 5 today → that day
> 6 will he or she win → he or she would win

► Focus Ss' attention on the Reference section on page 117.

9 ▶ Ss read the rules in the Active grammar box. Then Ss decide if the sentences in exercise 9 are correct or not. They identify the correct sentences and correct the incorrect ones. Ss compare answers with a partner.

Answers
1 ✓
2 ... ~~this~~ that evening. (change in time reference.)
3 ✓ (the 'back-stepping' rule is ignored here because the situation is still true)
4 She ~~said~~ told him ... (no object is used after said)
5 ✓
6 I asked her if she wanted ... (you need *if* in reported yes/no questions)
7 ✓
8 ✓ (the 'back-stepping' rule is ignored here because the situation is still true)

---

10 ▶ Ss rewrite the sentences and questions as reported speech. Ss compare answers with a partner.

Answers
1 ... me that he really wanted to win the race the following day.
2 ... if he/she/they was/were going to watch the rugby final on TV that afternoon.
3 ... (that) he would give him/her/them a lift to the football stadium.
4 ... what he/she/they did to prepare himself/herself/themselves before an exam.
5 ... me that she had been playing tennis for two hours.
6 ... (that) she could concentrate much better when she listened to music.
7 ... if he/she/they liked watching athletics on TV.
8 ... me (that) she was going to pay a sports psychologist to help her.

OPTIONAL EXTENSION

Put Ss in pairs (A and B). Ss A ask: *How competitive are you?* Ss B must give a detailed answer, giving examples. Ss A listen, asking further questions and taking notes of what B says. Then Ss B ask: *Do you prefer team or individual activities?* Ss A must give a detailed answer, with examples. Ss B listen, asking further questions and taking notes.
Then, Ss write a short summary of their partner's response to their question, reporting what they said. Ss then exchange summaries and check if their partner had listened well and reported their views accurately or not.

Pronunciation | intonation: reporting

11a ▶ ● 2.24 Explain that our intonation changes depending on whether we are quoting exactly what someone says using direct speech, or reporting what someone said using reported speech. Ss look at the two pairs of sentences. Play the recording. Ss listen and decide whether higher intonation is used in direct or in reported speech. Ss compare answers with a partner.

Answer
higher intonation for quoting direct speech

---

b ▶ Play the recording again. Ss listen and practise saying the sentences with a partner.

Speaking

12 ▶ Put Ss in pairs. They take turns to ask and answer the questions in the quiz. Each student must make notes about what their partner said.

13 ▶ Put Ss into new pairs. First they look at the sample dialogue given, then they use their notes from exercise 12 to discuss to what extent their respective partners from exercise 12 are 'born to win'. They must report what their previous partner said in order to do this.

14a ▶ Ask Ss to look at the points about successful language learning in the Lifelong learning box. They identify what they consider to be the three most important points with a partner.

b ▶ Ss work with a partner and discuss the questions. Get feedback from the whole class. Write Ss' suggestions about how to become more successful language learners on the board.

8.3 Tot.com

In this lesson, Ss read an article about the advantages and disadvantages of toddlers attending computer classes and listen to two people's reactions to this phenomenon. Ss discuss their own reactions to the article. Ss listen to the results of a survey on computer usage among young people and then do a similar survey in groups and report their findings.

Reading and listening

OPTIONAL WARMER

Write the following two headings on the board: *Parts of a computer* and *Verbs associated with computers*.
Ask Ss to work in pairs and to write as many words/phrases for each heading as they can. Give them a time limit of two or three minutes. Get feedback from the whole class and write suggestions on the board (possible answers: Parts of a computer: *mouse*, *keyboard*, *printer*, *hard drive*, *software*, *monitor*, *modem*; Verbs associated with computers: *download/upload*, *log on/log off*, *copy*, *cut*, *paste*, *print*, *drag*, *click*).

1 ▶ Ss discuss the questions in pairs. Get feedback from the whole class.

2 ▶ Ss read through the list, then read to find out which two are mentioned in the article. Ss should read the article quite quickly. Explain that they should read just to get the general idea of what is mentioned; they will have an opportunity to read for more detail in the next exercise.

```
Answers
2, 4
```

3 ▶ Ss read the statements, then read the article again to find out which ones are true and which are false. Encourage Ss to highlight where they found the answer and to correct the false statements. Ss compare answers with a partner.

```
Answers
1  F (they hope to introduce this in the future)
2  F (some children are put forward for exams at seven
   years of age; the normal age when children take the
   exams is 16)
3  T
4  T (parents are encouraged to do this)
5  T
6  F (there are many negative effects associated with
   looking at computer screens for long periods)
7  T
8  T
```

4 ▶ Ss discuss statements 3–8 with a partner. Get feedback from the whole class. Ask: *Do you agree more with Judy or with Alan?* Encourage Ss to explain their reasons in more detail.

OPTIONAL EXTENSION

Write the following definitions on the board. Ss find the words in the article which correspond to each one.
1 *reasonable and rational (logical)*
2 *an early advantage (a head start)*
3 *a suitable reward for the money and effort put into doing something (worthwhile)*
4 *use a person or thing for your own advantage (exploit)*
5 *a new pattern of behaviour or fashion (trend)*
6 *the state of being very overweight (obesity)*
7 *cause strong feelings of disapproval (to appal)*
8 *strong feelings of guilt and regret (ashamed)*

5a ▶ 🌐 2.25 Play the recording. Ss listen and answer the question. Explain that they will have an opportunity to listen for more detailed information in the next exercise but for now, they should listen for the general idea only. Ss compare answers with a partner.

```
Answers
Woman: a
Man: c (he expresses mixed feelings and sees both sides
      of the argument)
```

b ▶ Ss read through the quotations. Demonstrate and explain the use of *would* in 3. (*would* is stressed and describes typical or predictable behaviour of someone – usually in a critical way). Play the recording again. Ss listen for the quotes and decide in each case who says it and what is being referred to. Ss compare answers with a partner.

```
Answers
W = woman; M = man
1  W (the trend for providing special computer classes
   for toddlers is ridiculous)
2  W (What is the point in taking national exams at seven
   years of age?)
3  M (it is predictable that the director of the college
   would say that there were no negative effects at all –
   she would say that)
4  M (making money comes into the positive feelings the
   director of the college has towards the programme)
5  W (what the educational psychologist said confirmed
   what the speaker felt about toddlers having computer
   lessons)
6  W (the speaker feels the man should read the article)
```

6 ▶ Write the headings *Advantages* and *Disadvantages* on the board. Ss answer the question in pairs. Get feedback from the whole class. Write Ss' suggestions on the board as bullet points under the headings. Encourage Ss to give reasons for their ideas.

Grammar | reporting verbs

7a ▶ Ask Ss to read sentences 1–8 in the Active grammar box. Explain that one of the reporting verbs from the box goes in each gap. In pairs, Ss complete the sentences with the correct form of the reporting verbs. Ss check their answers in the audioscript on page 171.

Active grammar

1	claimed	5	suggested
2	explained	6	confirmed
3	denied	7	warned
4	admitted	8	remind

b ▶ Ss complete the rules of form A–C. Ss compare answers with a partner.

Active grammar

2	explain	6	suggest
3	confirm	7	warn
4	deny	8	remind
5	admit		

▶ Focus Ss' attention on the Reference section on page 117.

8 ▶ Ss rewrite the sentences using a reporting verb. Ss compare answers with a partner.

Answers

1 He admitted dropping the laptop by mistake the day before.
2 The teacher reminded us to give her our homework the next day.
3 He suggested looking for a course I could do in the evenings.
4 She claimed (that) her son had taken his exams a year earlier than his classmates.
5 They confirmed (that) the school would be closed until the following Monday.
6 She warned us not to be late for our exam that afternoon.
7 He denied copying his essay from the Internet.
8 He explained (that) he was doing the course because he needed to improve his English.

Listening

9a ▶ Focus Ss on the survey. Explain that 20 Ss aged between 16 and 24 participated in the survey. Ask Ss to look at questions 1–4 of the survey. With a partner, they predict what the results of the survey might be for these questions. Focus Ss' attention on the sample answer given before they start so that they are clear about what they have to do.

b ▶ ● 2.26 Play the recording. Ss listen to see if their predictions were correct. Get feedback from the whole class. Ask: *Were you surprised by any of the results?*

Answers

1 13 out of 20 people spend three or more hours a day on the computer; studying and for fun (playing games and communicating with friends)
2 most said that one hour a day was the maximum time children under 12 should spend on the computer
3 most people thought children under five should not use computers at all
4 80% agreed that there was a link

10 ▶ Ss focus on the precise language used to describe the results of the survey. Play the recording again. Ss listen and complete the sentences in the How to... box. Ss compare answers with a partner. Help Ss with the pronunciation of *majority* and *half*.

Answers
Thirteen **out of twenty** ...
75 percent of the group ...
Everyone suggested ...
Nobody thought that children ...
Most people said that ...
A few people, however, ...
The (vast) **majority** confirmed ...
Only a (small) **minority** were ...
Nearly half the group ...

Speaking

11a ▶ Put Ss in groups of four or five. First, they add one more question to the two sections of the survey in exercise 9.

b ▶ Ss discuss the survey questions in their groups. One member of the group makes notes about the other Ss' answers.

c ▶ When the groups have finished discussing the questions, they prepare how they will report the results back to the class. Encourage Ss to use reporting verbs where appropriate and the language from the How to... box.

d ▶ Go through the survey questions one at a time. One student from each group describes their results for each question. Ss compare their answers with other groups. Collate the answers for the whole class on the board as the Ss report their findings. Finally, ask about the additional survey questions. Ask: *Are you surprised by any of the results?*

OPTIONAL VARIATION

Give each student one of the questions from the survey. Ss mingle, asking their question of as many other Ss as possible in the time given and answering other Ss' questions. Ss make notes of the responses given to them and then report their findings to the whole class. Finally, Ss write a short report on the results of their survey.

---

8 Vocabulary | Phrasal verbs with three parts

OPTIONAL WARMER

Ask Ss to look back at the article *Technology for toddlers* on page 112 and to find a phrasal verb with three parts (*catch up with*). Ask: *What does this phrasal verb mean?*

1a ▶ Ss match the underlined phrasal verb with the correct meanings a–j. Ss compare answers with a partner.

Answers
1 b
2 d
3 f
4 i
5 e
6 h
7 j
8 a
9 g
10 c

---

b ▶ Ss look at the example, then test each other on the phrasal verbs in the same way.

2a ▶ Ss choose the correct option for each of the sentences. Don't ask for feedback at this point.

b ▶ ⏺ 2.27 Play the recording. Ss listen and check their answers. Explain that the three-part phrasal verbs are inseparable. Ask: *Can you say 'You won't catch up them with?'* (no, only *You won't catch up with them*).

Answers
1 looking forward to
2 coming up with
3 cut down on
4 look up to
5 make up for
6 got away with
7 keeping up with
8 putting up with
9 put in for
10 catch up with

Pronunciation | stress on phrasal verbs

3a ▶ ⏺ 2.27 Play the recording again. Ss listen and decide which part of the phrasal verb is stressed. Ss compare answers with a partner.

Answer
The second part of each phrasal verb is stressed.

---

b ▶ Play the recording again. Ss listen and repeat the questions.

4 ▶ Ss discuss the questions from exercise 2a in pairs. Get feedback from the whole class. Ask: *Were your answers mostly similar or different?*

OPTIONAL EXTENSION

Put Ss in pairs. Elicit main verbs often used in phrasal verbs (e.g. *go, come, take, bring, put, make, look,* etc.). Give each pair a dictionary and ask them to find two more phrasal verbs with three parts. They must write down the meaning and an example sentence for each one. Ss then form new pairs and explain the new phrasal verbs to each other. Write all the new verbs with the example sentences on the board during whole class feedback.

---

8 Communication

In this lesson, Ss listen to three people talking about the definition of success and discuss what success means.

OPTIONAL WARMER

Write the word *SUCCESS* on the board. Give Ss 20 seconds to write down the first thing that comes into their head when they see this word. Elicit the immediate responses of Ss and write them on the board. Compare Ss' list to the list in exercise 1.

---

1 ▶ Ss look at the photos in pairs and discuss how 'success' is represented in each one. They use the headings given to help them.

2 ▶ ◉ 2.28 Explain to Ss that they are going to listen to three people discussing the nature of success. Play the recording. Ss listen and answer the question.

Answers
First speaker: successful career; strong marriage/
    personal relationships
Second speaker: plenty of money; successful career;
    achieving your own specific goals; lots of loyal
    friends; a large close family
Third speaker: successful career

3a ▶ Focus Ss' attention on the question and the audioscript on page 172. They read through it and underline useful expressions for the discussion.

b ▶ Ss work alone and decide which three factors from the list in exercise 1 are most important in defining success. They note down their reasons but do not write full sentences at this point.

4a▶ Put Ss in small groups. They discuss the most important factors in deciding how successful someone is. Ss use their notes from exercise 3b to help them. Don't ask for feedback at this point.

b ▶ Put Ss into new groups with different Ss. They discuss the question again with new Ss. Get feedback from the whole class. Ask Ss: *How far do you agree/disagree about the question?*

OPTIONAL EXTENSION

Ss write a short essay outlining their views on the following topic: *Success can be measured by wealth and career.*

---

8 Review and practice

1 ▶

> **Answers**
> 1 I'd better ~~went~~ go to the shops now before they close.
> 2 ~~Had~~ Would you rather I didn't say anything to your boss?
> 3 ✓
> 4 I'd rather not ~~working~~ work this weekend if at all possible.
> 5 ~~Would~~ Had you better take a raincoat in case it rains?
> 6 ✓
> 7 What's that smell? I think it's time you ~~get~~ got the cake out of the oven.
> 8 I'd rather ~~took~~ take just hand luggage on the plane than a large suitcase.

2 ▶

> **Answers**
> 1 Tony asked me if I would like to play tennis this/that weekend.
> 2 They told me the best time to visit Egypt was in January or February.
> 3 Helen said she didn't know what time the firework display started.
> 4 He asked me when I wanted to go and see the London Eye.
> 5 My boss told me I would have to make a presentation at the sales conference in March.
> 6 The newspaper said one of our athletes had failed a drugs test.
> 7 She asked me if I had watched the football match the previous Saturday.
> 8 He told me he would arrive later that evening

3 ▶

> **Answers**
> 1 taking
> 2 he would be
> 3 us not to go
> 4 to go
> 5 she hadn't finished
> 6 being
> 7 that he hadn't heard
> 8 telling

4 ▶

> **Answers**
> 1 headstrong
> 2 proactive
> 3 ecstatic
> 4 opinionated
> 5 proud
> 6 exhausted
> 7 outgoing
> 8 devastated
> 9 single-minded
> 10 starving

5 ▶

> **Answers**
> 1 looking forward ~~with~~ to
> 2 ~~come~~ cut down on
> 3 catch up ~~for~~ with
> 4 ~~made~~ came up with
> 5 look up ~~with~~ to
> 6 ~~get~~ put up with
> 7 got ~~down~~ away with
> 8 make up ~~to~~ for
> 9 keep up ~~to~~ with
> 10 put me ~~on~~ in for

8 Writing bank

1 ▶

> **Answers**
> 1 Melanie is Head of the Department where Rebecca works; they are also close personal friends
> 2 to recommend her for a job
> 3 totally positive

2 ▶

> **Answers**
> 1, 2, 4, 6

3a ▶

> **Answers**
> A may concern
> B strongly recommend; no hesitation
> C further details

b ▶

> **Answers**
> very hard-working person; takes her responsibilities seriously; work efficiently under stressful conditions; (her ability to) meet difficult deadlines; her determination; (her) calm personality; is used to managing her own time which she does professionally and without fuss; an outgoing person; shows good leadership qualities; an excellent team spirit; (she demonstrates) sensitivity and awareness of other people; has an eye for detail; is good at using her initiative; a high-achiever; (is) single-minded in her attitude to professional development

4a/b ▶ Ss prepare and write a reference for someone they know.

Overview

Lead-in	**Vocabulary:** Crime
9.1	**Can do:** Tell a short anecdote **Grammar:** Participle clauses for sequencing **Vocabulary:** Law and insurance **Speaking and Pronunciation:** Consonant clusters (2) **How to...** tell a short anecdote **Reading and listening:** Crime stories
9.2	**Can do:** Speculate about past and present events **Grammar:** Deduction: present and past **Vocabulary:** Compound adjectives **Speaking and Pronunciation:** Stress: compound adjectives **Reading and listening:** Can you solve the mystery?
9.3	**Can do:** Take part in a discussion about crime and punishment **Grammar:** Relative clauses **Speaking and Pronunciation:** **How to...** start, move on and finish a discussion **Reading:** Was Sherlock Holmes a real person? **Listening:** My name is Sherlock Holmes
Vocabulary	News headlines
Communication	**Can do:** Solve problems with other people
Writing bank	Write a factual account **How to...** summarise clearly and concisely
Extra activities	ActiveTeach and ActiveBook

CEFR Can do objectives
9.1 Tell a short anecdote
9.2 Speculate about past and present events
9.3 Take part in a discussion about crime and punishment
Communication Solve problems with other people
Writing bank Write a factual account

CEFR Portfolio ideas
a) Work in pairs. You are probation officers. You have been asked to make recommendations for the judge in advance of sentencing the four people on page 128. Talk about possible punishments and outcomes and record the discussion.
b) Design and write a crime-prevention leaflet on protecting your home from theft while on holiday. Include suggestions on how to deter burglars.
c) Find a crime story in the news. Imagine you were an eyewitness to the crime. Write a witness statement for the police, giving details of what happened and what you saw.

Lead-in

OPTIONAL WARMER
Focus Ss' attention on the photo of the graffiti artist. Ss discuss the following questions in pairs: *How serious a 'crime' is this in your view? What would be a suitable punishment for this? How do you think local authorities should deal with this problem?*

1a ▶ Ask Ss to look at the photos and discuss the question in pairs. Get feedback from the whole class.

b ▶ Ss look at the columns and example words, then try to think of more words and expressions connected with crime and the law. Write Ss' suggestions on the board under the different headings.

Possible answers
law court: lawyer for the defence; lawyer for the prosecution; the accused
crime: murder; shoplifting; graffiti; arson
criminal: a murderer; a shoplifter; an arsonist
evidence: DNA; an eyewitness; CCTV footage
punishment: community service; life in prison; a sentence

2 ▶ Ss look at the underlined words and phrases and check the meanings of those they are unfamiliar with in their dictionaries. Get feedback from the whole class. Help with the meanings, word stress and pronunciation.

Answers
victim = someone who has been hurt or killed because of a crime
criminals = people who commit crimes
punishments = legal consequences of a crime
community service = a non-custodial punishment involving helping people or improving the environment
suspect = someone the police think might have committed a particular crime
innocent = when you did not commit the crime
guilty = when you did commit the crime
witnesses = people who saw or heard something related to a particular crime happen
evidence = one or more reasons for making you believe something is true or not true
petty crimes = non-serious crimes
suspended sentence = a period during which your punishment is not active, provided you do not commit another crime
prison = a place where guilty people are sent to live as punishment
graffiti = illegal artwork, usually drawings or words, in public places
vandalism = deliberate damage done to public places
forensic scientist = the person who examines the physical evidence connected to a crime

3 ▶ Ss discuss the statements in pairs. Ask: *Were there any statements you disagreed about?*

9.1 Legal madness

In this lesson, Ss listen to an amusing but true story about a crime involving cigars and an insurance company. Ss tell each other stories about crimes which went wrong

1 ▶ Ss discuss the questions in pairs. Ask: *What is your favourite police drama on TV? Why?*

2 ▶ Ss match the words/phrases from the box with the appropriate definitions.

> **Answers**
> to commit arson: b
> to commit fraud: h
> to be arrested: a
> to convict someone of: c
> to sentence someone to: f
> to get away with something: j
> to sue someone: l
> to be insured/to insure something: d
> to make a claim: g
> to pay a premium: e

3 ▶ Ss complete the sentences with the words/ phrases from exercise 2 in the correct form.

> **Answers**
> 1 sue
> 2 sentenced
> 3 premium
> 4 convicted
> 5 make a claim
> 6 insured
> 7 committed arson
> 8 get away with
> 9 arrested
> 10 committed fraud

4 ▶ Ss discuss the questions in small groups.

Listening

5a ▶ Tell Ss that they are going to listen to a story about a crime involving cigars, a lawyer and fraud. Ss work in pairs and suggest what the story might be using as many of the words in exercise 2 as possible. Don't ask for feedback at this point.

b ▶ ● 2.29 Play the recording. Ss listen and compare their ideas with the actual story. Ss should check in pairs what the actual story was and how similar/different it was from theirs. Ask: *Was your story similar to the real story?*

6a ▶ Ss read the sentences and try to put them into the correct order. Ss check answers with a partner. Don't ask for feedback at this point.

b ▶ ● 2.29 Play the recording again. Ss listen and put the sentences in the correct order.

> **Answers**
> 9, 7, 5, 3, 2, 8, 6, 1, 4

> **OPTIONAL EXTENSION**
>
> Write the following expressions on the board: *Fair enough*; *What on earth for?*; *You're kidding!*; *Cross my heart*. Ss work in pairs. They find the expressions in the audioscript on page 173 and decide what they might mean. (*Fair enough* = That sounds reasonable and fair to me. *What on earth for?* = I don't understand why. *You're kidding!* = You're joking. *Cross my heart.* = I promise)

Pronunciation | consonant clusters (2)

7a ▶ ● 2.30 Remind Ss of the work they did on consonant cluster at the beginning of words in Lesson 6.1. Explain that for this exercise they will focus on consonant clusters at the end of words. Focus Ss' attention on the table. Play the recording. Ss listen and write the words they hear in the correct place in the table. Ss compare answers with a partner. Ss take turns to practise saying the words with a partner.

> **Answers**
> *-st*: first; scientist; sentenced
> *-xt*: next; context
> *-nce*: evidence; insurance
> *-nst*: against; sentenced
> *-nts*: punishments; clients
> *-cts*: suspects; products

▶ Focus Ss' attention on the Pronunciation bank on page 161.

Grammar | participle clauses for sequencing

> **OPTIONAL LEAD-IN**
>
> Focus Ss' attention on the sequencing exercise in exercise 6a. Ss focus on the first two sentences of the sequence: *First a lawyer bought some rare cigars. Next, he insured the cigars against fire.* Elicit different ways of making these two sentences into one sentence. Then write on board:
> <u>After buying</u> some rare cigars, he insured them against fire.
> <u>Having bought</u> some rare cigars, he insured them against fire.
> Explain to Ss that these are both sequencing devises (ways of showing the order of events). Ask: *Which action happened first?* (buying the cigars) *Which action happened second?* (insuring the cigars)

8a ▶ Ss look at the first two sentences in the Active grammar box. Ss then complete sentences 3 and 4 with *cashing* or *cashed*. Ss compare answers with a partner.

> **Active grammar**
> 3 cashed
> 4 cashing

b ▶ Ss choose the correct option in the rules in the Active grammar box. Ss compare answers with a partner.

> **Active grammar**
>
> A   past participle
> B   present participle
> C   ether before or after
> D   first
> E   Past Simple

▶ Explain that the subject must be the same in both participle and main clause in these kind of sentences. (*Having made a claim, the insurance company did not pay* is not possible because the subject of the participle clause – the lawyer – is different to the subject of the main clause – the insurance company.)

▶ Focus Ss' attention on the Reference section on page 131.

9 ▶ Ss complete the sentences by writing the correct form of a verb from the box. Ss compare answers with a partner.

> **Answers**
> 1   going   4   read
> 2   promised   5   won
> 3   doing   6   staying

> **OPTIONAL EXTENSION**
>
> Focus Ss' attention on the sequencing exercise they did in exercise 6a. Ss work in pairs and make sentences based on the story using *After...* and *Having....* Ss will have to change some of the sentences in exercise 6a so that the subject is the same in both clauses.

10a ▶ Focus Ss' attention on the example in exercise 10b before they start so that they know what the activity involves. Then, each student thinks about three things that happened to them last week and what they did after each one.

b ▶ Put Ss in pairs (A and B). Ss A tell Ss B the first of the things they did. Ss B try to guess what Ss A did next. Ss swap roles and continue taking turns telling each other about what they did. Remind them to tell each other if they were correct or not.

Speaking

11 ▶ Explain to Ss that they are going to look at two picture stories about unlucky criminals and crimes that went wrong. Divide the class into As and Bs. Ss A work in pairs and look at the pictures on page 122. Ss B work in pairs and look at the pictures on page 148. Tell them that the pictures make a story (in the correct order) and they should work out the story with their partner.

12 ▶ Ss now read the story which goes with their picture story and check if their ideas were correct or not. Ss read their stories individually and then check with their partner. Student As read the story on page 149 and Student Bs should read the story on page 122.

13a ▶ Ss prepare their story. Point out the language in the How to... box, but remind them to adapt the language for their particular story. Ss should make notes about what they will say but they should not write full sentences.

b ▶ Put Ss in pairs (A and B). Tell them to show each other their picture stories and to tell their stories. Remind them to include the structures with *Having* + past participle and *After* + present participle as appropriate.

> **OPTIONAL EXTENSION**
>
> Ss look at the pictures for their partner's story and write the narrative in their own words without looking at the text. They then compare their version with the text (reading it for the first time) and check how much is similar and if they have missed anything out.

9.2 It's a mystery!

In this lesson, Ss read a short mystery which describes a number of suspects in a crime. Ss speculate about who committed the crime and listen to others discussing this and read the solution to the mystery. Ss discuss what is happening in a series of photos.

Reading

OPTIONAL WARMER

A national park is a reserve of natural or semi-natural land, set aside for animal and environmental protection and for human enjoyment. There are usually restrictions in place against development of the land. Elicit the names of famous national parks in the world (Yellowstone National Park (US); Everglades (US); Masai Mara Game Reserve (Kenya); Uluru-Kata Tjuta National Park (Australia); Teide National Park (Spain); Kruger National Park (South Africa); Valley of Flowers National Park (India); Snowdonia National Park (UK).
Teach the word *park ranger* (a person whose job it is to protect a forest or national park). Elicit the typical duties of a park ranger (e.g. making sure humans are not endangering the animals or damaging the environment, etc.). Ask: *Do you think a park ranger's job is also about solving crimes?*

1 ▶ Ss look at the picture and discuss the questions in pairs.

2 ▶ Explain to Ss that they are going to read the first part of a mystery story which takes place in a national park and is solved by the park ranger. Ss look at the questions, then read the text and answer them. Ss compare answers with a partner. Teach the word *tongue-tied* (when you find it difficult to express your views usually because you are nervous or shy).

Answers
1 intruders entered and vandalised the ranger's cabin in the park
2 three different couples (six suspects)
3 very confident – he doesn't need to check

Listening

3a ▶ Ss discuss which of the couples they think committed the crime in pairs. Don't ask for feedback at this point.

b ▶ 🔘 2.31 Play the recording. Ss listen and answer the questions. Ss discuss the questions with a partner. Ask Ss to give reasons for their answers.

4 ▶ Ss talk about who they think committed the crime again, having listened to the discussion. Don't ask for feedback at this point. Ask: *Do you think you would be a good detective?*

Grammar | deduction: present and past

OPTIONAL LEAD-IN

Write the following on the board: *Jan and Marek might be the vandals* and *Reg must be tired*. Ask Ss: *How sure is the speaker that Jan and Marek are the vandals?* (not sure – it's possible) *How sure is the speaker that Reg is tired?* (very sure) *Why is he so sure?* (Reg has been walking around the park looking for the vandals all day).
Now write the following on the board: *Jan and Marek might have committed the crime* and *Jan and Marek might be the vandals*. Ask Ss: *Are we talking about the past, present or future in each of these sentences?* (*might have committed* is talking about yesterday; *might be the vandals* is talking about now).

5 ▶ Ss focus on the extracts from the Listening, then complete the rules in the Active grammar box. Ss compare answers with a partner.

Active grammar

B	must + have	E	can't
C	might	F	can't/couldn't + have
D	might + have		

▶ Focus Ss on the Reference section on page 131.

▶ Ask what the negative of *Reg must be right* is (not *Reg mustn't be right* but *Reg can't be right*). Explain that for this particular use of these modals, the negative form of *must* is *can't* (not *mustn't*) and the positive form of *can't* is *must* (not *can*). This can be confusing for Ss who may be tempted to say Adam and Jean can be the vandals. Explain that we do not use the positive form of *can* to make deductions.

6 ▶ Ss choose the correct word in each sentence. Ss compare answers with a partner.

Answers
1	couldn't	5	can't
2	might	6	must
3	must	7	might
4	must	8	couldn't

7 ▶ Ss complete the sentences as directed. They check answers in pairs, then as a whole class.

Answers
1 can't have forgotten
2 must have seen
3 might have gone
4 must have told
5 must be
6 can't/couldn't have spent
7 might be
8 can't/couldn't have left

8a ▶ Ss discuss the reasons each of the couples might have had for committing the crime with a partner, using modals of deduction (e.g. *Jan and Marek might have stolen the food in the cabin because they were hungry. They only caught two fish all day so they mustn't be very good fishermen*).

b ▶ Ss read the solution to the mystery on page 147. Get feedback from the whole class. Ask Ss: *Were you right? Are you surprised? Why/Why not?*

Answers
Adam and Jean Wisemen are the vandals. Reg knew they were lying because the ground was wet inside their tent. They claimed to have put up the tent the previous night but the rain didn't start until that evening.

Vocabulary | compound adjectives

9 ▶ Ss read the sentences and think about the meaning of the words which might go in the gaps. Then, they combine a word from column A with a word from column B to form a compound adjective to go in each of the gaps. Ss compare answers with a partner.

Answers
1   middle-aged (aged approximately between 40 and 60)
2   well-dressed (had nice clothes on)
3   tongue-tied (nervous about speaking)
4   far-fetched (difficult to believe)
5   red-handed (found in the act of doing something illegal)
6   fire-proof (protected against fire and heat)
7   gift-wrapped (covered in wrapping paper)
8   pig-headed (stubborn)
9   colour-coded (sorted according to colour)

OPTIONAL EXTENSION

Ss find and learn some more compound adjectives. Divide the class into two groups (A and B). Group A should look at the following list A and Group B should look at the following list B.
A: *big-headed*; *two-faced*; *well-off*; *sugar-free*
B: *colour-coded*; *absent-minded*; *hard-up*; *off-peak*
Give Ss dictionaries to use in order to find the compound adjectives, checking the meaning and pronunciation. Tell them to write an example sentence for each too.
Then put Ss in pairs (A and B). Tell them to teach each other their adjectives, focusing on meaning and pronunciation and giving their partner an example sentence.

Pronunciation | stress: compound adjectives

10 ▶ ⏺ 2.32 Play the recording. Ss listen and write down the questions which they hear. Ss compare answers with a partner. If possible, have a slide or handout prepared with the questions written on it so that Ss can check their answers for spelling and punctuation. Although the audioscript is provided in the Students' Book, it is important that Ss do not look at this yet.

Answers
1   When you were a child, were you ever caught red-handed doing something you shouldn't?
2   In what situations have you found yourself tongue-tied?
3   Between what ages is someone middle-aged do you think?
4   What things do you have in your house which are colour-coded?
5   How often do you get things gift-wrapped professionally in shops?
6   Has anyone ever told you a story you thought was really far-fetched?

11a ▶ Play the recording again. Ss listen and decide whether the first or second part of each compound adjective is stressed. Ss compare answers with a partner.

Answers
stress on first part: tongue-tied, gift-wrapped, colour-coded
stress on second part: red-handed, middle-aged, far-fetched

b ▶ Ss read the rules and decide on the correct option in each. Ss compare answers with a partner.

Answers
1   first
2   second

c ▶ Play the recording again. Ss listen and repeat the questions.

12 ▶ Ss take turns to ask and answer five of the six questions. Encourage them to ask for and give details.

Speaking

13a ▶ Focus Ss' attention on the photos and ask them to discuss the questions in pairs. Don't ask for feedback at this point.

b ▶ ⏺ 2.33 Play the recording. Ss listen to see if they were right. Ss compare answers with a partner.

Answers
1   he is a burglar
2   in someone's house
3   he is stealing computer equipment but is caught red-handed

14a ▶ Ss discuss the questions with a partner.

b ▶ ● 2.34 Play the recording. Ss listen to see if they were right. Ss compare answers with a partner.

> **Answers**
> 1   The householder had set up a webcam which started recording when it detected movement and then sent the pictures automatically to a private email address.
> 2 & 3 Ss' own answers.

c ▶ Ss discuss the first question in pairs. Elicit adjectives to describe how the burglar felt during whole-class feedback.

▶ Then for the second question, write the following headings on the board: *burglary*, *vandalism* and *graffiti*. Ss discuss ways of preventing these crimes with a partner. Get feedback from the whole class.

> **OPTIONAL VARIATION**
>
> Write the following words on the board and ask Ss what they have in common: *guard dog*, *security camera*, *caretaker* (they are related to the theme of home security – all ways of protecting your home/property). Then ask them to work in pairs and continue the list, adding more ways of protecting your home against burglars and intruders. (Possible answers: *burglar alarms*, *remote-controlled gates*, *combination locks*, *padlocks*, *deadlocks*, *window locks*, *door chains*, *window bars and grilles*, *shutters*, *peepholes*, *CCTV/video surveillance*). Ask Ss: *Which are the best ways to prevent a burglar coming into your home?*

9.3 The real Sherlock?

In this lesson, Ss read a short article about the inspiration for the Sherlock Holmes character in real life and listen to someone describing what it is like to be called Sherlock Holmes. Ss discuss the seriousness of different crimes and what punishments might be appropriate in each case.

> Sir Arthur Conan Doyle published the first Sherlock Holmes story in 1887. The popularity of the character grew rapidly as he appeared in an ongoing series of self-contained stories. Soon people loved Holmes so much that they refused to believe he wasn't a real person; letters addressed to 'Sherlock Holmes, Consulting Detective' arrived daily at 221b Baker Street, each begging him to take on a real case. Although Holmes is, of course, a fictional character, he was largely based on a real person: Dr Joseph Bell, who met Conan Doyle at the University of Edinburgh Medical School.

Reading

> **OPTIONAL WARMER**
>
> Introduce the topic of detective stories. Write the word *Whodunit* on the board and ask Ss to discuss what it is (= 'who done it' and is another way of describing a detective story or a murder mystery book).
> Ask Ss to discuss the following questions in pairs.
> *Do you like reading 'whodunits'? Why/Why not?*
> *Can you name any authors or characters of famous detective books/films? Which is your favourite? Why?*

1a ▶ Ss look at the photos. Ask: *Do you recognise the character?* (Sherlock Holmes). Ask: *How do you know?* Ss answer the questions in pairs. Don't ask for feedback at this point.

b ▶ Ss read the article quickly and check their answers.

> **Answers**
> 2   No, he is a fictional character (but he was inspired by a real person).
> 3   He is famous for being a fictional detective in the stories by Arthur Conan Doyle, starting with the first book in 1887 and continuing today.

2 ▶ Ss read the article again and complete the notes. Ss compare answers with a partner.

> **Answers**
> 1   professor – student
> 2   University of Edinburgh Medical School
> 3   1877
> 4   playing sport
> 5   bird-watching
> 6   tattoos
> 7   hands
> 8   1887
> 9   Baker Street and Scotland Yard

3 ▶ Ss work together and read the article again to find words that mean each of the definitions given.

▶ Tell them that the paragraph numbers and word form are given to help them find the words.

Answers

1	intelligent	3	remarkable
2	admiration	4	innovation
		5	popularity

4 ▶ Ss discuss the first question in pairs. Write the following headings on the board to focus the discussion: *his creator, who SH is based on, the public reaction*. Elicit Ss' views about the second question as a whole-class discussion.

OPTIONAL EXTENSION

Tell Ss that there is going to be a film based on the student days of Arthur Conan Doyle. Ss discuss which actors should play the parts of Conan Doyle and Joseph Bell in the film.

Grammar | relative clauses

5 ▶ Ss read the information in the Active grammar box and decide which of the examples contain 'defining relative clauses' and which contain 'non-defining relative clauses'. Ss compare answers with a partner.

Answers

1	Defining	4	Non-defining
2	Non-defining	5	Non-defining
3	Defining	6	Non-defining

▶ Focus Ss' attention on the Reference section on page 131.

6 ▶ Ask Ss to look at the example, then to re-write the sentences to make one sentence using either defining or non-defining relative clauses. Remind them to think about the use of commas and that. Ss compare answers with a partner.

Answers

1 John, who has been my best friend since school, is helping me to start a new business.
2 The flat that I've been in for a couple of years, needs redecorating.
3 Tamsin, whose parents emigrated to Australia last year, is going there for the winter.
4 My neighbour, who I've always liked, has given me his old computer.
5 The family at the end of the road, whose dog barks constantly, are thinking of moving.
6 The car that she's had for years is for sale.

7 ▶ Ss complete the sentences in a way that is true for them.

Listening

8a ▶ Tell Ss that they are going to listen to an interview with an ordinary man whose name is 'Sherlock Holmes'. First, ask them to discuss the questions in pairs. Don't ask for feedback at this point.

b ▶ ◉ 2.35 Play the recording. Ss listen and see if their ideas were right. Ss compare answers with a partner.

Answers

1 Because his parents were great fans of the original Conan Doyle stories.
2 People don't forget you. People make funny comments. People think you can solve mysteries.

9 ▶ Play the recording again. Ss listen to find out the significance of the things in the list. Ss compare answers with a partner.

Answers

1 His friends and family call him 'Holmes'.
2 His parents were great fans of these.
3 This is the type of name his parents wanted to choose for him.
4 This is what people sometimes ask him when they're trying to be funny.
5 People think he can explain what TV magicians do.

10 ▶ Put Ss in small groups. Get feedback from the whole class. Ask: *Who likes/doesn't like their first name? Why/Why not?*

Speaking

11a ▶ Ss look at the four descriptions. Ask: *What crime did each person commit?* (Paulo – identity theft; Jenny – shoplifting; Akio – spraying graffiti; Teresa – speeding)

b ▶ Ss discuss the questions with a partner. Get feedback from the whole class on the seriousness of each of the crimes.

12 ▶ ◉ 2.36 Explain that Ss will hear two friends discussing the same questions as they did in exercise 11b. Play the recording. Ss listen and decide if they agree.

Answers

they agree that Paulo committed the most serious crime and Akio the least serious

13 ▶ Ss read the How to... box and think about what words might go in the gaps. Play the recording again. Ss listen and complete the sentences. Ss compare answers with a partner.

> **Answers**
> Why don't we **start** ...
> Let's **go** for it.
> So, **moving on** to ...
> Let's **come back** to ...
> What **else** do we have to decide?
> I think **that's** it.

> **OPTIONAL EXTENSION**
>
> Teach the phrase *mitigating circumstances,* which comes up in the listening (reasons which might explain bad behaviour). Play the recording again. Ss identify any possible mitigating circumstances for each of the crimes (Paolo – unemployed, so he was desperate; Jenny – she might be addicted to stealing things; Akio – his graffiti is not offensive but quite artistic; Teresa – perhaps rushing to a medical emergency).

14 ▶ Ss discuss appropriate punishments for the four people in exercise 11. Encourage them to use the language in the How to... box and to give reasons for their opinions. Get feedback from the whole class. Ask: *What did your group decide for Paolo? Does everyone agree? Why/Why not? What about Jenny?*, etc.

> **OPTIONAL EXTENSION**
>
> Ss imagine that they are the lawyer for either the defence or the prosecution at the trial of one of the people from exercise 12. Ss choose which person. They write the speech which will be delivered to the judge before he decides on the sentence at the end of the trial, arguing for or against a tough sentence and providing details of mitigating circumstances, if any. Encourage Ss to invent details which have not been provided.

9 Vocabulary | News headlines

> **OPTIONAL WARMER**
>
> Ss list the different parts of a newspaper in pairs (e.g. *headlines*; *main story*; *front page*; *editorial*; *sports section*; *entertainment section*, etc.) Write the word *headline* on the board. Make sure Ss understand what it means. Ask: *What is the purpose of a headline? Are they sometimes difficult to understand? Why?* Explain that headlines are usually short, to create more impact. In order to achieve this words are often missed out (e.g. articles, pronouns, auxiliary verbs, etc.).

1a ▶ Explain that headlines often use a particular vocabulary, often dramatic, shorter words in order to achieve maximum impact. Ss match the words 1–12 (from headlines) with the meanings a–l using dictionaries if necessary. Ss compare answers with a partner.

> **Answers**
>
> | | | | | |
> |---|---|---|---|---|
> | 1 | i | | 7 | f |
> | 2 | d | | 8 | g |
> | 3 | j | | 9 | k |
> | 4 | h | | 10 | b |
> | 5 | c | | 11 | e |
> | 6 | l | | 12 | a |

b ▶ Ss discuss, in pairs, what they think the headlines mean. Get feedback from the whole class.

> **Answers**
> A A well-known Hollywood actor has been involved in a tense situation in a bank, maybe a robbery.
> B A very successful sports personality is going to leave the sporting life.
> C A politician has been involved with a spy in some way.
> D A prince and a shop assistant are planning to get married.

2 ▶ Ss choose the most likely alternative in each headline. Get feedback from the whole class.

> **Answers**
> 1 Key
> 2 axes
> 3 blaze
> 4 back
> 5 drama
> 6 clash
> 7 bids
> 8 quits

3 ▶ Ss look at the headlines. Ss discuss what each one might be about and whether they would continue reading the article or not with a partner. Get feedback from the whole class. Ask: *Which is the most interesting headline?*

Suggested answers

1   Manchester United football team have lost heavily in a tournament
2   There is a development to a story about a painting by Van Gogh.
3   A bomb has exploded in northern India.
4   There has been a problem with recording the votes in an election in California. Some may have been stolen or changed.

OPTIONAL EXTENSION

Put Ss in pairs. They imagine they are about to read a big Sunday newspaper containing many sections. They tell each other which part they would read first, second and so on (e.g. *I would skip the news section and look first at the sports results. Then I would read the reviews of new films*, etc.).

---

5 ▶ Focus Ss on the tip in the Lifelong learning box. Then, they discuss the questions in small groups. Get feedback from the whole class. Write Ss' ideas on the board.

---

9 Communication

In this lesson, Ss discuss six lateral thinking puzzles with other Ss. They try to solve the puzzles by asking *Yes/No* questions and guessing the answers.

Lateral-thinking puzzles are stories in which you have some basic clues to a realistic scenario, but the clues don't tell the full story. You need to work out the full story using problem-solving that involves looking at the situation from unexpected angles. You need to think 'outside the box'.

OPTIONAL WARMER

Demonstrate a lateral-thinking puzzle with the whole class. Give the following basic scenario: *Anthony and Cleopatra die inside their house during a storm but their bodies are never found. The only clues to what happened are a wet patch of carpet, a cat and some broken glass. What happened?* Ss can ask *Yes/No* questions only and try to solve the puzzle. Explain that you will only answer correctly formed *Yes/No* questions and remind Ss of the intonation patterns for questions which were covered in Unit 7. Tell Ss that if they already know the solution, they should just remain quiet for now.
(Solution: *Anthony and Cleopatra are goldfish. Their goldfish bowl fell and shattered during a storm. The cat ate the two goldfish.*)

---

1 ▶ Tell Ss that they are going to try to solve six lateral-thinking puzzles. First, they read all six scenarios and note down any vocabulary they don't understand. Then, they discuss the meanings of the unfamiliar vocabulary with a partner, using a dictionary if necessary. Finally they think of possible explanations for the six problems in pairs.

2 ▶ Divide Ss into six groups (1–6). Each group corresponds with one of the puzzles. Ss 1s work in pairs, 2s work in pairs and so on. Each pair finds and reads the solution to their problem. Ss read the explanations on the relevant page. Explain that the solution to one of the other puzzles might be on the same page so they must be very careful to only read the solution to their own puzzle.

▶ Next, Ss look at the sample sentences and then each pair tries to think of two Yes/No questions to ask about each of the other five puzzles.

▶ Put Ss in groups of six, including at least one student from each group. Ss take turns to ask Yes/No questions about one of the puzzles. Encourage them to keep the answers simple and not give any more information than is necessary to answer the question. When the other Ss have asked their questions, they try to guess what the solution might be. Get feedback from the whole class.

OPTIONAL EXTENSION

Write the following types of puzzle on the board and ask Ss to explain to each other what they are: *crossword, sudoku, wordsearch, jigsaw puzzle, anagram.* Ask Ss to discuss the following questions.
Can you add any more types of puzzle to the list?
Do you like these types of puzzle? Why/Why not?

9 Review and practice

1 ▶

Answers
1 After travelling/Having travelled for hours to get to the village, she thought she should stay there for at least a couple of days.
2 After seeing/Having seen his neighbour struggling with a lot of heavy bags, he offered to help her.
3 After coming/Having come first in her university exams, she was approached by a top firm of lawyers.
4 After taking/Having taken home an injured cat she had found by the side of the road, she felt she had to keep it.
5 After seeing/ Having seen a young man take a CD without paying, he told the security staff.
6 After speaking/Having spoken to his father, he told his boss he wanted a raise.
7 After getting/Having got a long letter from their cousin, they decided to go and see him.

2 ▶

Answers
1 He might have stayed late at the office.
2 I can't have left my gloves in the car.
3 She might be at the station already.
4 She must have shown me her holiday photos at least ten times.
5 She can't have finished all her homework already.
6 They must have been really pleased to be the winners.
7 My letter might have got lost in the post.
8 He can't be serious about getting a dog.

3 ▶

Answers
1 No commas necessary.
2 I'm going to spend a few days in Seville, where I first met Raquel.
3 No commas necessary.
4 No commas necessary.
5 We decided to stay at the Regina Hotel, which some friends had recommended to us.
6 Tim, whose job involves a lot of travelling, has offered to let us use his flat for a few weeks.

4 ▶

Answers
1 Steve works for a small company which/that makes kitchen equipment.
2 ✓
3 Did you hear exactly ~~that~~ what he said?
4 The demonstration, which had been going on for several days, ~~is~~ was finally over.
5 ✓
6 My sister, ~~that~~ who speaks French and Italian fluently, wants to be an interpreter.

5 ▶

Answers
1 witness
2 arson
3 far-fetched
4 punishment
5 sued
6 community service
7 tongue-tied
8 convicted

9 Writing bank

1 ▶

> **Answers**
> 1 He had thought through some things but not others.
> 2 not successful at all

2 ▶

> **Answers**
> 1 readers who like an amusing story in the newspaper
> 2 to make it believable
> 3 a, d, e

3 ▶

> **Answers**
> A 3
> B 1
> C 2

4a/b ▶ Ss prepare and write a factual account of a news story.

Overview

CEFR Can do objectives

10.1 Discuss your beliefs and opinions
10.2 Persuade someone to do something
10.3 Talk about wishes and intentions for the future
Communication Describe what kind of person you are and how you think/learn
Writing bank Write a 'for and against' essay

CEFR Portfolio ideas

a) Read the article. You are planning a trip to Florida for a month. Write an email to a friend and try to persuade them to go with you.

b) Imagine you keep a 'lifelog'. Choose a significant event from your past and prepare an entry'. Use photos and other images for the entry and write about how the event has shaped you as a person.

c) Prepare a five-minute presentation entitled 'How I see myself in five years'. Think about your plans for your studies/career, travel plans, personal ambitions, etc. Use the language on page 142 to help you. Give your presentation to the class.

Lead-in

OPTIONAL WARMER

Write the following words on the board: *think, leap, hop, tickle, mull over, pat, march, thump, clap, forget, wonder, skip, rub, stroke, contemplate, stamp, ponder, kick*. Ask Ss to categorise the verbs under the following headings: *mind, feet, hands* (mind: *think, mull over, forget, wonder, contemplate, ponder*, feet: *leap, hop, march, skip, stamp, kick*; hands: *tickle, pat, thump, clap, rub, stroke*).

1 ▶ Ss look at the photos and discuss the questions. Don't ask for feedback at this point.

2a ▶ Ss work with a partner and match the photos with the quotes. Ss explain to each other what they think the underlined phrases mean. Get feedback from the whole class. There is no quote to match the larger picture at the top of the page.

Suggested Answers

Top photo: walking on hot coals = *mind over matter* (using your thoughts to control physical feelings or an unpleasant situation)
Middle photo: great leaders = *the power of persuasion* (the skill of persuading someone to do something)
Bottom photo: not eating sweet things = *willpower* (the ability to not give into temptation in order to achieve something you want to do)

b ▶ Ss discuss the questions in pairs. Get feedback from various Ss.

3a ▶ Ss read the questions and discuss the meanings of the underlined phrases with a partner. Encourage Ss to use dictionaries to help with meaning, word stress and pronunciation. Focus Ss' attention on the use of the prefixes *un-* and *sub-* (in *unconscious* and *subconscious*).

Answers

1 a strange feeling that something bad is going to happen
2 a feeling that what is happening now has happened to you before
3 to base decisions about events or people on feelings and instincts rather than considering the facts
4 a special ability to know things without using your five ordinary senses
5 unable to see, move, feel, because you are not conscious
6 fears that are hidden in your mind and which affect your behaviour, but you are unaware of these

b ▶ Ss take turns to ask and answer the questions in pairs. Encourage them to ask for and give additional details. Get feedback from the whole class. Ask Ss about their experiences of these phenomena.

10.1 Head games

In this lesson, Ss read an article about Derren Brown, his work as a mind-reader and listen to three people describing their reactions to this phenomenon. Ss give their own opinions on a variety of topics.

Reading

Derren Brown is a well-known British illusionist, particularly famous for his 'mind-reading' and 'mind-persuasion' acts on stage shows and television specials, where he appears to be able to predict and manipulate what people think. Although his magical feats appear to be the result of paranormal powers, in fact he says he possesses no such abilities at all and claims that he achieves his results through a mixture of subtle suggestion, psychological insights and showmanship. He frequently explains how he did a particular trick afterwards.

OPTIONAL WARMER

Ask: *Have you ever heard of Houdini? What was he famous for?* (the well-known magician/escapist from the early years of the 20th century, famous for escaping from chains, ropes, straitjackets, etc. on stage). Conduct a whole class discussion on the topic of famous magicians and illusionists and their stage shows. Ask: *Have you ever seen a show like this? Did/Would you enjoy it? Why/Why not?* If the magician asked a member of the audience to participate on stage, would you do it?

1a ▶ Ss discuss the questions in pairs.

Answers
2   *an illusionist* = a performer who seems to make things appear and disappear
    a magician = an entertainer who performs tricks
    a hypnotist in this context = an entertainer who seems to be able to manipulate the behaviour of ordinary people by putting them into a trance

b ▶ Ss read the article quickly and answer the questions. Remind them not to worry about unknown words at this stage but just to focus on answering the questions. Explain that they will have an opportunity to read in more detail in the next exercise. Ss compare answers with a partner.

Answers
1   both
2   No

2 ▶ Ss read the article again and decide if the statements are true, false or not given. Ss compare answers with a partner, giving their reasons.

Answers
1   NG (the text mentions how famous he is in Britain but does not say if he is famous elsewhere or not)
2   F (the writer can't help being fascinated by how Brown does the tricks)
3   F (this is not the most important thing for Brown; he is more interested in the relationship between the magician and the audience)
4   T (he tells people how many fingers they are holding up behind their backs; he beats six world-class chess players in simultaneous games; he predicts the winning lottery numbers; he states how many of a number of salesmen are lying about their pasts; he draws an almost exact replica of a secretly drawn picture in a sealed envelope)
5   T
6   NG (the writer is very impressed by the skills of Brown but does not say they are the best he has ever seen)

OPTIONAL EXTENSION

Put Ss in pairs and ask them to find the following phrases in the article. Tell them to look at the context around each phrase and try to explain to each other what they mean. Give them dictionaries to help if necessary.
sleight of hand (speed and skill using the hands when performing tricks, often used figuratively to describe skilful manipulation of facts and figures)
seemingly impossible feats (a very difficult action requiring great skill, strength or bravery)
in awe (filled with feelings of admiration and respect)
the key to his success (the reason why he is so popular and achieves what he does)

3 ▶ Ss discuss the questions in small groups.

Grammar | reflexive pronouns

OPTIONAL LEAD-IN

Write the following two sentences on the board.
1   *He asked him a question.*
2   *He asked himself a question.*
Ask Ss: *What is the difference?* (1: *He* and *him* are two different people, one man asking another man a question; 2: *He* and *himself* are the same person).

Write the following words on the board: *me, myself, I* and ask Ss: *What is the difference grammatically between them?* (*me* = object pronoun; *myself* = reflexive pronoun; *I* =subject pronoun).

Then ask Ss to work together to list subject pronouns, object pronouns and reflexive pronouns (subject pronouns = *I, you, he, she, it, we, you, they*; object pronouns = *me, you, him, her, it, us, you, them*; reflexive pronouns = *myself, yourself, himself, herself, itself, ourselves, yourselves, themselves*).

4 ▶ Ss read the two examples given, then match them to the correct rule A or B in the Active grammar box.

> **Active grammar**
>
> A 1   B 2

5a ▶ Ss match the examples 1–6 with the correct rule A or B in the Active grammar box.

> **Active grammar**
>
> A: 1, 3 and 5   B: 2, 4 and 6

b ▶ Ss discuss the question in pairs.

> **Active grammar**
>
> Sentence 1 means: I taught you a magic trick and you taught me a different one.
> Sentence 2 means: nobody else taught us or helped us learn the trick.

c ▶ Ss find one example of each rule in the article.

> **Answers**
> A   ... Brown taught himself standard forms of magic and hypnotism ...
> B   ... I myself am sceptical ...
> C   Even when he tells the audience how something is done, they still look at each other in disbelief.

▶ Focus Ss' attention on the Reference section on page 145.

6 ▶ Ss complete the sentences with a reflexive pronoun, an object pronoun or *each other*.

> **Answers**
> 1   myself   5   each other
> 2   each other   6   himself/herself
> 3   me   7   us
> 4   myself   8   itself

Pronunciation | stress: reflexive pronouns

7a ▶ ⬤ 2.37 Explain that the reflexive pronoun is used to give emphasis and that we also use stress to emphasise the meaning even more. Play the recording. Ss listen and identify the part of the reflexive pronoun which is stressed in each case.

> **Answers**
> my<u>self</u>, him<u>self</u>, it<u>self</u>

b ▶ Play the recording again. Ss listen and repeat.

8a ▶ Ss look at the first part of the sentences, then complete them so that they are true about themselves.

b ▶ Put Ss in small groups. They compare the sentences they prepared in exercise 8a. Encourage them to ask for and give more details and to discuss whether they agree or disagree with each other's views.

Listening

9 ▶ ⬤ 2.38 Tell Ss they are going to listen to three people talking about Derren Brown and mind-reading. Play the recording. Ss listen and choose which statement best summarises each person's opinion. Remind them that one statement cannot be used. Ss compare answers with a partner.

> **Answers**
> Person 1: statement 4
> Person 2: statement 3
> Person 3: statement 1

10a ▶ Explain to Ss that the phrases in the How to... box are all verb phrases about giving your opinion or stating your beliefs. Play the recording again. Ss listen and complete the gaps in the sentences. Ss compare answers with a partner.

> **Answers**
> I **reckon** he's probably ...
> I'm **in favour of** ...
> I've always **believed** that ...
> I have my **doubts** ...
> I'm **sceptical** that ...
> I'm **against** people paying ...
> I **doubt** anything he does is real.
> I'm **convinced** that he ...
> I **suspect** that a lot of ...

b ▶ Ask Ss to work in pairs and answer the questions about the meaning of the verb phrases. Demonstrate the intonation and stress patterns typically used with these expressions during whole class feedback. Remind Ss how to use intonation to sound tentative or sure.

> **Answers**
> 1   I've always believed that/I'm convinced that
> 2   I have my doubts about/I'm sceptical that/I doubt
> 3   I reckon/I suspect
> 4   I'm in favour of
> 5   I'm against

11 ▶ Ss rewrite the sentences using the words in brackets and adding other words to complete the appropriate verb phrase. Ss compare answers with a partner.

> **Answers**
> 1   I've always believed that there is life on other planets.
> 2   I doubt that ghosts really exist at all.
> 3   I'm convinced that I knew what she was thinking.
> 4   I'm in favour of people trying all sorts of different treatments.
> 5   I reckon that some people have supernatural powers.
> 6   I have my doubts about the existence of UFOs.
> 7   I'm against paying someone for a service I don't understand.
> 8   I'm sceptical that anyone can predict the future.

Speaking

12a ▶ Read through the topics from the box with the class, checking that Ss understand them all. Ss choose one of the topics to talk about. They can choose a different topic if they wish.

b ▶ Focus Ss' attention on the three questions given to help organise their ideas. Ss prepare to give a one-minute talk about their chosen topic. Encourage them to use the phrases from the How to... box.

13a ▶ Put Ss in small groups. When setting up the groups, try to ensure that a range of topics are covered in the groups. Ss take turns to talk about their topics for one minute. Encourage Ss to ask for further information/clarification and give more details in a short question-and-answer session after each talk. Ss compare views on each topic before moving on to the next one.

b ▶ Get feedback from the whole class. Ask: *Which topic was most controversial in your group? Why? Did you agree on any of the topics in your group? Which one?*, etc.

OPTIONAL EXTENSION

Give each student a topic (e.g. *using mobile phones in restaurants*; *eating in cinemas*; *parents slapping children who misbehave*; *buying first-class airline tickets*; *testing cosmetic products on animals*; *nuclear power plants*; *fast-food restaurants*; *the death penalty*; *organic food*, etc.). Ss mingle asking as many other Ss as possible about their views in relation to their topic in the time given. Don't worry if one or two Ss have the same topic. Ask Ss to make notes under the following headings as they mingle: *strong views for/against the topic*; *mixed feelings about the topic*; *no strong feelings about the topic*. When the time is up, Ss prepare a short report on the views of Ss in relation to their topic to present to the class. Remind them of the language used in surveys which was covered in Lesson 8.3 (e.g. *Most Ss spoken to have strong feelings against using animals to test cosmetic products. A small minority felt this would be OK if the animals were treated well.*).

10.2 Persuasion

In this lesson, Ss listen to an extract from a radio programme on persuasion tactics in advertising and retail. They listen to two dialogues where someone tries to persuade a friend to do something. Ss practise persuading each other to do things.

OPTIONAL WARMER

Tell Ss they are the marketing team responsible for a new shampoo for men. Put Ss in small groups. They have to decide on the following in order to appeal to their target audience: men aged 18–30. They must choose: *the colour and shape of the bottle*; *the name of the product*; *the price range* (top of the range/mid-range/cheap); *a celebrity to use in the adverts for the product*; *where to advertise* (e.g. magazines, TV, billboards, etc.); *where to sell the product* (supermarkets, hair salons, pharmacies; etc.). Get feedback from the whole class.

Listening

1 ▶ Ss look at the photos and discuss the questions in pairs. Get feedback from the whole class.

2 ▶ ● 2.39 Tell Ss they are going to listen to an extract from a radio programme. Play the recording. Ss listen and answer the question. Explain that they will have an opportunity to listen in more detail in the next exercise. Ss compare answers with a partner.

Answers
advertising and supermarkets

---

3 ▶ Give Ss time to read through the notes. Play the recording again. Ss listen and use one or two words to complete the sentences. Ss compare answers with a partner.

Answers

1	entrance	6	emotional
2	fresh bread	7	cleaning products
3	manipulated	8	friends
4	time-consuming	9	celebrities
5	bargain		

---

4 ▶ Ss discuss the question in small groups. Get feedback from the whole class.

OPTIONAL EXTENSION

Write the following heading on the board: *GROCERY SHOPPING*. Ss then discuss this topic in small groups with the following questions: *Who does it in your household? Do you make a list? Do you go to one supermarket or lots of different shops? Do you buy the same products each week or different ones?*
Get feedback from the whole class. Ask: *Who likes grocery shopping? Why/Why not?*

Vocabulary | advertising

5 ▶ Ss decide on the difference in meaning between the pairs of words in the box. Encourage them to use dictionaries to help.

> **Answers**
> *advertising* = to make a product known to the people in order to sell it
> *marketing* = planning how best to advertise a product in order to maximise sales
> *commercial break* = a short break for advertising during programmes on TV or radio
> *target market* = the audience the advertising is aimed at
> *brand* = label (e.g. Levi's and Lee Cooper are both brands of jeans)
> *hype* = positive media and public attention
> *slogan* = a catchy phrase which goes with an ad
> *logo* = an image associated with a brand
> *advertisement* = a piece of advertising on TV or on a billboard
> *trailer* = an advert for a film which includes short clips in order to encourage people to go to see it in the cinema

6 ▶ Ss choose the correct option for each sentence. Ss compare answers with a partner.

> **Answers**
> 1 advertisements
> 2 brands
> 3 marketing
> 4 slogans
> 5 commercial breaks
> 6 trailers
> 7 hype
> 8 target market
> 9 advertising
> 10 logo

7a ▶ Ss choose five questions from exercise 6. They then take turns to ask and answer them. Encourage Ss to ask for and give further details in their discussion.

b ▶ Get feedback from the whole class. Extend the discussion to a whole-class discussion on the extent to which we are influenced by advertising. Ask: *Do you think advertising should be aimed at children? What do you think about cigarette companies sponsoring sporting events? What do you think of 'shock' adverts to discourage people from speeding or drinking and driving?*

Grammar | conditional structures (2): with conjunctions

8a ▶ Ask Ss to look at sentences 1 and 2 in section A of the Active grammar box. Ask: *What type of conditional is sentence 1* (First Conditional) *and sentence 2* (Third Conditional)? Ss complete the sentences with the correct form of *stay* or *come*. Ss compare answers with a partner.

> **Active grammar**
> 1   will come   2   had stayed

b ▶ Focus Ss' attention on the first words of the five sentences in section B of the Active grammar box. Explain that these are all alternatives to if in conditional sentences. Ss complete the rules. Ss compare answers with a partner.

> **Active grammar**
> 1   unless
> 2   even if
> 3   provided that, as long as, supposing

▶ Focus Ss' attention on the Reference section on page 145.

9 ▶ Ss match the first and second halves of the sentences. Ss compare answers with a partner.

> **Answers**
> 1   c
> 2   e
> 3   a
> 4   f
> 5   b
> 6   d

10 ▶ Ask Ss to read the Reference section on Conditionals in Unit 5 if they need extra help. Ss complete the sentences with the correct form of the verbs in brackets. Get feedback from the whole class. Ask Ss: *What type of conditional is this?* for each sentence.

> **Answers**
> 1   find (First)
> 2   wouldn't buy (Second)
> 3   hadn't gone (Third)
> 4   wouldn't have bought (mixed Second and Third)
> 5   I'll watch (First)
> 6   She'll buy (First)
> 7   hadn't seen (mixed Third and Second)
> 8   would you do (Second)

11a ▶ Ss choose the correct conjunction for each sentence. Then they compare answers with a partner.

> **Answers**
> 1   as long as
> 2   even if
> 3   Supposing
> 4   provided that
> 5   Unless
> 6   If
> 7   As long as
> 8   Unless

b ▶ Ss rewrite the sentences so that they are true of themselves. Some sentences may remain unchanged depending on the view of the student.

c ▶ Ss compare their sentences in pairs. Encourage Ss to ask for and give further details as they discuss their sentences. Get feedback from the whole class. Ask: *Which sentences did you agree/disagree about?*

Listening

12a ▶ Teach the word *persuasive* (someone or something who/which is persuasive makes you want to do or believe a particular thing: a persuasive advert makes you want to buy the product; a persuasive politician makes you want to vote for him/her).

▶ Get feedback from the whole class. Brainstorm a list of factors which might persuade you to buy something and write them on the board.

b ▶ ● 2.40 Tell Ss they are going to listen to two dialogues where one person is trying to persuade another person to do something. Play the recording. Ss listen and answer the questions. Then they compare answers with a partner.

> **Answers**
> 1 Both Anna and Zoë (dialogue 1) and Jamie and Alex (dialogue 2) are friends
> 2 to buy a particular mobile phone (dialogue 1); to go and see a Woody Allen film (dialogue 2)
> 3 Yes

13 ▶ Ss read the phrases in the How to... box. Play the recording again. Ss listen and number the phrases in order in which they hear them. Then they compare answers with a partner.

> **Answers**
> 1 Go on ... treat yourself!
> 2 You should just do it.
> 3 Go for it then
> 4 Supposing you don't get it, how will you feel?
> 5 If I were you, I'd just do it!
> 6 You deserve it!
> 7 I'm sure you won't regret it.
> 8 I'm sure you'll enjoy it.
> 9 There's nothing else unless you want to get a DVD?
> 10 What have you got to lose?
> 11 Come on!
> 12 It'll be fun.

Pronunciation | intonation: sounding enthusiastic

14a ▶ Ask Ss: *How do the people sound when they are saying these expressions: bored? enthusiastic?* (enthusiastic and persuasive). Explain that they are going to focus on how to use your voice to sound this way. Ss discuss the questions in pairs. Don't ask for feedback at this point.

b ▶ ● 2.41 Play the recording. Ss listen and check their answers. Then ask them to practise saying the expressions.

> **Answers**
> 1 a broad intonation range is used
> 2 Go on ... treat yourself!
> You should just do it.
> Go for it then.
> Supposing you don't get it, how will you feel?
> If I were you, I'd just do it!
> You deserve it!
> I'm sure you won't regret it.
> I'm sure you'll enjoy it.
> There's nothing else unless you want to get a DVD?
> What have you got to lose?
> Come on!
> It'll be fun!

▶ Focus Ss' attention on the Pronunciation bank on page 161.

Speaking

15a ▶ Explain to Ss that they are going to practise persuading their partner to do something. First, Ss choose one of the ideas from the box.

b ▶ Next, Ss prepare how they will persuade their partner to do this. Encourage them to make notes under the following headings: *when?*; *where?*; *why will your partner enjoy this?*; *any other benefits?*.

c ▶ Ss take turns to persuade their partner to do something. Remind them to use the language in the How to... box. Ss decide whether to agree to do it. Get feedback from the whole class. Ask: *How many agreed to do what your partner wanted you to do? Why/Why not?*

> **OPTIONAL EXTENSION**
>
> Put Ss in small groups. They prepare an advert for one of the ideas in the box in exercise 15b (e.g. a health campaign to encourage people to cycle to work; an advert for salsa dancing classes; a camping holiday in Italy, etc.). It can be an advert in a magazine or on radio. Ss choose a product, decide who their target market is and create the advert. Ss perform/show their adverts to other Ss.

10.3 My digital memory

In this lesson, Ss read a blog entry about 'lifelogging' and the plans the writer has to start making a digital record of important events in his life. Ss discuss their own future plans, wishes and intentions.

Reading

OPTIONAL WARMER

Tell Ss to imagine they have been given a frame which can hold five photos. Give them a few minutes to think about their favourite photos from the past and present and to choose which five photos they would put into the frame. Explain that the photos must represent different times in their lives and that they themselves must be in each photo. Ss then work in pairs. They explain their choice of photos to their partner. Encourage Ss to ask questions and give as much detail as possible about the photos they have selected for the frame.

1a ▶ Ss read through the sentences and decide which are true of themselves. They then re-write the other sentences to make them true.

b ▶ Ss compare sentences with a partner.

2 ▶ Ss read the blog entry and answer the questions. They compare answers with a partner. Explain that they will have a chance to read in more detail in the next exercise.

Answers
1 a way of digitally recording the main events and stages of your life, through photos, video clips, recordings, blog entries, etc.
2 that his life will not be interesting enough

3 ▶ Ss read the blog again and answer the questions. They compare answers with a partner.

Answers
1 he forgets things easily
2 he would like to have more photos and video recordings of when he was younger, particularly of his schooldays and family holidays
3 a researcher at Microsoft has recorded all aspects of his life over the last few years, including his communications with others, sounds he has heard, images he has seen and websites he has visited
4 it can provide an ongoing health record of a person and give early warnings of many illnesses
5 one terabyte at the moment but this will grow to 250 terabytes in the next 20 years
6 he writes a blog and uploads photos on it but he feels this is not enough

4 ▶ Write the following headings on the board: *Advantages* and *Disadvantages*. Ss discuss 'lifelogging' in relation to the three categories given. Ask Ss to think of the advantages and disadvantages for each one. Get feedback from the whole class.

Vocabulary | verb phrases with *mind*

5 ▶ Ss look at the underlined expressions which contain the word *mind*. In pairs, they work out the meanings of the phrases using the surrounding context and dictionaries if necessary.

Answers
1 I made up my mind = I made a decision after thinking about it first
2 things slip my mind = I forget to do things
3 change my mind = reverse my decision
4 it crossed my mind = I thought about it briefly
5 nothing springs to mind = I can't think of any ideas at this moment
6 I'll keep it in mind = I will consider this when I make a decision/do it
7 it's hard to keep my mind on it = it's hard to concentrate on it
8 he speaks his mind = he says what he thinks, even if it offends other people

6a ▶ Ss choose the correct option in each sentence.

Answers
1 crossed
2 make
3 slipped
4 keeping
5 change
6 speaks
7 keep
8 spring

b ▶ Ss ask and answer the questions from exercise 6a.

Grammar | futures (2)

OPTIONAL LEAD-IN

Write the following headings on the board: *definite plans* and *uncertain plans*. Say the following sentences to Ss and ask them to decide whether they are definite or uncertain plans for the weekend: *I might go to the cinema on Saturday afternoon* (uncertain); *I'm meeting Julia for dinner on Friday evening* (definite); *I'm thinking of going shopping on Saturday morning* (uncertain); *I've made up my mind to go to the gym on Sunday afternoon* (definite); *I'd like to go to the football match on Friday afternoon* (uncertain – a wish).

7 ▶ Explain to Ss that they are going to focus on the language we use when we are describing definite and uncertain plans. Ask: *Is a wish a definite plan?* (no, it is something you would like to do or to happen but it might not). *Is an intention a definite plan?* (yes)

▶ Ss look at sentences a–i. First, they decide whether each one is a definite or an uncertain plan and then they write them in the correct place in the Active grammar box.

Active grammar

1	b		6	c
2	f		7	i
3	e		8	a
4	d		9	g
5	h			

▶ Focus Ss' attention on the Reference section on page 145.

8 ▶ Ss identify the two correct sentences and correct the other six.

Answers
1 I wish I ~~have~~ had …
2 ✓
3 If I have time this weekend, ~~I put~~ I'll put …
4 I'm intending to ~~having~~ have …
5 ✓
6 ~~I study~~ I'd study really hard …
7 I've decided ~~buying~~ to buy …
8 If ~~I'll~~ I save up …

9a ▶ Give Ss a minute or so to think of definite plans and intentions and uncertain plans and wishes for the next six months. Ss then complete the sentences.

b ▶ Ss compare their sentences and discuss their plans. Encourage Ss to ask for and give as much detail as possible. Get feedback from various Ss.

Speaking

10 ▶ Ss read the extract and discuss the questions in groups of three or four.

11a ▶ Elicit the headings which are given in the extract for types of intentions people make and write them on the board: *exercise more*; *eat better*; *save money*; *get a better job*; *get better grades*; *learn something new*; *become more organised*; *reduce stress*; *become less grumpy*. Give Ss a minute or two to make notes on their intentions.

b ▶ Ss tell each other about their intentions. Encourage Ss to ask for and give as much detail as possible about what they would like to do, why they want to do this and how they will go about doing it.

OPTIONAL EXTENSION
Ask Ss to think of three things they are happy about (e.g. they are happily married; they enjoy their job) and three things they would change if they could (e.g. earn more money). Ss compare their lists with a partner.

10 Vocabulary | Commonly misspelt words

OPTIONAL WARMER
Write the following words on the board, one group at a time. Elicit which one is correct each time and give feedback.
1 a acomodation b accomodation c accommodation
2 a there b they're c their
3 a practise b practice
4 a colour b color
(1 Only *accommodation* is correct.
2 All are correct depending on the context.
3 *Practise* is the verb and *practice* the noun in British spelling.
4 *Colour* is British spelling and *color* is US spelling.)

1a ▶ Ss discuss the questions in pairs. Don't ask for any feedback at this point.

b ▶

Answers
1 c
2 c
3 a

2 ▶ Ss decide which is the correct spelling for each pair of words. Ss compare answers with a partner.

Answers
1 believe
2 intelligence
3 subconscious
4 psychologist
5 doubt
6 existence
7 successful
8 responsibility

3a ▶ Remind Ss that they may be actual mistakes or they may be words which are spelt wrong because of the context (e.g. *there/their*, *where/wear*).

b ▶ Ss check answers with a partner.

Answers
great, generous, foreigner, weird, beginning, weather, definitely, changeable, accommodation, interesting, restaurants, library, necessary, usually, occasionally, friends, their, separate

4 ▶ Ss discuss the questions in small groups. Get feedback from various Ss.

10 Communication

In this lesson, Ss do a quiz and discuss different ways in which people think and approach life. The quiz is based on the idea that there are at least five types of thinkers/learners and that each type approaches life and its problems in slightly different ways. The five types of thinker/learner that are used in this quiz are: linguistic; logical-mathematical; interpersonal; existential; and kinaesthetic.

OPTIONAL WARMER

Write the following headings on the board: *theoretical, mathematical type subjects*; *humanities subjects (History, Literature, etc.)*; *language subjects (English, Chinese, etc.)*; *creative subjects (Art, Technical Drawing)*; *practical subjects (Business, Home Economics)*; *physical activity subjects (Gymnastics, etc.)*. Ask Ss to work in pairs and discuss which type they liked most and why.

---

1 ▶ Ss look at the photos and discuss the questions in pairs.

Suggested answers
Teacher: patient, able to explain things clearly, approachable
Nurse: kind, good at science
Sculptor: artistic, imaginative, able to see things spatially

---

2 ▶ Tell Ss that they are going to do a quiz to find out how they like to think, learn and approach life. First, they have to match the six questions in the quiz to the correct answer box. Ss compare answers with a partner.

Answers
1 B
2 E
3 D
4 F
5 A
6 C

3a ▶ Ss then take turns to ask each other the questions from exercise 2. They can choose answers from the box or give different answers. Encourage Ss to ask for and give as much detail in their answers as possible. Ss take notes of their partner's answers.

b ▶ Focus Ss' attention on the descriptions on page 147. They read about the five different types of learner/thinker and then discuss the questions with their partner. Explain that one type is not better or worse than another. It is also possible to be a mixture of different types but usually one or two predominate. Get feedback from the whole class. Ask: *How many of you are linguistic/logical mathematical/Interpersonal etc.? What kind of thing do you like doing?*

10 Review and practice

1 ▶

Answers
1 burn yourself
2 felt
3 expresses herself
4 relax
5 hurt himself
6 meet
7 enjoyed ourselves
8 concentrated

2 ▶

Answers
1 unless
2 provided that
3 Supposing
4 Unless
5 Even if
6 as long as
7 provided that
8 Supposing

3 ▶

Answers
1 I wish I had more willpower.
2 I'm determined to go for a run every morning.
3 If only I could travel more this year.
4 If the weather is good, I'll go to the beach.
5 If only I had enough money to pay for you.
6 I wish I was/could be a professional musician.

4 ▶

Answers
1 slipped
2 déjà vu
3 make
4 springs
5 intuition
6 subconscious
7 keep
8 premonition

5 ▶

Answers
1	hype	4	logos
2	brand	5	slogans
3	breaks	6	trailer

6 ▶

Answers
1	definitely	5	separate
2	accommodation	6	their
3	responsibility	7	✓
4	✓	8	successful

10 Writing bank

1 ▶

> **Answer**
> The writer agrees that advertising during children's programmes should be banned.

2a ▶

> **Answers**
> c, a, b, d

b ▶

> **Answers**
> 1 Parents have responsibility for what their children watch on TV; many children like to watch adverts to find out what is available in the shops.
> 2 Companies are using children because they know that they will pester their parents to buy them things which are advertised on TV; children are exposed to too much commercialism on TV.
> 3 In this essay, I will consider the question of ...; It is an important issue and there are strong feelings on both sides ... ; In conclusion, I am convinced that ... ; On balance, I think it is wrong ....

3a ▶ Ss choose one of the statements and prepare notes for and against it.

b ▶ Ss write their essay.

Audioscripts

Track 1.2

S=Sarah, F=Fiona

S: Hello. My name's Sarah. Pleased to meet you.

F: Oh, hello. A pleasure to meet you, too. My name's Fiona. It's really nice to see a friendly face actually. I'm feeling a bit nervous.

S: Oh, don't worry. There's no need to be nervous. I've been to this class before and everyone is really nice. The teacher really makes you feel at ease. Have you done any Spanish classes before?

F: Just a bit, but not for ages. I feel like I've forgotten everything!

S I know what you mean. So, do you live near here?

F: Erm, not too far. I live in Wood End …

S: Oh really? That's not far from where I live … I live in Whitefields, you know, just at the top of the hill.

F: Oh yes, that's really near me actually!

S: So, how did you get here today? Did you come by bus?

F: Yes, I did. I got the 17 all the way. It took me ages though because there was so much traffic. What about you?

S: Yes, I got the 17 too. The traffic was awful, wasn't it?

F: Yeah, really bad. I was a bit late leaving the house as well, 'cos I didn't get back from work till after six …

S: What's your job?

F: I'm a teacher.

S: Are you?

F: Yes, I teach children. Primary school age, you know, mostly aged between 7 and 11. I love it, but it's really hard work! And you? What do you do?

S: Oh, well, I'm certainly not a teacher. I wouldn't have the patience for that! I work in advertising.

F: That sounds fun!

S: Yeah, it's OK. But I'd like to do something different now I think. Oh, here's the teacher. Well, it's been really nice talking to you. Maybe we could meet up after the class and … well, if you're going straight home, perhaps we could go together?

F: Yes, that would be great.

Track 1.3

And now a story about another large family. Being in a large family usually means learning to juggle several tasks at once – shopping, cleaning, making dinner, helping with homework, bandaging a knee and keeping an eye on the children playing outside. However, in addition to a normal family life, the Boehmer family juggle clubs, rings, torches, balls and anything else they can get their hands on. It all started while Larry Boehmer was working as a pipeline worker for Shell Oil. His job took him away from his wife Judy and the four children they had at that time. He had spent the first few weeks sitting in his motel room between shifts, when one day, while he was feeling bored, he decided to take up a new hobby. Using a book, he taught himself to juggle. When he had mastered the basics, he went home and showed his children what he could do. Immediately, they wanted to learn too. Larry is a big family man, so he was only too happy about that, and soon the whole family was juggling. Larry and three of the children gave their first family performance at an amusement park, and from there it all went

from strength to strength. Now, there are four sons and seven daughters in the family, and they are the largest family of jugglers in the world, working together and performing regularly as a family. As Judy puts it, they didn't plan on this happening. When the kids saw each other, they picked up on different things. One would do rings, another would do clubs, acrobatics or the unicycle. Before they knew it, they had everybody doing something. Even Casey, the second son, who was born with only one arm, is a champion juggler in his own right, as well as part of the family troupe.

Larry insists the children's talents aren't inherited, it's simply a matter of practice and persistence. This is a skill that basically anybody can do – you just have to put your mind to it. It's just that most people who try to learn juggling give up too soon. Each member of the family has a speciality but they all have to practise … a lot! Each member of the family not only takes part in the show, they also help with preparing the costumes, transporting everything and setting up the show. In the end, though, performing in the show makes all the practise and hard work worth it. It's great fun and they all love it.

Track 1.4

J=Julia, A=Andrew, M=Maria

J: So Andrew, how many people are there in your family?

A: Erm, there are … well there are three really. I have … I have an older brother, he's about two years older than me, and I have a younger brother, he's about a year and a half younger than me.

J: Mm, so you're the middle child then?

A: Yeah I'm the middle child …

J: A lot of people say that middle children have the worst time. What do you think about that?

A: It's, ah, it depends, erm, I think, erm, there's, ah – you end up, I suppose, looking up to your older brother, ah, as a kind of a leader, you look to him for guidance …

J: That's quite interesting. I've got an older brother and I definitely don't look up to him …

M: I have an older sister and I don't look for gui … to her for guidance for sure, no.

A: I think, erm, when I was young I did, yeah. Definitely to my older brother, yeah. And your older brother does certain things first – first to ride a bike, pass a driving test, first to university. Ah – so maybe they get more attention than the middle child.

J: Yeah, I suppose. And I suppose parents kind of spoil the younger children because they've had the toughest with the older children and then by the time they get to – for me, there's five children in my family – so by the time my parents got to the fifth child they were kind of ready for her to just let herself go.

M: That's not the experience that … that I had, my parents were quite liberal with … I have one sister who's only a, a year and a bit older than me, and, and, ah, my parents were quite liberal with both of us and we grew up …

J: Oh right, you were lucky.

M: … kind of as friends, yeah, it was great.

J: Mm, I don't know, and did you have lots

of, do you think everyone in your family has a lot of friends, or is it different depending on which, which, erm …

M: No, I think it's, it's quite similar. I suppose my sister maybe has a, a wider network and perhaps I have a slightly smaller network but, of very close friends maybe … But I don't think it's connected to position in the family at all.

J: Mm. What about only children, I mean none of us are only children but …

M: No, well …

J: Do you think they need more friends or less friends?

M: I don't know about needing friends but I do think that sometimes they … they can need a lot of attention. I think maybe if they've been the sole … yeah.

A: But they … they're used to the attention.

M: Exactly.

J: I mean, I guess though, it depends on how much attention they get. Do all parents give, you know, if they have one child, do they all give them loads of attention or just only children? Are they quite lonely and do they want more attention? I don't know.

M: I suppose it must, must be the case for some but I, I … I don't know anybody like that.

Track 1.6

Before I had my mobile, my parents worried about me all the time because they couldn't contact me when I was out. You know, I wasn't able to tell them where I was or what time I was coming back. There was one particular time when I lost track of time … I know I should've been more careful but I ended up missing the bus. I wanted to let my parents know that I was going to be late, but I couldn't phone them. In the end, I got to a friend's house and I was able to phone from there … but they had been very worried because I was already 45 minutes late. I felt really bad – I knew I shouldn't have put them in that situation. After that, they bought me a mobile phone, which was good – except, at first, I had to phone them every half an hour to tell them where I was – which was a real pain. After a while, they changed their minds and I didn't have to phone them so much, but I had to have it turned on all the time. I don't find it too annoying – in fact, I like having a phone and it makes me feel safe, knowing that I can phone my parents at any time.

Track 1.9

M=Morgan, F=Friend

M: Look – have you seen this great website? It's about genealogy, you know, family history …

F: Family history? What … your family?

M: Yes, well, any family. It basically helps you to find old relatives and build a family tree. Actually, there are loads of websites like this now. It's quite popular now – lots of people are doing it.

F: Oh really? I've always thought I'd like to know a bit more about my family in the past.

M: Well, this is just the thing. It's great. Even before I found this website, I had started putting together my own family tree – but the website really helps.

F: So, how far back can you go?

M: Well, I'm pretty confident about as far back as my great-grandparents, Cicely and John.

F: You didn't actually know them, did you?

M: No, unfortunately, they died in the 1970s. By all accounts they were an amazing couple, devoted to each other ... and of course they'd lived through two World Wars.

F: Yes ... that generation went through such a lot ... Do you know when they were actually born?

M: Well, yes, I do. My great-grandfather, John, was born right on the turn of the century in 1900. And my great-grandmother, Cicely just a year before that in 1899.

F: Wow ... So did they have children?

M: Yeah, they had two children, Laura and Ben, both were born around 1930 I think.

F: So, Laura's your grandmother, isn't she? I've heard you talk about her.

M: Yeah, that's right. I get on really well with her. My mum says I take after her in lots of ways. I even look quite like her ... same nose!

F: Really?

M: Yeah. I usually go and visit her about once a month, up in Leeds. I'm going up there this weekend, actually ...

F: Is her husband still alive?

M: Julian? No, he died a couple of years ago. So, she's on her own now.

F: So, obviously Laura is your ...

M: ... my mum's mother. Laura and Julian had three children: my mum, Alison, and my aunts, Sue and Deborah.

F: Three girls!

M: Yeah ... but all very different in character!

F: Really?

M: Oh yes ... have I never told you about Aunt Sue?

F: I don't think so.

M: Well she was ... is ... an anthropologist, a kind of adventurer really. She's spent most of her life in and around Borneo, studying the culture, religion and so on. She's quite an expert apparently.

F: And have you got any cousins?

M: Yes, my aunt Deborah had a son and a daughter, Leon and Esther. Esther's a year or so older than me ... and I'm a few years older than Leon. We all got on really well with each other. We saw each other a lot when we were growing up, you know – we'd see them at weekends, and we also used to go on holiday quite a lot together.

F: And do you see them now?

M: Well, I try to keep in touch as much as possible, but it's not as easy as it was ... I mean, Esther lives in New Zealand now ...

F: Oh!

M: ... and Leon divides his time between being a diving instructor in the summer mainly around Egypt and Turkey ... and a skiing instructor in the winter.

F: Hard life!

M: Yeah, I know ...

Track 1.10

I was about 25 and I'd been with the same company for five years. A friend showed me his photos of an amazing holiday he'd had in Central America. One photo in particular really struck me. It was when he went diving and saw the most beautiful fish you've ever seen! I began to have itchy feet and wanted to leave work and do something exciting. I'd never been out of Europe before then and I was a bit worried about going straight into uncharted territory! I mean, I didn't know anything about countries so different and far away from mine. So, I decided to go to Spain first, to learn a bit of Spanish and get used to being away from home. I went as an independent traveller on my own, because I really wanted to do it all by myself. I spent a month wandering around the town where I was living, learning Spanish and loving every minute! I was bitten by the travel bug then and wanted to explore lots of other places. About six months later, after saving up some money, I went off to Guatemala, feeling very confident and pleased with myself. The first two months were difficult and I experienced real culture shock, I think. It seemed that everything was different. Lots of things went wrong too, like I was robbed twice, I couldn't find anywhere to live and I was really homesick and missed my family like mad! So I had a bit of a bumpy ride to start with, but after a while, I found a job teaching English, made some friends and started to really enjoy myself. In fact, I grew to love it so much I stayed there for three years!

Track 1.12

I=Interviewer, O=Oliver

I: So, Oliver, just to remind the listeners, let me ask, what have you been doing here?

O: Erm ... yes, OK ... well, basically I've been living with a family in a small village. I've been here for about a month and a half now.

I: Mmm ... a month and a half ...

O: Yes, since about the beginning of July. And ... erm ... I've been teaching in the village school ... I've been teaching maths mostly, but other things as well. It's all part of a bigger project ... a lot of university students from the UK come for a couple of months at a time. It's voluntary work, you know ... in the university holidays ... to help people here and get some work experience.

I: So, it's all coming to an end now ... how do you feel about leaving?

O: Oh, well, mixed feelings I suppose. I mean, I'll be really sad about leaving everyone here. I've had such a good time. You know, it's been challenging at times ... especially the heat. It's so hot here! But I've had a great time ... really fantastic. Kenya is a really inspiring place.

I: Mixed feelings though?

O: Well, yes, I mean, I'm looking forward to seeing my family. I've missed them while I've been here. Everyone in the village has been really friendly though and really looked after me.

I: And what will you miss about this place when you leave?

O: I'll definitely miss the children in my class ... all the children in the village actually. They're great.

Track 1.13

1 The summer is generally hot and very <u>humid</u> and you are often quite uncomfortable. It's often <u>overcast</u> too and there is no <u>breeze</u> to cool things down. It's very different in the winter, when it's <u>cool</u> and the sky is <u>clear</u>.

2 I'm not so keen on <u>mild</u> weather – when it's not really hot or cold. I much prefer it when the weather is quite dramatic. Like when you are somewhere with <u>scorching</u> days and then it suddenly <u>pours</u> for hours. Or when it's hot in the day and you get <u>sub-zero temperatures</u> at night.

3 The weather is very <u>changeable</u>. In the summer, the days are often <u>bright</u> but can be <u>showery</u> and the nights are sometimes <u>chilly</u> but not very cold. In the winter, it seems to <u>drizzle</u> a lot and the sky is often grey.

Track 1.15

P=Presenter, J=Jamie, W=Woman, M=Man

P: Hello everyone. I think we'll make a start as it's 7.30 already. Let me introduce Jamie. He's our 'Bhutan expert' ... He's spent a substantial amount of time in this amazing country and I'm sure he'll be able to help you with whatever queries you may have.

J: Hello. Thank you. Well, I'll do my best ... Please feel free to ask whatever you want and if I can't answer anything, well, I'll say so! So, fire away ...

W: Erm ... yes ... when is the best time to go?

J: Well, in the winter it can be up to about 15°C in the daytime, but you often get sub-zero temperatures at night. There is a lot of snow in winter, which can make travelling difficult. It's hot in the summer, sometimes really scorching, but it's often very wet too. In my experience, the best seasons to visit are spring and autumn. Spring is beautiful with wonderful flowers and lovely sunny days. And autumn is fantastic too with mild weather and clear views of the Himalayas ... Yes?

M: What activities do you recommend?

J: One of the most popular activities for visitors to Bhutan is to go trekking in the Himalayas. The high mountains and deep valleys are truly spectacular and you can sometimes walk for several days before coming to the next village. You'll see a huge variety of plant life ranging from dense forest to tiny mountain flowers. I've been many times ... You won't be disappointed, I can assure you!

M: Thank you.

W: Excuse me ... I'd like to know whether we need to take anything special.

J: Ah yes, good question. The changeable climate means that you will need an assortment of clothes, including rain gear and good walking boots. The sun can be very strong especially up in the mountains, so you'll need a hat and sunglasses. I'd also recommend warm clothes for the evenings ... it can get pretty chilly, even in summer.

M: Would we need to carry all our equipment on a trek?

J: No. Trekking is done in organised trips and they provide yaks to carry your luggage. They also carry the food and camping equipment, which is all provided. I've always found them very well-equipped and helpful.

M: And who goes with the trekking group? I mean do they provide a guide?

J: Oh yes ... There's always a guide who speaks English and a cook and other assistants to help make the trek run smoothly. They're all very friendly ... you really don't need to worry about getting lost or anything ...

W: Could I ask you what the food is like?

J: Mmm ... interesting, yes. The Bhutanese eat a lot of meat, dairy foods, vegetables and rice. The national dish is a fabulous chilli-pepper and cheese stew called Emadatse. In fact, chillis are very common in Bhutan and you'll find that a lot of their dishes are flavoured with spicy chilli peppers. I love the food, I must say.

M: I'm thinking of going in the autumn. Do you know if there are any interesting festivals at that time?

J: Well, yes, this year there are, although the dates of festivals vary according to the moon. The most popular one for tourists is held in Thimphu, the capital, and this year it's in October. People dress in their colourful, traditional clothes and there is a lot of music and dancing, including the masked sword dances. All the festivals are important religious events for the people to offer thanks to their gods.

M: I've seen pictures of strings of flags in the mountains. Can you tell me what they are?

J: Yes, they are prayer flags. As I said, the Bhutanese people are very religious and they use the flags as a way of communicating with the heavens …

Track 1.16

N=Natalie, M=Man

M: Natalie, you've lived abroad, right?

N: Yeah, yeah, I've lived in Italy.

M: And when you went to Italy, how did you find it? Was it easy to integrate or more difficult than you thought it was gonna be?

N: Oh it was easy actually. Erm, I think once you learn the language then, erm, things just come naturally. And it took me a long time to learn the language but, erm, I don't think it's such a big issue that many people think it is.

M: Do you think that many people think it's a big issue?

N: Yeah I think it's a lot easier than … than people, than most people think. Because it's maybe the fear of the unknown, people haven't tried it, they think it will be more difficult.

M: I think you're right, I think the more time you spend abroad, the easier you'll find integrating in to new places. But it's that first, first step the first time you go and do it, it seems quite daunting.

N: Definitely, but then you have … I don't know … less fun if you stay in your own country or you, erm … I think it's quite safe to stay in your own country, too.

M: Yeah I completely agree, I mean, we only get one life right, so might as well see as much as you can.

N: Exactly, and there's nothing more interesting than getting to know other cultures and finding out about another language or … I mean, how did you find moving here?

M: Erm, for me moving here was a lot easier than, for example when I moved to South Korea but, erm, obviously I needed to learn the … a new language in Korea, but al … but also I think Canadian and British culture are a lot closer than Canadian and Korean culture are to each other.

N: Do you find that you're more adventurous, erm, in Britain than in Canada?

M: Yes I think once I'm at home I'm much more in a routine. Erm, but then again I'm only home for brief periods of time so I just go home and spend it with my family.

N: See the family, yeah.

M: Whereas, if I was living there, maybe I would venture out and travel more in Canada.

N: Mm, but I think the more you, erm, explore a country, the more you find out about it and the more you learn … I mean, for me it's, you can learn so much more living abroad from different people, and maybe you're more open too, I don't know.

Track 1.17

Well, I'm sure that many people have different definitions of what a hero is, and in most cases we see it in the context of war. Erm, if I had to think of the people who I consider heroic in my life, I would think of people who do things, erm, that we can learn from and things that give us inspiration for how we can

react in times of pressure and times of crisis. Erm, and in that sense my father is probably one of my big heroes. Erm, he wasn't famous, erm, although he travelled internationally and, erm, he achieved a fair high degree of success in his job. He was actually born, erm, not in poverty, but he was born in a mud brick house in the Kalahari, erm, in a family of farmers, sheep farmers, erm, living in the desert. And when I was a young man he told me – and he didn't tell me this as a lesson really, he was just telling me about something that mattered to him – he told me that his father had once explained to him that a person, a man or a woman, should want no more in life than the satisfaction of being able to rest with their head on a stone. And it sounds perhaps a bit clichéd but I do think, erm, my father actually believed in that, erm, and lived by that. Now what did he do? Well, he was a human rights activist. Erm, his job was mainly to help people who were confronted, erm, by social injustice in one form or another. So, in a way he – he did fight wars, but he didn't fight his wars with weapons, he fought his wars with words and public opinion, information and at times, erm, the legal system.

Track 1.18

P=Presenter, M=Mei

P: Hello, welcome to *Then and Now*. Today we're talking about an incredible country, with a fascinating culture and a long history going back over 3,000 years. China is hugely rich in art and culture, and its food and traditions are well-known around the world. But two aspects of China are perhaps lesser known. Firstly, this vast country has a long history of inventing things and secondly, it is now the third-biggest economy in the world, with ultra-modern cities and many booming industries. Today we've got China expert Mei Zhang here to tell us all about this flourishing 'Land of invention'. Hello Mei.

M: Hello.

P: Well, this programme is called *Then and Now*, so let's start with 'Then' – China's history, and this idea of a 'land of invention'. I knew that the Chinese invented paper, but I must admit I didn't know that they invented so many other important things. Before we talk about those, can you remind us about the story of paper?

M: Yes. It was in 105 AD that paper-making was perfected in China. The first paper was made of silk. Well, it was really the waste from silk-making, which they pulped up to make paper.

P: Of course, paper had an enormous impact on China, didn't it?

M: Yes, with paper and then printing, it meant people could get information much more easily.

P: Mm. So, what else did the Chinese invent?

M: Well, quite a few simple but important things. I think one of the simplest inventions was the wheelbarrow, invented around 220 AD, which meant that enormous loads could be carried by just one person – as well as other things that we take for granted today like silk, porcelain, the kite and even the umbrella!

P: And we have the Chinese to thank for fireworks, don't we?

M: Yes, that's right! In the 8th century, the Chinese discovered gunpowder. And by the 10th century, it was being used to make fireworks, the gun, the rocket and the bomb – so, it eventually had a huge influence on the whole world of course. Another major invention was a machine

for making cast iron, which they first developed in the 6th century BC.

P: Wow! That really is a long time ago! That must have made a big difference to people's lives too.

M: That's right. A lot of iron was used for agricultural tools, so production was increased hugely, which brings me quite nicely to the present really – to the 'Now' – to present-day China.

P: Mm. Is agricultural production big in China now?

M: Well, yes, there's a lot of agriculture – about 15 percent of the economy is based on agriculture. You know, things like rice, tea, cotton and fish. But, it's certainly not just countryside and agriculture. There are some massive cities in China, like Shanghai, whose population is around 20 million. And, as I said, China is now the third-biggest economy globally. Industry is huge and expanding all the time. Production of iron, for example, is growing at a rate of about 22 percent a year at the moment.

P: That's certainly a booming industry. So, what other industries are important now?

M: Well, so many of the things we buy are made in China, aren't they? Industrial production accounts for over half of China's economic wealth, including such consumer items as toys, clothes, shoes, cars and electronic goods, as well as the heavier industrial products like iron.

Track 1.20

C=Carla, J=James

C: So James what do you think, what's the most important invention?

J: Well, perhaps gunpowder.

C: Why do you think that?

J: Because it's … even though it's had quite a negative influence on world history it has had a significant in … influence on world history. It changed, um, the power in … in global communities …

C: But it only changed, erm, in some countries. I don't think you can really say that that has had the biggest effect in every single nation or every single country. And also, I mean if you take into account what a negative influence it's had too, I don't think it is the most important, because the most important is more influential and … and therefore positive.

J: Right OK, so we could argue that importance … or that we want to look at importance from a positive perspective, yeah.

C: I think so, yeah.

J: So what would you say?

C: Well I would actually say paper. I think paper really changed, ah, changed the world. Changed how the fact that we, ah … you can document history, can communicate, that was really the first way of … of communicating something, ah, in a concrete way rather than just word of mouth.

J: Communication, yes … and communication which you can hold on to rather than … yes, as you say, rather than just anecdotal.

C: And we … and we would never have had computers if we hadn't had paper I think. And it's a knock on effect.

J: Although, ironically we possibly don't need paper now that we have computers.

C: I still write letters.

J: Yes we're sat here with paper in front of us, both of us, yeah.

C: Exactly, I don't think …

J: You write letters?

C: Of course. Do you not?
J: I don't, no, I only write emails now.
C: I send birthday cards and …
J: Birthday cards yeah, yeah you're right.
C: What about the computer, then? Was that really as fundamental as the others?
J: It's changed our lives, hasn't it … our generation?
C: Unfortunately, yes.
J: Erm, for work it's something that we use all day every day.
C: Mm … But then again, so is the light bulb.
J: Yes the light bulb is something, the light bulb … and what's the other one and the wheel, and paper to an extent, you don't even notice them any more, whereas a computer, a telephone you would … you would notice.
C: Yeah, because they were all invented before we came along.
J: Yeah, they've become normalised.
C: Exactly.
J: So, what would you say, what would you say is the most important, pa … would you stick with paper, or the computer?
C: I … No, I think paper.
J: Yes I like the communication idea. It has, it has, erm, changed the way that communication happens throughout the world yeah OK, paper it is.

Track 1.22

There's a saying that your school days are the best days of your life. Well, I definitely wouldn't agree with that. My life since leaving school has been much more interesting and rewarding and I definitely wouldn't want to live my school days again. But that said, my memories of school were pretty good, and I've still got really good friends that I went to school with, you know, 30 years ago. When … when I was at school, there was some idea that if you studied hard and you passed your exams and maybe went to university and got a degree that somehow you were, you know, guaranteed to get a good job and a good salary. But with the benefit of hindsight I've realised that while that's true to an extent, success in life is really about what you can do, not what you know. And I think that in schools these days with … with teaching these days across all subjects, they have a much greater emphasis on vocational skills where school children learn to think and they learn to apply their knowledge, which I think can only be a good thing. When I was at school the most important subjects were English and maths, and I don't really think that's changed. Of course it's essential to have, you know, good language and communication skills, and a good grasp of, you know, at least basic mathematics, whatever you end up doing in life. But, erm, in addition to English and maths, I think it's become more and more important to learn a foreign language. I think it really opens up opportunities for work and travel, and I really regret not studying harder in French class at school. I left school without any foreign language qualifications which, erm, which is a real shame. But you know I shouldn't complain, I ended up with a career in marketing which is stable and yes, you know, I find it interesting and enjoyable, and you know I'm … I'm quite good at it. But looking back, I wish I'd followed my heart a bit more and not just my head. When I was at school, I was really passionate about drama and the arts, but I never studied it or pursued it. My parents always encouraged me to be, you know, sensible and study maths and sciences, which I did, and you know I … I was quite good at those subjects … but now, now I'm, you know, I'm a bit older and wiser, one of

the biggest lessons I've learned in life is that you can … if you can find your passion in life, you should follow it whether it's art or science or sport or economics, whatever, it will inspire you and it will energise you and you're more likely to be happier and fulfilled in life, and you're more likely to be good at it too.

Track 1.23

1 Recently, I've realised that investigating and writing about important issues is what I really want to do, so I'm now considering a change of career. I'd like to get a job with a newspaper or perhaps a specialist magazine.
2 You could call my job a labour of love, I suppose. I don't get paid much and it's very hard work, but I really love working with children and I really wouldn't want to do anything else.
3 There's a pretty strict career path for my field of work. After the basic five-year training, you have to work in various different hospital departments to build up experience. That's what I'm doing now, but eventually I'd like to specialise in heart operations.
4 I used to work in an office but it was really boring, so I left and took a year out to retrain. The training I did was hard but I like the fact that this job is physically challenging and that we're providing a really vital emergency service for people.
5 What I really like about my job is being able to help people. I mean, I get a great deal of job satisfaction from knowing that I've helped individuals and families with some pretty serious problems – like having nowhere to live.

Track 1.24
Dialogue 1
M=Mark, J=Julia

M: Hi Julia. What's the matter? You look a bit upset.
J: Oh I don't know. I'm so fed up with work at the moment. It's so stressful here … I'm supposed to do a nine-to-five day, but I'm working longer and longer hours. I'm not being paid to do all this extra admin. Basically, I'm totally overworked and underpaid – and I'm on the verge of collapsing with sheer exhaustion!
M: I know. It's been awful for ages, hasn't it?
J: I'm thinking about leaving … Actually, I'm on the point of leaving really. You know, I'd like to have a complete break … really soon.
M: That's a good idea. That would be great. Have you got any plans?
J: I'm not sure yet but as I say, I think I'll leave … in the next month or so, even. I can use the time to think about what to do next … perhaps I'll do some voluntary work or something. One idea is to do some voluntary work abroad. I've seen an ad recently and I'm going to get some more information about it …
M: You could research some stuff on the Internet …
J: Yes. That's a good idea! I think I'll go to the library now and do it there. It's my lunch break and I've got at least half an hour.
M: Good idea! Let me know how you get on …

Track 1.25
Dialogue 2
J=Jane, A=Andreas

J: How are you, Andreas? What have you been doing?
A: Oh I'm fine. I've been making plans! I'm really excited.
J: Oh? Really? What's going on?
A: I've decided I'm going to leave work and

go back to college. I'm planning to retrain and do something completely different.
J: Retrain? Really? What are you going to do?
A: Well, I've always wanted to be a vet … And life's too short … you know, I want to get on and do it now! I know it's going to be tough. You know, it's sure to be really hard work, but I've decided I'm just going to do it.
J: Wow, that's great. When are you going to start?
A: Well, it depends on being accepted on the course this year. I have to take an exam first. I'm doing that in about three weeks' time … and then, if it all goes to plan, if I pass … , I'll probably start the course this coming September.

Track 1.26
Dialogue 3
H=Helen, C=Cassia

H: Hi, Cassia. Do you fancy coming out for a meal tonight?
C: Well, I'd love to, but I can't I'm afraid. I'm having an interview tomorrow, so I'm about to have dinner and then have an early night.
H: An interview? What for? I thought you liked working for yourself from home.
C: Well, it's been OK, and I suppose I like the flexible hours and not having to commute and stuff, but to be honest, I'm feeling a bit isolated.
H: Yes, I know what you mean.
C: I really miss having colleagues, you know – not going to a sociable workplace every day. So I've applied for this job – it's to work for a small firm of architects. It's a small open-plan office and they seem really friendly on the phone. I'm meeting them at 10 o'clock tomorrow morning and then having the interview in the afternoon.
H: Oh, well. Good luck. I hope you get it.

Track 1.27
Dialogue 4
T=Tom, J=John

T: I think I'm going to try and look for another job.
J: Why? Don't you like where you are?
T: Yes, it's OK. But I want to be promoted and take on more responsibility. I really want a more senior position now and there are lots of other people who I work with who are certain to get those jobs before me.
J: Oh, you don't know that.
T: Well, I do. I think they'll offer Ania the job of departmental manager. She's really good and she's been there ages.
J: OK … but what about assistant manager?
T: No, Dominic's going to be assistant manager. He's a workaholic and a bit of a rising star, isn't he? He's bound to get the job. It's obvious. He's being fast-tracked for it … you can tell … I heard him talking to Miguel about it.
J: That's just because he wants the job … you don't know if he'll get it.

Track 1.29

I'm standing in the extraordinary Rock Gardens of Chandigarh in India. And I've spent the morning talking to Nek Chand, India's most visionary artist and creator of these gardens. He is a small, elderly man with a wrinkled face and silvery hair, and is extremely modest about his work. I've been trying to find out what has driven him to create these gardens, but he told me, simply, one day I started, and then I continued. His modest manner, however, hides an incredible story.

Audioscripts

Nek Chand was the son of a poor farmer and in 1958 he started work as a government road inspector. At that time, his city, Chandigarh was being designed and built by a famous Swiss architect. Chand was fascinated by the process of design and construction using concrete, and decided to build his own 'kingdom'. He started to collect rocks and other bits of 'rubbish' from the building sites. Secretly, he took these things to a forest area outside the city and began to build his garden. It had to be done in secret because he was building on land which belonged to the government. At first, he spent time making walls and paths and buildings. And then he moved on to the second phase, creating over 5,000 sculptures. These sculptures provide an incredible array of different figures: people, animals, birds and many other strange and wonderful creatures. Each one is different and they are all made of material that had been thrown away. Chand recycles anything he can find – old bicycles, bricks, lumps of concrete, broken plates, old sinks, electric plugs, pebbles … the list goes on.

Many people find that they waste a lot of time, but it's amazing what you can do when you really want to. For 18 years, Chand worked on his secret garden. He made time to do a bit more every day after work and every weekend. In fact, whenever he had time to spare he worked on this huge project that nobody else knew about. Then after 18 years, the garden was discovered by accident. At first, Chand was afraid that it would be destroyed as he had built it illegally on government-owned land. But quickly, people became interested in it and the government realised that the garden could become a tourist attraction. They paid Chand a small salary to work full-time on the project and one year later the Rock Garden was officially opened. Now it is one of India's most popular tourist attractions with 5,000 visitors every day. His huge achievement doesn't seem to have changed Chand at all, however. He told me, 'I am just doing my work. Everyone has work they do. This is mine.' He says his life is utterly regular. 'I eat. I sleep. I work.' Tomorrow morning, he will be doing the same as he's doing today. And the day after, he will be doing the same. He says it makes him happy, just doing it. Which is a good thing, because soon, he will have spent half a century just doing it.

Track 1.30
M=Man, W=Woman

M: Well, what's interesting about the whole work-life balance thing is that most of us only spend more or less a third of our day in work. So, actually, there's plenty of time for other things … and if you're organised, you can have a very good work-life balance. I mean, I'm not the best organiser in the world, but I think I can organise my time pretty well … and divide my time between work and other things.

W: Mmm … yes, I know what you mean, but although in theory, people spend about a third of their day at work … eight hours or something… in reality, it's often much longer. Your time gets swallowed up by having to work longer hours. The fact is, I have a really busy work schedule. I really do. You know, there are pressures of deadlines and things, and I end up coming to work earlier and staying later … so the work-life balance gets a bit lost.

M: Yes, true. Believe me, I know, it's not easy, but I do think it's possible to improve it.

It's something that people need to work at, in a sense. You know, it might not just happen, if you don't work at it – you need to be quite disciplined, in a way. My non-work life is really important to me, so I make sure that I prioritise it. Without a doubt, I'd say that I 'work to live' and not the other way round. I want to be able to have spare time, you know, leisure time, and not be too tired to do anything with it!

W: Yeah. What do you like doing in your spare time?

M: Well, I think it's important to make time for the fundamental things in life: family and friends, and relaxing on your own too, sort of recharging your batteries.

W: Yes, I agree. Family and friends are the most important, for sure. What do you do then, you know, to recharge your batteries?

M: Well, I go to the gym a lot. I find it a really good way of relaxing, and keeping fit, of course. If I don't have time to fit in at least three trips to the gym every week, I begin to feel a bit anxious, I must say.

Track 1.32
M=Marc

M: I started learning English when I was about 15 and my main goal was to have a chance to study in the UK. I wanted to do a course in London and I had to get to a good level of English so I studied really hard to get the right grades. Then when I first arrived in the UK, and I was around a lot of native speakers, I became quite self-conscious of my accent. So, although I had a good level of English in general, my aim became to sound like a native speaker. I think that I really wanted to fit in and sound like one of them … I didn't want to sound different. However, I found it very difficult to change my accent, and more importantly, maybe, I found that it didn't really matter. Nobody seemed to have a problem understanding me. And anyway, at the school there were lots of native speakers, but there were also lots of non-native speakers from lots of different countries. It was a multi-cultural community and people had different accents and sounding like a native speaker didn't matter. We tried to communicate with each other and we could all understand each other – I'm happy with my English and my accent … it isn't a problem.

Track 1.33
Dialogue 1
I=Interviewer, S=Susanna

I: It's Susanna, isn't it?

S: Erm … yes …

I: Hello Susanna. Pleased to meet you. My name's Michael Harrison. Come and sit down.

S: Thank you.

I: So, thank you for applying for the job and coming to the interview today. First, I'd like to ask you about your experience. In your letter, you say you've worked in an office before. Tell me about that.

S: Oh well, it was ages ago actually.

I: OK, well, what did you do there?

S: Nothing much really … I was just an assistant. You know, answering the phone and stuff …

Track 1.34
Dialogue 2
I=Interviewer, J=Joana

I: Ah, here you are …

J: Oh dear. I'm so sorry …

I: Let's see … You're Joana, aren't you? Joana Mendes?

J: Yes, that's right.

I: Well, come in Joana. I'm Peter Manning, head of the economics department and I'll be interviewing you today. Very nice to see you. Thank you for coming.

J: I'm really very sorry. I thought it would be a much quicker journey. The traffic was terrible and then I couldn't find the building.

I: OK. Can I start by asking you about your reasons for applying for the course? What do you think you'd get from studying economics in this particular university, Joana?

Track 1.35
Dialogue 3
I=Interviewer, K=Karema

I: Well, thank you very much for talking to me today, Karema. We're coming to the end of the interview now. Is there anything that you'd like to ask me?

K: Yes, I do have a question, if that's OK.

I: Of course. Fire away.

K: Well, I was wondering about promotion prospects. Obviously I'm keen on staying in the journalism business and I'd like to know what kind of opportunities there might be.

I: That's a good question. We are very interested in the professional development of our staff and offer many opportunities for further training and promotion within the company. The right person can be promoted to a position such as senior editor and we are always looking for people to manage completely new magazines. Anything else?

K: Could you tell me when you're going to make your decision?

I: I've got some other candidates who I'll be interviewing this afternoon, but we'll let you know by tomorrow afternoon.

K: Thank you very much.

Track 1.37

I guess I am what you call an adrenaline junkie … a bit of a risk taker. I love to challenge myself but more in the outside world away from work. Erm, I like to try and give myself things that I wouldn't normally do that might be a bit scary at the start, erm, to try and see whether I can do them or not. This has included jumping out of an aeroplane, erm, doing rap jumping in Aus … in New Zealand, which is like running down the front of a building face first, kind of like abseiling but in reverse. Erm, swimming with sharks, all of those kind of things. I think it's just the thrill of doing something that you're so scared of in the beginning, to accomplish it and do it is quite an achievement. And in that sense, erm, I definitely think it's good to take risks. Erm, I try and do some things at weekends as well, erm, like sea kayaking, abseiling, just to give myself a bit of excitement, and to be in an environment that isn't as controlled as, ah, working life, which has so many rules and regulations it gets a bit boring.

Track 1.38
M=Man, W=Woman

M: I've decided to leave my job soon … maybe, even, this coming summer. I'm fed up of working for a big company and I think I'd like to be my own boss.

W: Really?

M: Yes, I'm thinking about starting my own business.

W: That's brave, I mean, it's a bit of risk, don't you think? What would happen, for example, if things got difficult? You would have nobody to fall back on.

M: Well, I suppose it's brave, but actually it feels like totally the right thing to do. To be honest, I really like working on my own, well, in fact, I like being on my own, generally. You know, I'm somebody who enjoys my own company, in a way.

W: Do you? I'm not like that. I like being with other people. I get really lonely, I mean, if I had to be alone for a long period of time, I would get really miserable. I need people to talk to, I think. And if I had to work on my own, I'd hate it! It would be so boring.

M: I don't mind. I like it. I find that I can concentrate on my goals more easily, and I'm in control of everything. Also, with my own business, if things go well, I think I'll feel really good about it. You know, it'll be my own achievement and nobody else's.

W: True, but it's still a big risk, leaving a secure job and the salary that goes with it. Are you really prepared for that?

M: Yes, I think I am. I've got the experience and the motivation, and I really want to go for it.

W: Well, I'm impressed! Your confidence is inspiring me! Maybe I should be braver with things and take a few more risks. I've always thought that if I were a different person, the characteristic I'd like to have would be to be more of a risk-taker – to have more confidence in my own abilities and just go for things more.

M: Well, you could. Just think about what you really want to do, and really get yourself well-prepared. You know, don't rush into things, but get prepared and do your research – and I'm sure you can do anything you want, if you want it enough.

Track 1.39

M=Man, W=Woman

W: Hey, Daniel, I'm dying to hear about your hang-gliding. How did it go?

M: Oh yeah, it was fantastic, really amazing actually.

W: Oh really? I think it looks really scary … !

M: Well, the place I went was very organised and the instructors were really good, and I just felt very safe. I got there quite early. You could arrive anytime after 8.00 in the morning – and I got there soon after that, you know, I wanted to do as much hang-gliding as I could.

W: Did you have to do a lot of training before you could go up? Or were you allowed to just start without doing any training?

M: Well, I couldn't go straight up without any training at all. But there wasn't much – just information really. The amount of training you have depends on what kind of hang-gliding you're doing. I mean, I didn't go up alone, you know, I went up with an instructor – so he was doing all the flying and the technical stuff, like steering, and knowing how and where to land. Basically, you can't go up alone on your first time. I'm not sure how many times it is, I think you can go alone after doing a few flights with an instructor and some longer training.

W: Oh, I see.

M: Anyway, I wasn't allowed to go up before having some brief general instructions. But that's all it was really – no training as such. Then I got into the harness, they attached me to the hang-glider. I was literally hanging in a lying-down position from the frame of the glider. It felt quite strange! Then a small plane pulled the glider – and me – to the taking off position, and then up into the sky. It's really simple.

W: But really scary!

M: Well, strangely, it didn't feel too scary at that point – just exhilarating. We climbed higher and higher, until the gauge said we were at 2,000 feet – that's about 600 metres! Then the plane let us loose and went back towards the field below. Once the plane had gone, everything was silent – you just hear the sound of wind rushing around your ears. It was amazing!

W: Did you look down? I mean, what could you see on the ground?

M: It looks incredible from up there – you can see beautiful fields and mountains, and lots of tiny specks which are houses and things! Anyway, at one point, my instructor explained how to steer. You just move your weight to one side in order to change direction.

W: Did you do it?

M: Yes, but, well yes I did, but it didn't just gently change direction. The hang-glider suddenly went veering over to the left.

W: Oh, maybe you should've moved a bit more gently.

M: Yes. I think so, I mean, I did what he said. I leaned to the left.

W: Mmm, maybe you shouldn't have leaned so far then.

M: Yes, anyway, it was fine. I just scared myself a bit! I was quite happy to give the controls back to the instructor!

W: Yes!

M: After that we circled around the valley for about 15 or 20 minutes. It was so beautiful and calm up there.

W: What about the landing?

M: Well, that was another bit that I was a bit scared about. As we got closer to the ground, I got a bit less calm! Suddenly the ground seemed to be rushing up towards me really quickly! But the instructor was really good and he landed the glider really smoothly. And once the glider has stopped, you just stand up and take off the harness.

W: Wow, great.

M: Yeah, it was really good. I loved it. I did two more flights that day. I can see how sports like this are addictive. I'd definitely like to do it again. Next time, I think I'd like to do some training and go up alone. You should come with me next time …

W: Erm, well, sounds a bit too scary for me.

M: It's not really. If I were you, I'd just go for it. It's not scary once you're up there – being a spectator is probably worse!

W: Could you do a really low flight? I mean, are you allowed to go up just a little way above the ground – not go up so high?

M: Erm no! I don't think so. I think that would be much more dangerous. I mean, think of all the things in your way – buildings, trees …

W: I suppose so, yes. I hadn't thought of that.

Track 1.41

P=Paul, L=Lidia

P: So, did you go and see it?

L: See what?

P: *Million Dollar Baby* … you remember, you said you were going to get the DVD …

L: Oh, yes, *Million Dollar Baby* … you were right … it was quite good.

P: Quite good!? Come on, it was really good. I think it's a brilliant film.

L: Do you? I do like Clint Eastwood but I suppose I've never really been that into films about boxing.

P: OK, but it's not really about boxing is it?

L: Isn't it? But one of the main characters runs a boxing gym, and the other wants to be a boxing champion.

P: That's all true, but there's a lot more to it than that. There are so many different themes running through the film. I mean, I thought the whole theme of risk was so interesting.

L: Risk?

P: Well, you know at the beginning of the film, one of Clint Eastwood's most promising boxers leaves him just as he has a chance to make the big time.

L: Oh yes, that's right. Doesn't he go off with another promoter or something?

P: Yeah, after years of training in the gym with the Clint Eastwood character. And actually, it's because Clint won't take a risk with him.

L: He won't put him up for a big championship fight – and the other promoter will.

P: Exactly. The Clint character plays it safe. He's just too cautious. And then this young woman turns up and she turns out to be a really good boxer – and then he faces another risk.

L: You mean, he'll train her up and then she'll leave him.

P: Exactly – and that nearly does happen, doesn't it?

L: Oh yes, that's right, but she does stay with him in the end thank goodness!

P: Then there's a kind of emotional risk he takes too. You remember how he keeps writing to his daughter and never getting any replies? He's upset about something, which we never really find out about.

L: Mmm. I couldn't work out what all that was about.

P: No, it's not really clear. Anyway, I think there's a growing emotional connection between him and the woman boxer, and because of whatever's happened with his daughter it feels like there's a big emotional risk too.

L: I see what you mean. I hadn't really looked at it like that before, but now you say it. Actually, it reminds me of another Clint Eastwood film, *Gran Torino*. Have you seen that?

P: Oh no, I haven't. Why, is that about risk too?

L: Well, it's very different, but yes, I think there's quite a lot about risk. Basically, it's about an old guy called Walt – played by Clint Eastwood – who is an old war veteran. He's quite bad-tempered and bitter about the world. His wife has just died, he's fallen out with his family and doesn't get on with his neighbours or anything. The only thing he likes is his car – a beautiful *Gran Torino* – which he mostly keeps in his garage. You know, he likes his car, but he doesn't like, or trust, people.

P: So, where's the risk?

L: Well, he gets to know his neighbour – a teenager originally from South-east Asia. He gets to know him by chance, really, when the boy tries to steal his beloved car. The risk then comes – the emotional risk, as you say – when Walt decides to become friends with him and help him in various ways.

P: Help him?

L: Yes, he gradually takes the boy under his wing in a way. He teaches him a few things about life and helps him get a job. It's a risk, partly because of the violent gangs around, but I think mostly it's a risk because the old man has to confront his own prejudice and racist ideas and get close emotionally to someone who previously, he had felt angry towards.

P: Mmm. It sounds interesting.

L: It's a really, really good film. I'd definitely recommend it. In fact, I think it's the film I've enjoyed most this year. I think Clint Eastwood is an amazing actor – and he's also an incredible director. He directed and acted in both *Million Dollar Baby* and *Gran Torino*, didn't he? They're such great films.

P: Yes, well, I definitely want to see *Gran Torino*. It sounds like such an interesting film. I think I'll try and get the DVD of it tomorrow.

Track 1.43
H=Heather, E=Eben

H: OK, so which movie do you wanna see?

E: Well, looks good, you ... you've taken two Clint Eastwood ones, I love Clint Eastwood as a director. He's brilliant.

H: I do too ... he's so good.

E: Yeah. Did you see *Bird* by the way?

H: No I haven't seen that one.

E: Really, really good about Charlie Parker jazz musician.

H: OK.

E: Incredible music, incredible acting, erm ...

H: Really? I'll have to try that one out some time.

E: So which one do you ... do you wanna go for?

H: Mmm. I don't know, I mean I think I like the look of *Mystic River*, just because it's a bit mysterious and ...

E: Yeah.

H: You know, I really like Tim Robbins.

E: Yeah so do I. Sean Penn as well, and ...

H: Mm, they're both so ... such good actors.

E: Yeah, and Madison ... *The Bridges of Madison County*.

H: Yeah.

E: Judging by the cover, it looks like a romance.

H: Yeah, I think so.

E: And it's got Clint Eastwood in it as an actor.

H: Yeah, I mean Meryl Streep's really good. She ... she is really, really ... and so is ... obviously so is Clint Eastwood.

E: But, I have a hard time seeing him as a romantic lead.

H: Yeah ...

E: I wonder what he plays?

H: I have to agree with you there.

E: Also, *Madison County*, OK *Madison County*, that's not necessarily Wisconsin but it makes me think of Wisconsin.

H: Mm.

E: I don't know, to- ... today that sounds a bit tame to me, rated 12 years old, *Mystic River*, 15. Two Academy awards.

H: Yeah.

E: Sean Penn, Tim Robbins.

H: Oh, and Kevin Bacon's in it too.

E: Oh yes.

H: Oh he's rea- ... oh, and Laurence Fishburne, OK, definitely *Mystic River*.

E: I think that's the one. I think that one sounds really good.

H: Yeah, I agree.

E: I wonder what it's about?

H: Mm ...

E: Have you seen any ... you haven't seen any reviews or trailers?

H: I heard something about, that it's based on a book and it's about three brothers.

E: OK.

H: So ... but I don't know much else about it.

E: OK. But you, like you say, you know, great actors.

H: Mm.

E: Good title.

H: Yeah.

E: Sounds like it could be intense.

H: Yeah definitely not boring, the other one has potential to be boring.

E: Yeah it does, I think maybe not today, the other one looks kind of tame. Another day.

H: Alright then, well let's get *Mystic River* then.

E: OK, *Mystic River* it is.

H: Yeah? Alright.

E: Good.

Track 1.45
M=Man, W=Woman

M: Thank you very much for coming to the meeting today. My name is Liam Davidson and I am here to represent the views of the local government on the proposal to build a nuclear power station on the edge of our town. So, I'd like to introduce the other people here today. We have Mr Daniel Hawke, representing the local businesses, Ms Sarah Holmes, representing a local group of environmental campaigners and Mrs Laura Franks, representing local people living in the area. Welcome to everybody. I will outline some of the issues, then everybody will get a chance to put their ideas and concerns forward. We will then have time for further debate and questions. OK, so, first of all, I'd like to say that I'm very pleased that this area has been chosen as a possible site for the development of a new nuclear power station. It is a fantastic opportunity not only to produce cheaper, more efficient energy, but also for us to regenerate the area, by creating a lot of job opportunities for local people.

W: Excuse me, if I could make a point here. My name is Laura Franks and I'm representing the local people, as you said, and yes, we need jobs in the area, but the last thing we need is a nuclear power station in order to create jobs ... I mean ...

M: Sorry, I'd just like to interrupt you for a minute. As I said, everyone will get a chance to put their point of view ...

W: OK, but if you could let me finish my point.

M: Erm ... everyone will get a chance ...

W: I'm sorry but I haven't quite finished ... because already what you're saying is wrong. What I mean is, you're introducing this by saying local people want this project. We don't! You are here representing the local government. In other words, you are obviously FOR the whole project and you will say anything you can think of to make it sound like everyone is with you on this. I want to say, right from the outset, that's wrong. Most people are against the idea. I mean, the health implications are huge. Local people are rightly concerned about the health of our children. And what about the effect on the environment and local wildlife?

Track 2.4
W=Woman, M=Man

W: Oh ... look at these photos of Brad Pitt ... He used to look so different – I'd forgotten that he used to have a beard!

M: A beard? Did he?

W: Yeah, look. In this photo, he's got a really long, scruffy beard ... and long, scruffy hair too. I think he looks awful! What was he thinking of? Do you think it was for a film or something?

M: No, I don't think it was. I mean, I don't remember him looking like that in any films.

W: No ... nor do I ... Hmm. I mean, he's so good-looking in this picture. I think he looks great when he's clean-shaven and with short hair ... He looks great. I really can't understand why he grew that beard. I mean, I don't mind the long hair so much ... although I do think he looks better with short hair ...

Track 2.5
E=Eben, I=Interviewer

E: Well, I'm sure you've all heard that Switzerland is ... is as beautiful as a postcard or one of those famous Swiss chocolate boxes with all the postcard pictures on it. Well, I actually grew up in Geneva, Switzerland. I lived there for all of my teen years starting at the age of 11. And like most teenagers, I wasn't terribly happy. The other reputation, of course, that Switzerland does have is, you know, that it's, it ... it's like clockwork. It's the perfect place, natural beauty and lots of things to do. And as an adult, I suppose I sometimes regret that I didn't appreciate it when I was a teenager, when I was younger. I had all the opportunity to live there. I could've stayed there and finished my university there, erm, but I chose not to. I'd ... I was more interested in going to North America. But as a parent, and going there, and that's what this picture's about. This picture was actually only taken a few years ago, of my family, standing, not at one of my favourite spots, but certainly a spot that repre- ... represents Geneva to me. It's the lake, it's the boats in the background, and the Salève, that's the mountain. Well, in many ways I feel that if I'd settled there, you know, as an adult, as a parent, that would've been the ideal place, and ... to raise my children. All the things that I took for granted, that I couldn't quite appreciate as a young person, I appreciate as a parent, and would've wanted, in a way, to give my kids the opportunity to ... to experience life there. I suppose what it comes down to is, you know, although I'm not Swiss, having lived there for so many years, there is so much that I'm attached to, including things, that you know, are part of the community, the people. And those are the things that I would've wanted to share with my kids and my wife, I guess.

Track 2.6
J=Jeanette, I=Interviewer

I: Well Jeanette, these photographs on your wall are really interesting. Can you tell me where they're from?

J: Ah, they're from, ah, Kyoto actually. I used to live, erm, very close to Kyoto and I'd often go at the weekends and visit the temples and the shrines and the gardens, and they were absolutely exquisite. They were so beautiful, I loved them so much. In fact I was going to create, ah, a Japanese garden when I came back to the UK, ah, but unfortunately, erm, we didn't and I, I ... When I was there I would ... would, ah, often take photographs, and to remind me of different features and, erm, I often, erm, bought ... looked for and bought, erm, bamboo ornaments and, erm, things that I would put in the garden. And in fact I ... I always knew that my parents were going to, erm, design and create a Japanese garden, and they have, so I ... I also bought those things for them. Erm, yes, erm, I would have liked to, ah, create a pool with carp in and have, erm, bamboo and azalea and Japanese pines and, erm, but unfortunately, it never really happened because when we came back, erm, we had the children very quickly and somehow the garden just became filled with things for the children to play on, trampolines and play houses and so on, and there was never any room for a Japanese garden. I do have some, I did buy some bamboo and azaleas and so on but, erm, yeah unfortunately … well, maybe in the future some time.

I: Yeah maybe yeah, well the … the water is very calming as well isn't it, it's very serene looking.

J: Yeah. It's, it's beautiful, really relaxing.

Track 2.7

1 Some of my happiest memories are from when I used to go on holiday. We often went to the same place … I went with my parents, my grandparents and my brother. I can remember that place so clearly … it was such a lovely beach, and in my mind, it was sunny all the time. I don't know if it was, really! It makes me feel really nostalgic about my childhood … I can picture it so well. I tell you, in a way, it feels like last week … even though I was about six … I can still smell the sea and … oh, I would've liked to live there all the time …

2 Well, if we're talking about great memories … well some of my best memories are of playing football with our team. Just thinking about it … well, it brings back so many memories. We'd get together every Sunday and play down at the park. And we'd also play matches against other local teams. We had such a good time … I mean, we weren't very good … we didn't win much, but that wasn't really the point. We were all friends at university together … it was about five years ago, I suppose … Those were the days! I wish I hadn't lost touch with so many of them … We just had such a laugh together …

3 I found a photo the other day of when I was living in Italy and my friend Siena and I used to have breakfast at the weekends in this lovely little café on the main square … It was so nice. It reminds me of one of the best times of my life … I regret leaving that place in a way. I loved living in Italy. The people were so friendly and the town where I lived was so beautiful. It doesn't feel that long ago really, although I suppose it must be about, what … nine or ten years ago now … yes, about ten years ago.

Track 2.9

1 This year hasn't been great but I'm sure things will be better next year.

2 A: I saw this great film last night.
B: Oh yeah …

3 … but I don't really understand what you're saying. Do you mean that …

4 Kate … Kate … thank goodness you're home … I've been so worried …

5 Listen … I think we're lost … and we shouldn't be walking round here late at night … I'm not sure that it's safe, you know …

6 So, go on, why exactly did you agree to go out on a date with him?

7 Well, of course, he said that was why he was late home but you don't believe him, do you?

8 I can't believe it. We're flying off to Australia for a month on Monday to see my twin sister. I can't wait …

9 You're always late … why can't you be on time for once in your life?

10 Can you see that young guy … standing … looking into that car? What on earth do you think he's doing?

11 She said what?! I can't believe it. That's terrible …

Track 2.10

Well … where shall I start? Well … the basic story is that a girl, Catherine, is left a box by her mother, who died when she was a baby. Catherine discovers the box when she's 31, the same age as when her mother died. Inside the box are 11 objects, like a red hat, a map of part of England and so on … all of them meaningless at first, but when Catherine begins to examine each object, she finds new truths not only about her mother but also about herself. Through these objects Catherine finds that her mother was not the sweet and innocent woman that everyone likes to remember her as.

So, what did I think of it? Well … overall … I really enjoyed it – it's a really interesting idea for a story – and I thought it was very well-written. Not only that but there are lots of aspects of Catherine's life that I can totally relate to – different events, feelings and thoughts which so accurately mirror my own life that I found myself constantly underlining parts of the text.

However, sometimes I found it a bit slow. I wanted to know about the objects and it seemed to take ages to work out what they were all about. Still … apart from that one small thing … it was very easy to read and I'd certainly recommend it.

Track 2.11

M=Man, W=Woman

M: Hi … what are you reading?

W: Oh, it's *1984* by George Orwell. It's really good. Have you read it?

M: No I haven't. I've heard of it … but I haven't read it. I would like to read more books in English though … My teacher is always saying that it's a really good way of improving your English.

W: Yes, that's true… Obviously, you can improve your reading skills by reading a lot, but you can also learn a lot of vocabulary … and improve your writing.

M: The problem for me is that I find extended reading in English very difficult – there's always so much I don't understand that I get frustrated and then give up.

W: Yes, me too … I think a lot of students feel like that … It's really frustrating when you want to look everything up in a dictionary all the time! But there are some techniques you can use … some ways of improving your reading so you won't find it so difficult …

M: Mmm? Like what?

W: I used to try to read and concentrate on every single word … but it makes it so slow and boring. Now, I've really increased the speed of my reading by reading in chunks.

M: Reading in chunks?

W: Yes … try to look at about four or five words at once before you move your eyes to the next group of words. You'll find it much easier to understand because you're looking at words more in context. If you only look at one word at a time, it often doesn't really have any meaning on its own.

M: Oh, I see what you mean. Yes, that makes sense.

W: I think the other thing you can do is time yourself. You, know, you can test yourself by seeing how fast you can read something … a newspaper article, let's say. Give yourself five minutes or something to see how much you can understand.

M: Yes, I suppose you get more aware of your level then … and you can focus on how much you do understand instead of all the words you don't understand!

W: Yes, that's right.

Track 2.12

M=Man, W=Woman

M: OK, well, this is fun, it's quite exciting to think that someone might open this up in 100 years' time.

W: Yes, and see what kinds of things we had. I wonder if they would be able to work out what the things were …

M: Mmm … well, what things shall we put in? I mean, five things … that's not many. We have to try to decide on five really good things to try and show our world as it is now.

W: Yes. OK, well, I think we should include a globe so that they can see what the world looked like. I mean, whoever opens this thing up can see how the world was divided up. I mean, because in 100 or 1,000 years' time, the world might look very different.

M: OK, yes, good idea. And in my opinion, we should also include a sort of everyday thing. You know, like, maybe some typical clothes in order to show something about daily life.

W: Like a pair of jeans, or something?

M: Yes, jeans would be good, since most people nowadays own at least one pair of jeans, don't they?

W: Yes, true. OK, well, what else then?

Track 2.13

C=Carol, S=Sarah

C: Do you have any plans for today?

S: Erm, yeah I'm going to make a special meal for some friends tonight.

C: Oh that sounds good. What … what are you going to make?

S: Erm, it's my grandma's, ah, pancake recipe, it's quite unusual.

C: Oh. How is it different from normal pancakes?

S: Erm, well what you do is, first, you, erm, make a pancake mix, erm, you must make sure it's not too thick, the pancake mix … and then you fry lots of pancakes. When you've done that, you put one pancake in the pan … And then in the other pan, you cook, erm, onions and spinach and tomatoes and herbs and …

C: Oh, so, it's a savoury pancake?

S: Yeah.

C: OK.

S: Yeah, so it's savoury … And then you put a layer of, erm, the … the spinach mix on top of a pancake. You know, to make another flat layer … You should be careful not to put too much spinach mix in one layer.

C: Right. Is that because there are lots of layers?

S: Yes, you put another pancake on top flat, and then you put more spinach mix on top. Then you put another pancake on top, and you keep doing this, layering spinach mix and pancakes … and then on the top you put lots of cheese and a sort of white sauce.

C: Mmm. So, you mean you pour the sauce over the whole thing?

S: Yes, that's right.

C: And, erm, what's the white sauce made of?

S: Erm, I think it's just, ah, usually I use it from a jar, but I think it's just flour and eggs and butter and that sort of thing.

C: OK, OK.

S: And cheese sometimes.

C: So, it sounds like there are quite a lot of layers.

S: Yeah, it's a bit, it looks like lasagne but it's not.

C: Do you put it in the oven?

S: Yeah. Finally, you bake it in the oven, erm, for a little while and the top goes sort of crispy ... the important thing is not to overcook it at this point. And ...

C: OK.

S: ... you cut it into slices.

C: Interesting. And so did your grandma make this for you a lot when you were young?

S: Yeah she did.

C: OK. OK, so it's quite a traditional thing in your family?

S: Yeah ... I still cook it quite a lot ... I love it....

C: Yeah, it sounds really delicious ...

Track 2.15

P=Presenter, E=Expert

P: Today, on *It's a Buyer's World*, we're talking about buying things at the top end of the market ... Julia Taylor is with us, from *Everyone's Auction Magazine* and we'll be looking at some of the incredible prices people pay for celebrity items, pop and film memorabilia, as well as fine art. Hello, Julia.

E: Hello.

P: So, first, one story to hit the headlines recently was the record sale of the Giacometti sculpture ... Tell us about that.

E: Yes, well, a life-sized bronze sculpture, called *Walking Man I*, by the Swiss artist Giacometti was sold at auction for a record $104.3 million, making it the most expensive piece of art ever to sell at auction.

P: Wow, 104.3 million, that seems incredible. Who has that kind of money?

E: I know, it's amazing. We don't actually know who bought it, as the winning bid was made by an anonymous telephone buyer after just eight minutes of bidding!

P: It's not just fine art, though, is it? Some people spend huge amounts of money on quite ordinary things.

E: Yes. There was another record set recently, when an original comic book was bought for one and a half million dollars. It was issue number 1 of *Action Comics* which came out in June 1938, and it was the first time Superman had appeared in a comic, and you know, comic books like these are extremely popular at the moment.

P: Mm. If you're lucky and you happen to have something like that, you can make a lot of money.

E: Mm. That's right. One of the six storm trooper helmets used in the original *Star Wars* films was found by chance at a second-hand sale and bought for just $75. The owner then sold it at an auction and ended up getting around $25,000 for it!

P: Amazing! What about celebrities, too? They can make a lot of money, can't they? You know, selling their clothes or other items. Huge sums of money have been paid for all sorts of things.

E: Absolutely, yes. Some huge numbers which spring to mind are: something in the region of $1,200,000 was paid for one of Marilyn Monroe's dresses, and erm, oh, one of Michael Jackson's gloves, covered in jewels, was bought for $350,000 by 36-year-old Hong Kong businessman

Hoffman Ma. Apparently, it will now be displayed in a hotel in China.

P: Sometimes, things really do get a bit ridiculous, though, too. I mean, you hear about people paying huge prices for, well, crazy items,

E: Well, that's right. When it comes to being a superfan, people want everything and anything. Erm, for example, a clump of Elvis Presley's hair, which they say was cut from his head when he joined the Army in 1958, well, it was sold for $15,000!

P: Really? 15,000?

E: And apparently, this is amazing. When Justin Timberlake finished a breakfast interview at a New York radio station, the interviewer put the left-over toast on the Internet auction site, eBay. Lots of people bid for it, and in the end it was bought by a fan for $3,154!

P: That's just mad!

E: Yes, although I think the worst one I've ever heard of is a used tissue, yes, a used tissue, which the actress Scarlett Johansson used to blow her nose on was sold on eBay for $5,300!!

P: Wow, yes, I think that is the worst. That's really ridiculous and quite disgusting!! What on earth would you do with that?!

Track 2.16

M=Man, W=Woman

M: Hello, Electrical Solutions?

W: Hello my name's Ella Fernandez and I recently bought a TV from your website.

M: Mmm?

W: It was the Panasonic 32-inch widescreen, and it was delivered yesterday.

M: Oh, yes, I hope there are no problems?

W: Well, first of all, I'd just like to complain about how long it took to deliver ... I mean, you promised on the site that delivery would be within three days... but in the end, I waited two weeks ... and to be honest, I don't think that's acceptable.

M: Oh, I'm terribly sorry about that ... we did have some problems with the stock and so it took a little longer than usual ... I can only offer my apologies for that.

W: Well, it would've been better if you'd let me know beforehand about any possible delays.

M: Yes, I do apologise for that.

W: Well, anyway, I would've been OK with the delayed delivery if the TV had been in perfect condition when it arrived, but I'm afraid to say that it is far from perfect.

M: Oh?

W: Yes, the top left corner of the TV is slightly damaged and the on/off switch is loose.

M: Is the TV itself working? I mean, can you turn it on and is the picture clear?

W: Yes, it is. It's fine in that respect ... but given that this is a brand new TV and cost a lot of money, I'm not prepared to accept damaged goods, and I'd be grateful if you could send a replacement as soon as possible please.

M: Well, we'll send someone to pick up the faulty TV as soon as possible and then when we've got that back in the warehouse, I'll send out a replacement.

W: Well, OK, but when could you pick this TV up?

M: Erm, let me look, erm, next Thursday ... we could do it next Thursday ...

W: Next Thursday? That's over a week from now! Can't you do it any earlier than that? I mean, I've already waited nearly two weeks ... And how can I be sure that you'll come on Thursday? I don't want to be waiting around and then nobody turns up.

M: I can assure you that we'll definitely stick to the appointment ... and I'll send you an email to confirm it.

W: Oh, well. OK. If that's all you've got, yes, next Thursday, and yes, could you send me an email, please, confirming that?

M: Yes, of course. So, next Thursday between 8 and 6 ... someone will come and collect the faulty TV ... That's all booked for you. And then, as I say, we'll contact you to arrange a time to deliver the replacement TV ...

W: OK, fine. Well, thank you for your help.

M: And thank you. And once again, I can only apologise for the problems you've had.

W: OK. Thank you. Goodbye.

M: Bye ...

Track 2.18

1 I can't believe the trouble I've had over this jacket I bought on the Internet. It was unusual because I've ordered stuff from the same company before and never had one single problem. But this time, I ordered a waterproof rain jacket and when it came it was an extra-large, even though I'd ordered medium. When I sent it back, the same thing happened. I sent it back about three or four times. So, eventually I phoned the customer services department, but the man I spoke to was so rude I couldn't believe it. Throughout the whole conversation, he spoke to me in a sort of bored, monotonous voice and clearly wasn't interested in my problem at all. He didn't even apologise!

2 I'd forgotten to set the alarm clock that day, so I overslept and woke up three hours later than I was supposed to ... Then, I'd seriously underestimated the time it would take me to get there. On the way, it started pouring with rain and I got completely soaked to the skin. In the end, it took me nearly two hours which meant that I was really, really late. When I did finally arrive – wet through – I walked into the interview room and who was sitting there, waiting to interview me, but my ex-boss from my previous job! I felt so awful because I know for a fact that he hates me and I'd made such a fool of myself.

3 A couple of years ago, I decided to have a change of career. Having been a Spanish teacher for nearly 20 years, I decided to retrain as a translator and interpreter. It's a really difficult job and I found the training very hard work, but I'm really pleased with myself for having done it. I was brought up bilingual so the language itself wasn't difficult for me, but you have to learn completely different skills. I now work for a huge multinational holiday company specialising in organised trips around South America and I really love it! It's the best job I've ever had.

Track 2.19

B=Boss, E=Employee

B: So, Will ... generally, it seems that things are going fine. We've talked about your attitude to work, which is very good ... And, over the three years that you've worked here, you've shown a consistently professional approach to your work.

E: Thank you ... I must say that I've enjoyed it very much. My colleagues are very helpful and supportive ... and testing computer games is great fun. I must say, it's great doing something you love in a job.

B: So, well ... the next part of this appraisal is to think about the future. What do you see yourself doing next?

E: Well, as I say, I've really enjoyed the games testing work that I've been doing, but I feel that it's time I moved on now … I mean I think it's time I had a bit more responsibility, perhaps.

B: Yes, I think we need to think about that. You've shown some good leadership skills and I wonder how you would feel about becoming a team leader. You know, then you'd be supervising a team of games testers and making sure everything gets done properly. Or maybe you'd be interested in the marketing side of things?

E: Oh, well … Marketing is interesting, but I think I'd rather stay in the same department and become a team leader. Yes … I'd be very interested in that … though I'm not sure that I've got all the necessary skills to be honest. I mean, I'd like the responsibility, but erm … would there be any management training?

B: Yes, of course. We run some excellent in-house courses which I think would give you confidence. There's one coming up next week and then another in two months' time. And I think I'd rather you did the first course. You know, I'd rather we didn't waste any more time than we have to. What do you think?

E: Well, yes. I'd be very interested. It would be great to get some training underway as soon as possible. I mean, I'd rather not wait for two months, if that's OK with you. I'd like to be as prepared as I can.

B: OK. Great. In that case, I'd better get your name on the list for the one next week immediately. I hope it's not full up already. I don't think it will be but I'd better not promise anything before checking with my secretary … Erm …Perhaps I'll do that right now. Excuse me just one minute … Oh, hello Jeannie. I just wanted to check if you've still got places on the Management Skills course for next week … ah, you have … great … Could I put Will Scott's name down please? … Yes, S-C-O-double T …

Track 2.21

M=Martin, E=Evan

E: You know, Martin, I was reading this interesting article the other day, and it said that people had different personalities in different situations. So the way you behave in one given situation would be different than how you would behave in another situation. Do you think that's true?

M: Yeah I really do think it's true because, erm, I mean most of the time I'm quite a calm person but, erm, yesterday I had to make a complaint in a shop, I had to take something back.

E: Right.

M: And, erm, I actually became quite aggressive with the person because I wanted my money back and they wouldn't give it and I, suddenly, I just changed into this aggressive person and I think most of the time I'm … I'm pretty calm. What about you?

E: Yeah I think there's definitely some truth in that, erm, for example, generally at work I think that I'm fairly confident in that I don't have trouble speaking to people or leading discussion … or a presentation, or something like that, but if I don't know people or it's a social event then I find that I'm a lot, a lot less confident, erm, and more introverted, I … if I had to speak to a crowd of people at a party then I would say I'd be very nervous and would find it difficult to speak to people I didn't know.

M: Oh right. What are you like with the presen- … at giving a presentation

because I'm s- … quite calm when I have to give a presentation, is it the same for you or do you … ?

E: Yeah, I think it's because I know exactly what has to be done. Erm, whereas in a social situation, it's maybe, you have to improvise a little bit more and feel it out, whereas at work you have to get a task done, so you do what you have to do.

M: I can understand, if I have to give some kind of presentation I find you've got, you've got, ah, ah, something to follow, so you know what you're going to say.

E: Right.

M: So it's better.

E: Absolutely.

Track 2.22

P=Presenter, T=Tony

P: Today on *Sports Alive*, we are talking about success and achievement in sport. Who are the most successful sportspeople in the world and just how do they achieve their success? There is a huge sports psychology industry working with almost all athletes these days. But does it work? Is it all really necessary? We've got sports psychologist, Tony Greenwood here to help us answer these questions. Hello, Tony. Welcome to the programme.

T: Hello …

P: So, first of all, Tony, let's think about that question. Is sports psychology really necessary? I mean, if I pay for a sports psychologist, will he or she really help me win? Some people would say that you've either got the determination to succeed or you haven't. What do you think?

T: Well, I suppose that's sometimes true. There are examples of sports people who are extremely successful and have never needed any help with their mental determination. You know, for some people, winning is vital. Mohamed Ali was probably the most famous of all those people. He had huge self-belief … he totally believed that he was the best and absolutely unbeatable.

P: That's right. Nobody needed to remind him to focus on his goal!

T: No … and then there are other examples of sportspeople who seem to be really committed to their own success: tennis player Roger Federer, racing driver Michael Schumacher and basketball player Michael Jordan to name but a few. But these people are actually quite rare … most sportspeople do a lot of work on mental preparation and get a lot of help with staying focused on winning.

P: OK, so what do the sports psychologists do? How do you help people to succeed?

T: Well, my basic job is to prepare the mind … and, well, I can do this in different ways depending on who we're working with. One of the most important things I do is that I can help people change negative thoughts into positive ones. I did some work with a footballer recently. He missed an important goal. You know, he missed a goal in a big match and he was devastated … and he started thinking that he couldn't do it anymore. I told him he could do it by thinking about something different, not on missing the goal. After practising thinking about the way the ball was turning instead, his whole game improved dramatically.

P: The British runner Kelly Holmes is a good example of that too, isn't she?

T: Yes, that's right. For much of her career, she was constantly getting injured and

then worrying that it would happen again. I remember that she admitted feeling really out of control when she got injured all the time. But the fact is, athletes have to get over that and start to take control mentally. That's exactly what she did – and then of course won two gold medals at the Athens Olympics … and she was absolutely ecstatic … I mean it was obviously a fantastic achievement!

P: Yes, she was really brilliant!

T: There are other things we can do to help with mental preparation too. Things like routines to get the players focused and working as a team can really help.

P: Routines? What do you mean?

T: Well, the New Zealand All Blacks rugby team do their Haka war dance to focus themselves and to try and worry the other teams. Then there are people who have their own personal lucky routines. Footballer Andy Cole said he always wanted to be the last player on the pitch. It might seem a bit silly, but if it works …

Track 2.25

W=Woman, M=Man

W: Your little brother spends so much time on the computer …

M: What? No, he doesn't … no more than any of his friends … Anyway, he's 14 … he's not so little…

W: True … but you know, it's not good for children … I read an article recently … it was on about computer classes for two-year-olds!! It's unbelievable what some parents do.

M: Computer classes for two-year-olds? Seriously?

W: Yes, I am totally serious. Apparently, it's a growing trend … special colleges which offer computer classes for toddlers … aged two and three. I'm sorry, but I think that's ridiculous!

M: Well, hang on a minute, it might not be so bad.

W: I remember the woman in the article. I think she was the director of technology in a college. Well, she claimed that some of their students sat the national school exams aged seven. I mean, what's the point?!

M: OK, but that's not toddlers.

W: Oh, I know, but she explained that the success of those exams led them to start children earlier and earlier. She said that the parents are really keen on their children getting a head start and denied having any problems. In fact, she denied that there were any negative effects at all …

M: Well, she would say that I suppose.

W: Yes, and she admitted feeling pleased that the parents gave her really positive feedback. I'm amazed. She actually admitted that it made her feel good. If you ask me, it's all about making her feel good, and making money, of course.

M: Yes, money. I'm sure that comes into it.

W: Well, yes, and without thinking about the effect on the children. As I remember from the article, she actually suggested encouraging toddlers to do homework too, you know, she suggested that parents should help them do more 'practice' on the computer at home.

M: Well, most kids don't need much encouragement!

W: That's right.

M: It doesn't sound like a very balanced article.

W: Well, it did have two parts actually. There was another person. I can't remember his name … but he was an educational psychologist, and of course, he confirmed what I feel. He confirmed that studies show too much time on computers is bad for young children.

M: Mmm. I'm sure I read something about one study which warned people not to let their children on a computer for more than an hour a day.

W: Exactly! Er … How long's your brother been sitting there?

M: Erm, oh, about two and half hours.

W: Two and half hours!! What?! Will you remind me to get that article for you? I think you should read it.

Track 2.26

Thank you so much for returning all the surveys to us. We have now had a chance to look at all your responses and here are the collated results. So, first, for question 1 … 13 out of 20 people admitted spending three or more hours a day on the computer, which adds up to over 20 hours a week. The majority claimed to use the computer largely for studying, although 75 percent of the group also said that they used the computer for fun, doing things like playing games and communicating with friends. Moving on to question 2 … for this one, everyone suggested restricting the number of hours that children spend on the computer. Most people said that an hour a day was the maximum amount of time that children under the age of 12 should be sitting in front of a computer. However, nearly half the group admitted that it was quite difficult to enforce this, and that many children had to do homework using a computer. Nobody thought that children should never use a computer at home. OK, so, now question 3 … computer classes for children under the age of five … for this one, only a small minority were in favour of computer classes for toddlers … The vast majority confirmed my own feelings on this one, and that is, that very young children should not use computers at all, and should be encouraged to be active and play with their friends. This leads us on to question number 4, and the link between obesity and computer use in children. Reports have warned us about the link and most people who answered the survey seemed to agree. 80 percent confirmed that they thought there was a definite link, and that the longer children spent in front of a computer, the more likely they were to be overweight. A few people, however, disagreed, saying that obesity is a complex issue with a number of contributing factors.

Track 2.28

E=Eliot, C=Caroline, P=Polly

E: For me, erm, Richard Branson would be someone I consider a success, considering he started off with a small company, and basically turned it into a huge multinational, erm, corporation, erm. How would you define success, would you agree with that statement?

C: Mm, yeah, I think I … I have similar, erm, ideas about success, erm, yeah I think it's definitely to do with your wealth and how far you progress in your career, erm, I think the best thing is probably when you attain the goals that you've set yourself which usually end up in success.

P: Well, erm, I kind of agree with you that, erm, it's about how … how well you do and, erm, how much you progress, but not necessarily about your wealth so, erm, Richard Branson has been really successful and because of the nature

of his business that's made him really wealthy but you could have, erm, say, erm, I don't know, erm, an artist who, erm, had a huge talent and made fantastic paintings and therefore they were successful but, erm, maybe they weren't gonna make any money until after their death. So they still have, erm, had a huge achievement but not be that wealthy, but maybe still as successful as someone who's made lots of money.

C: Mm, yeah you're right. I mean another, erm, means of success, obtaining success – success I suppose is, erm, through your family, erm, having loyal friends and, erm, a big family some people consider that being successful.

E: I think it's good to have, erm, strong relationships that you surround yourself with, erm, regardless of your social status or how well you do in a career, erm, for some people you know they're quite happy just to have a strong marriage or a strong personal relationship with a close knit of people. And money and, erm, social status really doesn't come into it.

Track 2.29

M=Man, W=Woman

M: Did I tell you about this really funny lawyer story that a friend of mine sent me on email the other day?

W: No, go on.

M: Well … the way it goes is that … there's this lawyer in the US … North Carolina or somewhere … and he buys this box of really rare and very, very expensive cigars.

W: OK.

M: And because they're so expensive he decides to insure them … against fire, amongst other things.

W: Fair enough.

M: Yes … except that, within a month, the lawyer made a claim against the insurance company, having smoked his complete collection of these fantastic cigars! You know, without having paid the premium … he hadn't even made his first payment to the insurance company … he made a claim against them.

W: What on earth for?

M: Well, in his claim, the lawyer stated that the cigars were lost in a series of small fires.

W: How ridiculous!

M: And unsurprisingly, the insurance company refused to pay for the obvious reason that the man had smoked the cigars in the normal way. But then, the lawyer sued the insurance company … and won! When he gave his decision, the judge agreed with the insurance company that the claim appeared ridiculous BUT … concluded that the lawyer had a policy from the company in which it said that the cigars could be insured against fire, without defining exactly what did or did not count as 'fire'. And so the company would have to pay the claim.

W: No! You're kidding!

M: But that's not all! You see, the insurance company wanted to sort the claim out quickly so they accepted the decision and paid $15,000 to the lawyer for his loss of the valuable cigars in the 'fires'. But now comes the best part!

W: Go on … I can't wait …

M: Then … after cashing the cheque, the lawyer was arrested! The insurance company had him charged with 24 counts of arson! With his own insurance claim and evidence from the previous case

being used against him, the lawyer was convicted of deliberately burning his insured property and so – can you believe it? – he was sentenced to 24 months in jail and a $24,000 fine.

W: No! Is that really true?

M: Cross my heart! My friend said he got it from a real newspaper.

W: How amazing!

Track 2.30

first, evidence, suspects, next, sentenced, punishments, products, scientist, insurance, clients, context, against

Track 2.31

M=Man, W=Woman

M: Well, what do you think?

W: Hmm, it's a hard one, I don't know, erm, well, the park ranger sounds quite sure. He must have a good reason to be so sure.

M: He might not be certain who it was. I mean, he says he knows who was lying, but he doesn't say that was definitely the person who committed the crime.

W: True, but they probably are. So, who then?

M: OK, well, the brothers, Jan and Marek, they were rather tongue-tied it says … that's a bit suspicious. But they had been hiking for two days, and then they'd spent the whole day fishing, so they couldn't have committed the crime.

W: What do you mean? It might be a big lie! You're too trusting. If you want to be a detective, you've got to spot clues, not just believe everything you hear!

M: Well, OK, I don't know. They might have done it, I suppose, but I'm not sure. What clues are there? He says that he asked them if they had fished in the rain. Do you think that's significant?

W: Yes probably, but it sounds a bit dodgy, and you can't prove anything. Let's think about the next lot of suspects, Adam and Jean. They're a middle-aged, well-dressed couple, it says.

M: OK, well, as you say, a middle-aged couple, they must be innocent, don't you think? I mean, they can't be guilty. A middle-aged couple wouldn't do that sort of thing. You know, they can't have stolen food, and vandalised a park ranger's cabin. Surely, they wouldn't do that!?

W: What?! There you go again! That is so prejudiced! You haven't got any idea what they would or wouldn't do just because of their age, honestly! You've got to look at proper clues, not just prejudices and things people say.

M: Proper clues? Well, what clues are there here then?

W: OK, well, they said they took shelter in a small cave when it started raining. I suppose that's possible …

M: Yes, and they set up camp the previous night. I can't see anything wrong with that.

W: No. OK, what about the last people, Lara and Pia?

M: Well, they sound very suspicious to me. Oh, no, wait, I shouldn't judge too quickly!

W: That's right. OK, they do sound a bit suspicious. I mean, firstly they parked in the wrong place … but that doesn't prove anything really.

M: No, but having a brand-new campervan, not in their name, that's a bit strange.

W: Hmm, true … it is a bit weird, but they do offer an explanation, and also their friend's phone number. Oh, I don't know. I'm sure it's really obvious. We're probably missing something really simple. Either that or it's something really far-fetched and we'll never get it.

M: Mmm. Are there any other details that we've missed? It's all in the detail, you know, when you're a detective!

W: Oh, I see, you're a professional now, are you?!

Track 2.32

1 When you were a child, were you ever caught red-handed doing something you shouldn't?

2 In what situations have you found yourself tongue-tied?

3 Between what ages is someone 'middle-aged' do you think?

4 What things do you have in your house which are colour-coded?

5 How often do you get things gift-wrapped professionally in shops?

6 Has anyone ever told you a story that was really far-fetched?

Track 2.33

W=Woman, M=Man

W: Did you see these photos in the paper?

M: Mmm?

W: Basically, they are pictures of a burglar … he broke into someone's house and he's in the middle of stealing that person's computer equipment … He was caught completely red-handed because they managed to take pictures of him in the middle of the crime …

M: Really? So, how did they manage to do that?

Track 2.34

M: Really? So, how did they manage to do that?

W: I'm not sure, I suppose they must have fixed up some kind of security camera.

M: What … inside their own house?

W: Yeah. Let's see … mmm … actually it says here that the householder had been burgled before so he set up a webcam which would start recording as soon as it detected movement in the room.

M: Hmm, that's a good idea. But the burglar can't have realised that he was being filmed, otherwise wouldn't he just steal the camera too?

W: Well, it says that he did take the computer and the camera, but that the homeowner had already thought of that.

M: Oh? So what did he do?

W: Well, the particularly clever thing in this case was that even though the burglar stole the computer and webcam, the images had already been sent via the Internet to a private email address …

M: Oh, that's very good, he really was caught red-handed …

Track 2.35

I=Interviewer, S.H.=Sherlock Holmes

I: Mr Sherlock Holmes, I must ask you first … How is it that you have the same name as Sherlock Holmes, the great detective from London?

S.H: Please, call me Holmes – that's what my friends and family call me – well, you see, my parents were great fans of the original Conan Doyle stories. They were the kind of parents who would spend hours reading to me … and my father, especially, would spend hours reading the Sherlock Holmes adventures to me – even as a child.

I: Really!?

S.H: Yes … and when I was born, they discussed a number of first names. They wanted to give their son a name that was uncommon – but also that represented something special. They

didn't take long to decide on Sherlock Holmes as he was their favourite literary figure – and they knew no one would forget me once they'd heard my name. And boy, were they right!

I: So, how do people in general react when you introduce yourself to them?

S.H: Well, I get all kinds of reactions really – everything from the usual 'Where's Dr Watson' type comments to people just thinking I'm being funny.

I: I can imagine … And do you mind?

S.H: No, not at all. I'm a pretty easy-going person and I've never minded … no. I think, the best reaction was when I was in San Francisco one time. I went into an electronic store to buy a TV. The clerk behind the counter was a young lady about eighteen or so. After noticing the name on my credit card, she stared at it for about ten full seconds. Then, she slowly lifted her face to look at me and she said, in all sincerity, 'I didn't know you were real! Wait 'til I tell my friends I saw the real Sherlock Holmes!'

I: No!

S.H: Yes! It may sound far-fetched, but it's absolutely true … You could have knocked her over with a feather. The expression on her face was as if she'd seen a ghost. It was very amusing.

I: Given your name, do you feel that you have any special talent or ability to solve mysteries in everyday life?

S.H: Well, I will say that having such a name does mean that people often turn to me if anything unusual happens. For example, if I'm watching TV with a friend or family member and a magician comes on and does some kind of trick – all eyes turn to me to explain how it's done.

I: Really? How funny!

Track 2.36

W=Woman, M=Man

W: So what do we have to decide?

M: We have to decide which of these crimes is the least serious and which is the most serious.

W: Right OK. Mm.

M: So, why don't we start by talking about them individually perhaps, first?

W: Yes that's a good idea. OK, erm, right shall we … shall we start with Paolo?

M: Let's go for it, yeah. Any thoughts?

W: I think this is quite a serious crime, hacking into somebody's bank account. Erm, for me that would rate quite highly on the scale of being one of the most serious crimes … and I haven't seen the others yet, but …

M: And it's not mitigated at all by the fact that he's unemployed? The man's desperate?

W: Not really, not in my opinion. No.

M: And I suppose thousands of euros' worth I suppose …

W: I'd like to suspend judgement until we've gone through the, you know, the other three.

M: So, moving on to Jenny who's 35 and married with two children. Sounds like it's gonna make a difference.

W: Well, if she's married then she's obviously got a husband who supports them.

M: Well presumably. I guess we don't know.

W: So why is she shoplifting, that's the … that's the question, erm …

M: Kleptomania perhaps, erm …

W: Shall we … shall we come back to this one? Let's come back to this one later.

M: Erm, yeah that's, ah … I'm wildly dubious. Akio.

W: Akio.

M: Erm, a graffiti artist, a young graffiti artist. Well …

W: For me this is not really a crime.

M: Really? Not at all?

W: No.

M: But the … depending on the type of graffiti, I suppose.

W: Oh I suppose, so if it's offensive, then that's a different matter.

M: His graffiti apparently is well done and quite artistic but, ah, beauty in the eye of the beholder and what not, so.

W: Mm, it is art though.

M: You think all graffiti is art?

W: Not all graffiti, not the offensive graffiti but if it's as it says here, erm, well done and quite artistic it can actually lift the urban environment.

M: Interesting.

W: So for me that's probably going to be one of the least crimes.

M: Yeah I probably … yeah I think I'd be inclined to agree. So Teresa, the successful doctor, erm, this to me, erm …

W: She's been spe- … speeding every day, my goodness.

M: Doesn't … ah. I guess in a 30, 40, 45 and a 30 zone I guess is pretty significant, it's certainly irresponsible but …

W: Well, it depends, I mean if she's going to an emergency case then, then I'd say it's quite alright for her to d- to speed, however, it does say every day.

M: Yeah.

W: Or most days, most days, so I'm sure she doesn't have emergencies most days.

M: Yeah, yeah. Maybe you need a little more context perhaps, but … bom, bom, bom, bom, boh … I mean doctors generally aren't responding to emergencies in their own cars are they?

W: No.

M: So, to me it seems pretty irresponsible, whether it's a terrible crime, yeah. So …

W: Oh let's come back to that one later. I'd like to go back to, um, Jenny.

M: Uhuh, OK, erm, Jenny, so we're thinking isn't too bad, then?

W: No.

M: Maybe the least, and then after that I would probably say, ah, Akio is the least … oh so probably Akio is the least offensive we would say followed by Jenny …

W: It really … it really depends doesn't it on people's opinion, I mean for me Akio is the least offensive, followed by Jenny. Erm …

M: Followed by … Teresa.

W: Teresa possibly.

M: And then probably Paolo …

W: I think Paolo is the most serious crime.

M: Probably no great excuses for what he's done. Erm, good.

W: So what else do we have to decide? I think we've agreed on everything.

M: I think that's it. Yeah.

Track 2.38

I=Interviewer, W=Woman, M=Man

Dialogue 1

I: How do you feel about Derren Brown?

W: Well, I reckon he's probably genuine myself. It sounds as if audiences love him. Whether it's magic or not, all his TV shows are completely compelling viewing – and you can't say that about much TV these days. So even if we don't really understand how he does it, if you ask me, it doesn't really matter. He must be doing something right! I think Derren Brown gives us real entertainment and there's nothing wrong with that. Some people want to know how everything works, but I'm in favour of just enjoying it as entertainment, and not analysing things too much!

Dialogue 2

I: What are your views on mind-reading and illusionists? Do you have any strong feelings about that kind of thing?

M: Yes, I do. I've always believed that people like Derren Brown are just good showmen. To my mind, it's all rubbish – he's just good at talking and charming people, and also filming things so they look spectacular. But, I have my doubts about how much mind-reading he actually does. I mean, what's the point of pretending to predict lottery numbers when really he's filmed himself picking out every number and then they've edited the correct ones together at the last minute? I'm sceptical that any of it is real and I'm against people paying for a show which is really just a con. I mean, I doubt anything he does is real ... it's just clever filming.

Dialogue 3

I: What do you think of mind-reading by people like Derren Brown?

M: From my point of view, I have to say that when I went to one of his shows, I thought it was fantastic. I loved every minute of it. I mean, at the beginning I was quite open-minded about it all but having seen him in action, I'm convinced that he really does have some kind of power. As I say, I've seen this man in action with my own eyes. He's a magician, I can tell you. Right in front of me, with absolutely NO special effects or pre-filming, he did mind-reading on me. He predicted my answers to every question he asked me. It was amazing and almost a bit scary. In fact, I suspect that a lot of people don't believe he's doing anything just because they are quite scared about the whole thing.

Track 2.39

I=Interviewer, E=Expert

I: Welcome to *Modern World*. On the programme today, we're talking to Jo Carlson about the power of persuasion. All around us, there are images on television, jingles on the radio, adverts in magazines, sound bites on the news, offers in the shops. They're all hard at work – trying to make us believe something or persuading us to buy something. Fear not, however, Jo Carlson is here to reveal their secrets and show us how to resist all this persuasion! Hello, Jo.

E: Hello.

I: First, persuading people is big business, isn't it? I mean, supermarkets and politicians, advertisers and salespeople, they all take it very seriously, don't they?

E: Yes. They spend a lot of money on marketing and on working out the best psychological tricks to guarantee that even the most cautious among us are open to manipulation.

I: Let's take supermarkets then. How do they make us buy things we don't necessarily want? What are some of their tricks?

E: Well, firstly, most supermarkets have a 'transition zone' as you enter the shop. You might have noticed that the entrances of most supermarkets are quite small and crowded ...

I: Yes ... ?

E: Well, this is a deliberate effort to slow people down. The supermarkets want you

to stop rushing around and take longer with your shopping ...

I: That's interesting ...

E: Yes, and ... they also try to relax you by playing music and by pumping the smell of fresh bread into the store. Studies have shown that the smell makes people buy more.

I: I know I've done that without even thinking about it ...

E: Exactly ... most of the time, we are completely unaware of what's happening. It's subconscious persuasion ...

I: There are also endless tricks when it comes to pricing, aren't there?

E: Yes ... there's the old one of putting the price at £3.99, or £9.99, or whatever ... Of course, we know about the trick, but it still works, because every time we see a price of £9.99 we are manipulated into thinking that it's a lot cheaper than £10 ... In our heads, we think £9.99 is £9 but in fact, of course, it's £10.

I: Yes ... it's simple, but it works ...

E: And, another trick which is used more and more is putting the produce, let's say, apples ... in bags of different sizes ... So, for example, they put the ordinary apples in a bag costing, say, £1.80 and the organic ones in a bag costing say, £1.90.

I: So, supposing you're a customer, you might think, oh, organic apples aren't so much more expensive – I'll have those.

E: Yes ... but what you might not realise is that the bag of ordinary apples contains six apples and the bag of organic ones contains only five ... so really, they are more expensive than you think.

I: Mmm, and unless you're really good at doing maths in your head, you won't want to work out the price of each apple all the time ... it's just too difficult and time-consuming.

E: That's right ...

I: And what about sales ... I mean, shops are always trying to attract customers by cutting prices, especially during end of season sales ...

E: Yes, and if there are large discounts on offer, customers will come to the shops in huge numbers. Shops know that people are tempted by lower prices ... even if you end up spending more in the end. You certainly wouldn't have spent as much if you had stayed at home and not bought anything!

I: Shops rely on customers' greed ...

E: Yes, people will buy something as long as it looks like a bargain ... though often they don't really want or need it at all.

I: So, what about the advertising industry? In what ways do they persuade us to buy particular products?

E: Well, adverts on TV in commercial breaks, or on posters, or in magazines ... all follow the same principles and basically, there are two types of ads ... those that appeal to the thinking part of our brain and those that appeal to the emotional part.

I: So, for what type of products would they advertise by appealing to the thinking part of our brain?

E: Well, they are mostly used for things which have little emotional appeal, for example, cleaning products. They give us information about the product and try to influence us that way. However, if an advert targets our emotions, it's likely to be much more successful. You don't have to believe the hype ... provided that you respond emotionally ... you know, on a

subconscious level, you'll probably want to buy the product ...

I: So, what kinds of emotions are used?

E: Well, adverts for different brands of clothes often want to make us feel that we belong, for example by showing us how to buy the right clothes to fit in with our friends. And adverts for insurance play on our need to feel safe. For example, they might show a family happily spending their insurance money buying new things when their house has been burgled.

I: Celebrities are used a lot too, aren't they?

E: Yes, that's very popular. Celebrities are often used as a quick way of getting the message across. Their success and familiarity makes them feel safe, interesting, cool ... whatever ... If we see our favourite pop star drinking a particular fizzy drink, we're immediately persuaded to buy it!

Track 2.40

Dialogue 1

A=Anna, Z=Zoë

A: Hi Zoë ... ?

Z: Oh, hi, Anna ... How are you? Are you OK?

A: Oh, yes, I'm fine ... I'm just phoning because, well, I need some advice ...

Z: Mmm? Advice? What about?

A: Oh, nothing major ... it's just that I've just been looking at phones ... and I'm trying to decide what to do ... I mean, there's a really nice phone I want ... and ... you've probably seen the adverts on telly ... You know, when all those people are running around trying to grab the phone.

Z: Oh yes, I know the one ... It looks really good ...

A: Yeah, well, I've just been looking at it in the shop ... and I really like it. But, you know, I don't really need a phone ...

Z: Oh, but you've had your phone for ages ... it's pretty out-of-date now, isn't it? Go on ... treat yourself!

A: Do you think I should?

Z: Yes, you should just do it. Don't worry about things so much. Is it really expensive or something?

A: Well, it's more than I'm paying at the moment. You know, I'm on a contract, so it would be a little bit more every month ... but you get the phone itself free, if you go on the contract...

Z: Well, go for it then! If it's only a bit more money ... well, it's not a huge deal, is it?

A: Mmm ...

Z: I mean, supposing you don't get it, how will you feel? If I were you, I'd just do it!

A: Yeah, maybe I should ...

Z: Definitely ... you deserve it! I'm sure you won't regret it.

A: OK then. I will. Thanks, Zoë.

Dialogue 2

J=Jamie, A=Alex

J: So ... Alex, what do you think ... I mean, there's so much on that I want to see at the moment ... We're spoilt for choice really!

A: Yeah, true ... erm ... well, let's look at the list ... OK ...screen 1, there's some kids' film ... I've seen the trailer for that one, and it looks really ridiculous. I mean, I like some kids' animations, but that one looks a bit stupid ... from what I've seen, anyway.

J: OK, what about screen 2?

A: Erm ... there's some boring romantic comedy ... I'm not that keen on films like that...

J: OK, so, screen 3 then?

A: Screen 3? Oh, there's the new Woody Allen film.

J: Yes, that's right. I haven't seen a Woody Allen film for years.

A: Well, let's see that then. I haven't seen a trailer, but I did read a good review though.

J: Oh, I don't know. I don't usually go for psychological dramas. It looks a bit weird.

A: It's a comedy. Don't be so negative! Anyway, what do you mean, it looks a bit weird? You haven't seen anything about it yet! I'm sure you'll enjoy it.

J: I'm not so sure …

A: Well, there's nothing else, unless you want to get a DVD?

J: No.

A: Well, what have you got to lose? Come on … it'll be fun … It might cheer you up a bit!

J: Oh, alright then. Let's go!

The ActiveBook component features the Students' Book pages in digital format and includes integrated audio and video as well as interactive exercises for students to do in class or at home. The ActiveTeach component will help you get the most out of the course with its range of interactive whiteboard software tools and extra resources.

ActiveBook

Students' Book pages and interactive activities

Audio bank (Class CD material)

Video clips

Interactive video activities

Phonetic chart and dictionary

Video clips to play on DVD player

ActiveTeach

Students' Book pages and interactive activities

Interactive whiteboard tools with save functionality

Audio bank (Class CD material)

Video clips

Interactive video activities

Phonetic chart and dictionary

Extra resources for the teacher:
- class photocopiables
- video photocopiables
- printable audio and video scripts
- editable tests

Video clips to play on DVD player

Pearson Education Limited
Edinburgh Gate
Harlow
Essex CM20 2JE
England
and Associated Companies throughout the world.

www.pearsonelt.com

First published 2011
Third impression 2013

ISBN:
New Total English Upper Intermediate Teacher's Book and
Teacher's Resource Disc Pack
978-1-4082-6730-1

Set in Meta Plus Book-Roman
Printed in Great Britain by Ashford Colour Press Ltd.